America
and the Reconstruction
of Italy, 1945–1948

America
and the Reconstruction
of Italy, 1945–1948

JOHN LAMBERTON HARPER

THE JOHNS HOPKINS UNIVERSITY
BOLOGNA CENTER

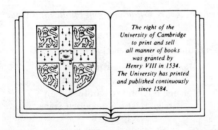

The right of the
University of Cambridge
to print and sell
all manner of books
was granted by
Henry VIII in 1534.
The University has printed
and published continuously
since 1584.

CAMBRIDGE UNIVERSITY PRESS

CAMBRIDGE
LONDON   NEW YORK   NEW ROCHELLE
MELBOURNE   SYDNEY

To my mother and father

Published by the Press Syndicate of the University of Cambridge
The Pitt Building, Trumpington Street, Cambridge CB2 1RP
32 East 57th Street, New York, NY 10022, USA
10 Stamford Road, Oakleigh, Melbourne 3166, Australia

First published 1986

Printed in the United States of America

Library of Congress Cataloging-in-Publication Data

Harper, John Lamberton,
America and the reconstruction of Italy, 1945–1948.
Bibliography: p.
1. Economic assistance, American – Italy.
2. Reconstruction (1939–1951) – Italy. 3. United States
– Foreign relations – Italy. 4. Italy – Foreign
relations – United States. I. Title.
HC305.H36 1986   338.91′73′045   85-30915

British Library Cataloguing in Publication Data

Harper, John Lamberton
America and the reconstruction of Italy, 1945–1948.
1. United States – Foreign relations
– 1945–1953. 2. United States –
Foreign relations – Italy. 3. Italy
– Foreign relations – United States
I. Title
327.73045   E183.8.I8

ISBN 0–521–32518–8

Contents

2298457

Preface		vii
Frequently used abbreviations		ix
1	Introduction and overview	1
2	Wartime diplomacy	22
3	Liberation and transition	37
4	The advent of De Gasperi	58
5	Clayton at bay	76
6	Corbino, UNRRA, and the crisis of the liberal line	88
7	The emergency response	105
8	The "whirlwind of disintegration"	118
9	The dilemmas of deflation	137
10	Conclusion: the Marshall Plan and after	159
Notes		169
Bibliography		201
Index		209

Preface

My original interest in this project arose from the somewhat simplistic conviction that some combination of American money, power, and idealism was responsible for the course of events in Italy during the years 1945–8. Indeed, my study of the period has confirmed that, understood as military occupation and financial support, the American presence affected in a profound if unmeasurable way the options and opportunities of the local forces competing to determine the political and economic identity of the new Italy. Those years also witnessed the consolidation of a bargain between the United States and a pro-Western center-right alliance. Subsequent life under the American umbrella has meant, to paraphrase Croce, a sort of parentheses from history, unimagined material well-being along with a respite from the trials and rigors of national independence. For the United States, the relationship has meant a faithful and compliant ally, providing control of the central Mediterranean.

The prospect that these happy arrangements may not last forever has in the past several years begun to provoke both anxiety and signs of independence among the pro-American political elites. Faced with a less predictable America and an uncertain international climate, some Italians have begun to ask themselves whether the declining benefits of continued passivity are worth the sacrifice of greater dignity and self-reliance. Perhaps both Italians and Americans would now do well to look again at the origins and consequences of their postwar special relationship.

The following study of the years 1945–8 demonstrates that regardless of the energy, will, and inspiration of its internationalist community, America lacked the necessary intellectual and political resources to address Italy's historic problems of poverty, disunity, and vulnerability. The crucial choices of the day were Italian choices, for which Italians alone were responsible. The choice to depend so utterly on the United States, while attractive and probably unavoidable in 1945–9, tended to become a way of postponing, perhaps even of forgetting, the path of national unity and

vii

independence. For the Christian Democratic Party, national political divisions and ideological tensions became a means of guaranteeing continuing American and domestic support, if not a necessary premise of their identity and survival. A largely unspoken assumption of the story that follows is that such a relationship, although comfortable and profitable at a moment of political, economic, and psychological recuperation, may become counterproductive and enervating at a time of maturation and transition. Aside from its attempt to explain the origins of the postwar economic–political relationship between the United States and Italy, an ulterior purpose of this book is to provoke discussion about how that relationship might change and evolve.

I am fortunate to have received criticism and material aid from many people during the writing of this book. The following people deserve my special gratitude: David P. Calleo, James Edward Miller, Charles Maier, David Ellwood, Paolo D'Attore, Steven Schuker, Giangiacomo Migone, Maurizio Vaudagna, Adrian Lyttelton, Vera Zamagni, Pierluigi Ciocca, Paolo Baffi, Egidio Ortona, and Spurgeon Keeny, Sr. I would also like to thank my typists Zilla Bristol and Janice Delbert, and finally my wife, Maria Belfiore, who has provided insights into the relations of Italy and America not to be found in any library or archive.

JOHN LAMBERTON HARPER

Washington, D.C.

Frequently used abbreviations

AC (ACC)	Allied Commission
ACS	Archivio Centrale dello Stato; Central State Archives
AFHQ	Allied Force Headquarters, Mediterranean Theatre
AMG	Allied Military Government
CCAC	Combined (British and U.S.) Civil Affairs Committee
CCS	Combined (British and U.S.) Chiefs of Staff
CF	National Archives Confidential File
CGIL	Confederazione Generale Italiana del Lavoro; Italian General Confederation of Labor
CLN	Comitato di Liberazione Nazionale; Committee of National Liberation
CLNAI	Comitato di Liberazione Nazionale Alta Italia; North Italian Committee of National Liberation
DC	Democrazia Cristiana; Christian Democratic Party
DL	Democrazia del Lavoro; Democracy of Labor Party
DOS	U.S. Department of State
ED	Division of Investment and Economic Development, Department of State
EUR	Office of European Affairs, Department of State
FEA	Foreign Economic Administration
IBRD	International Bank for Reconstruction and Development, or World Bank
IMF	International Monetary Fund
IR	International Resources Division, Department of State
IRI	Istituto per la Ricostruzione Industriale; Institute for Industrial Reconstruction
ITO	International Trade Organization
ITP	Office of International Trade Policy, Department of State
NA	National Archives

Frequently used abbreviations

NAC	National Advisory Council on International Monetary and Financial Affairs
PCI	Partito Comunista Italiano; Italian Communist Party
Pd'A	Partito d'Azione; Action Party
PLI	Partito Liberale Italiano; Italian Liberal Party
PRI	Partito Repubblicano Italiano; Italian Republican Party
PSIUP	Partito Socialista Italiano di Unità Proletario; Italian Socialist Party
PSLI	Partito Socialista dei Lavoratori Italiani; Socialist Party of Italian Workers
SACMED	Supreme Allied Commander, Mediterranean
UNA	United Nations Archives
UNRRA	United Nations Relief and Rehabilitation Administration

1

Introduction and overview

Soon after the collapse of the German army in April, 1945, Allied economic experts entered the industrial heartland of Northern Italy. Experts who had seen systematic German destruction in the South were stunned by the sight of Genoa, Turin, and Milan. Thanks in part to the local resistance, about 85 percent of northern plant capacity had survived, although damage varied from sector to sector. The war-related metallurgical industry had been reduced to 75 percent of its 1938 value, but losses in the wool and cotton textile sectors were a mere 0.5 percent.[1] Even though first impressions were comforting, calculations of physical damage revealed neither the true cost of Fascism, war, and foreign occupation, nor the size and complexity of the Italian economic problem at the time. That problem, it was generally agreed, had three fundamental and interrelated aspects.

The first and most pressing task was to restore production and employment. Industrial output stood at 29 percent of prewar levels at war's end; agricultural, at 63.3 percent. Estimates of unemployment were approximate, but most observers placed the number between two and three million in a population of forty-five million people.[2] Obviously, the production problem entailed much more than factory repair. The internal transportation and communications systems were shattered. Forty percent of prewar rail lines had been wrecked, along with half the country's rolling stock.

The main obstacle to increased production was lack of raw materials, especially coal. Italy had imported almost all of its coal from Germany and Britain before the war, but neither country was exporting in 1945. Italy needed foreign exchange to pay for fuel and other essential materials from other producers, but the Italian state was bankrupt at the time. Two traditional sources of hard currency, tourism and emigrant remittances, had evaporated, and the commercially vital merchant marine had ceased to exist. The imperative was to find raw materials and foreign exchange using any means available. The alternatives were starvation and collapse.

The second major task was to stabilize the internal monetary situation. Through forced saving measures, the Fascist regime had limited its recourse to the printing press early in the war. By the fall of 1942, however, the Bank of Italy could no longer reabsorb the vast purchasing power it was obliged to create at the state's behest. During the Allied bombings and great internal migration of late 1942 and early 1943, the public's need for cash increased dramatically and bank deposits were withdrawn. The system of wartime price controls collapsed, and local black markets developed in all essential commodities.[3]

Severe inflation began after the Allied invasion of Sicily in mid–1943. Its causes and character varied geographically. Inflation in the North was surprisingly mild due to the North's greater wealth and also to the strict controls maintained by the Germans and the Fascist puppet regime, the Italian Social Republic. By 1945, retail food prices had increased thirty-three times in Rome (liberated in June 1944) and nineteen times in Milan (liberated in April 1945). Conditions in the South were more severe. The battle lines had created an isolated economic unit out of the poorest part of the country. Into this zone, the conquering armies released a flood of overvalued paper money to pay the costs of war and occupation. Currency inflation increased demand, and severe shortages transferred income to those who controlled the market.[4]

The outstanding feature of the situation in April 1945 was the enormous liquidity in the hands of banks and private individuals. The money supply stood at 47 percent of the gross national product in 1945, compared to 28 percent in 1938.[5] The immediate tasks were to absorb this purchasing power and prevent prices from rising in proportion to the money supply. All, including the left-wing political parties, recognized that a stable currency was essential to the resumption of investment and exchange. The pernicious effects of inflation in the South were obvious, and Allied and Italian authorities hoped to avoid a similar unhappy experience in the North.

They also agreed that the Italian economic problem had a third, more basic, aspect, variously defined as historical, structural, or qualitative. The task at hand concerned not simply production and stabilization, but also reconversion and reform. In its most familiar dimension, the problem involved the long-standing disequilibrium between the North and South. The traditional problems of the South, underindustrialization, low agricultural productivity, and cultural and political backwardness, had been severely aggravated by war and occupation. The immediate

2

postwar period appeared to offer the chance to address the Southern Question in some systematic way. The structural problem involved the fate of Northern industry as well. Fascist monetary stabilization and depression had reinforced the concentrated, monopolistic character of private heavy industry. During the period of autarchy, chemical, mechanical, and metallurgical giants had consolidated their market power thanks to official protection and largesse. Their ability to survive and compete in an open postwar economy was questionable, at best. The elimination of excess capacity, technical innovation, and reconversion were universally accepted imperatives in 1945.[6]

The Fascists had also elaborated on the long-standing tradition of state intervention in the economy. The *Istituto per la Ricostruzione Industriale* (IRI) had come to life when the great banks that controlled much of Italian industry found themselves on the verge of collapse in 1933. IRI's original purpose had been to buy up the industrial securities of the banks, then to make long-term loans to Italian industry. It was generally assumed that IRI would sell off its new properties, but this was not the case. Private capital was not available, and the state soon realized that IRI could serve to rationalize production in the heavy, war-related industries it now controlled.[7]

IRI reorganized its huge patrimony into subsidary holding companies. In 1933, IRI created the Societa Torinesi per gli Esercizi Telefonici (STET). By 1939, STET controlled 53 percent of the country's telephones. In 1936, IRI set up Finmare to oversee the major shipping lines in its portfolio. By 1939, Finmare controlled 90 percent of Italian passenger tonnage. In 1936, IRI's long-term credit operations were transferred to the Istituto Mobiliare Italiano (IMI). IRI became a permanent agency and undertook a large-scale reorganization of Italian heavy industry. By 1939, IRI's Finsider holding controlled 77 percent of pig iron and 45 percent of steel production. IRI also controlled the nation's major shipbuilding, munitions, and machine industries. By 1943, IRI firms employed 300,000 workers and accounted for 20 percent of total industrial production. By 1945, this vast complex lay in ruins. As the heart of Italian war industry, IRI had borne the brunt of Allied bombing and German looting. As member firms pleaded with the government for support, the question of IRI's fate – of the principle of state intervention itself – demanded a clear response after April 1945.[8]

To a nation physically and psychologically ravaged by defeat, these tasks of economic renewal were a daunting yet welcome challenge. Each task required energy and intelligence, qualities Italy was fortunate to possess in abundance in 1945. Italians of passion, conviction, and ingenuity stood ready to begin the painful business of reconstruction and reform. Nor was there any lack of answers to the great economic questions of the day. The experience of Fascism, war, and resistance had spawned several conflicting visions of the future. Marxist, Catholic, and radical interventionists all foresaw some sort of rationally ordered economy based on planning, worker participation, and income redistribution. Economists of the classical liberal school, on the other hand, favored a far-reaching transformation along strict free-market lines. Each program drew particular lessons from the country's past and had its own solutions to the problems of production, stabilization, and structural change. The historian Piero Barucci has aptly called the two years after April 1945 the "heroic" period of Italian economic reconstruction. In contrast to the years following the Christian Democratic victory and stabilization of 1948, the immediate *dopoguerra* was a moment of intellectual ferment, political debate, and widespread expectation of renewal and reform.[9]

The years 1945–47 likewise constituted an heroic period for the foreign economic policy of the United States and witnessed a parallel debate on the questions of postwar economic recovery. The Wilson-inspired program of Secretary of State Cordell Hull aimed to release the constructive forces of American capitalism abroad, while the New Deal liberalism of Vice-President Henry Wallace and his followers envisioned worldwide economic planning and social change. Like their Italian counterparts, American proposals drew lessons from prewar experience and proposed a comprehensive solution to postwar economic and political problems.

American planners had no illusions about Italy's relative importance. Germany and the British Empire were the crucial testing grounds of American foreign economic policy. Yet given its Fascist–mercantilist past, Italy required attention as a matter of principle. Even though America's prewar interest in Italy had been slight, Italy would, as in the immediate post–1918 period, offer new opportunities for U.S. trade and investment. Finally, following the Anglo–American occupation of Southern Italy in 1943, it was clear that the United States would bear the major financial burden of Italian relief and rehabilitation. In view of Italy's strategic location and great importance to Italian-American voters, the fate of the peninsula was too important for Italians alone to decide.[10]

What follows is a history of American foreign economic policy in Italy during the years 1945–48. As such, it does not treat U.S. policy comprehensively nor does it provide another version of Italian economic reconstruction. Rather, this history traces the attempt of an internally divided and politically isolated foreign policy apparatus to hammer out and implement an American approach to postwar Italian reconstruction. The story of the gradual revision and adaptation of wartime plans for Italy provides a case study in the education of early postwar policy makers to domestic and European realities and in the limits of American power and pretentions in the early postwar years. The development and outcome of U.S. policy were decisively affected by the relationship of mutual dependence between the Americans and the local political class that emerged after Fascism and war. The formation of those lasting bonds, in particular between the U.S. government and the Christian Democratic Party, are a central theme of the discussion. The study does its best to avoid the twin pitfalls of determinism and counterfactual wishful thinking. Accounts of this period have tended, on one hand, to stress the inevitability and virtue of what happened or, on the other, to see the early *dopoguerra* as a tragic missed opportunity for some sort of lasting solution to Italy's historical plight. This study reaches more modest conclusions. It is hard to imagine an outcome to the Italian crisis much different from the one in fact achieved, yet the hybrid political-economic solution that emerged was neither foreseen nor really desired by any of the contending forces.

This opening chapter introduces those contending forces and their respective approaches to the Italian economic problem. The discussion also assesses the strengths and weaknesses of the postwar programs in relation to the balance of political forces in Italy and the United States. This introduction reveals the dynamics of the story contained in the body of the book, a story that begins with the Allied seizure of Southern Italy in 1943.

CLASSICAL IDEALS

In late May 1942, Italy's most eminent economists met at the University of Pisa for a special conference on the "Economic Problems of the New Order." After six days of debate, they issued a series of official-sounding resolutions endorsing the domestic and geopolitical objectives of Mussolini. However, the conference organizers could scarcely conceal an open break within the nation's scholarly elite. The only contribution destined for acclaim was Professor Giovanni Demaria's "Il problema industriale italiano." The paper was barred from the conference publication but gained attention in a separate volume issued by Demaria and his dissident friends. Its substance appeared four years later as the introduction to the report on industry of the postwar Constituent Assembly's Economic Commission under the chairmanship of Professor Demaria himself.[11]

The 1942 paper was a cautiously phrased critique of autarchy. The postwar version was a magisterial condemnation of the Fascist regime. In a nostalgic re-evocation, the author described the great spurts of industrial growth between 1900 and 1914, and 1922 to 1929. Those, according to Demaria, were the "golden years" of the individual entrepreneur, of limited state intervention, and an open world economy. Modern in-

5

dustry had arisen "according to pure economic principle . . . in harmony with the necessities of the time." In their misguided pursuit of autonomy, the Fascists had violated the laws of economics and condemned Italy to relative backwardness and stagnation. Why, Demaria asked, did growth of Italian per capita income compare unfavorably with that of other industrialized countries? "*In the first place,*" he argued, because of the "*failure to observe, for political-military reasons, the fundamental principle that a wide foreign trade contributes strongly to the development of national income,* a truth demonstrated not only in theory, but overwhelmingly proved by history, even by most recent history" (emphasis in original).[12] It was equally demonstrable that real per capita income was highest in countries with the lowest proportion of agricultural workers. Demaria's prescription emerged naturally from his historical analysis: rapid reintegration into the world economy along free-trade lines, a drastic reduction of the agricultural workforce via mass emigration, and a prompt end to activities that violated the principle of comparative costs.

Giovanni Demaria represented an honored tradition in modern Italian economic thought, the pre-Keynesian or classical liberal school that dominated academic circles in the early twentieth century, and formed a dissident stronghold at Milan's Bocconi University during the Fascist years. Other members included Luigi Einaudi, Gustavo Del Vecchio, Costantino Brescianni Turroni, and Epicarmo Corbino, all to become ministers in early postwar governments. All espoused free trade (the Italian term is *liberismo*) and abhorred outside interference in the market. The duties of the state consisted solely of balancing the budget and defending the currency in the interests of the small businessmen and farmers who formed the backbone of the economy.[13]

The classical liberals saw the collapse of Fascism as a heaven-sent opportunity to apply their elegantly simple recipe for the economy's short- and long-term ills. The problems of production, inflation, and structural deformation could be resolved simply and simultaneously by removing the state from the economic arena and allowing the market to do its work. Liberalization of trade and exchange would generate exports and hard currency, and dismantling price and financial controls would restore private investment and production. Increased output, along with a balanced government budget, would lead automatically to stable prices, and the end of tariff protection and government subvention would force industry to readjust on its own, according to the dictates of international competition.[14]

It is difficult to know whether Giovanni Demaria's manifesto crossed the desks of Washington's economic bureaucracy, but it would have aroused interest and satisfaction at the U.S. Department of State.[15] Demaria and the department had a similar vision of the postwar world. The

State Department's version was inspired by Wilson's Fourteen Points, later invigorated by the Southern free trade doctrine of Secretary Cordell Hull. Hull's outlook also bore the stamp of more recent 1930s experience. He was deeply convinced that economic nationalism had caused the war. Therefore, the elimination of economic blocs was the sole guarantee of future prosperity and peace.

The Roosevelt administration's vision of the postwar era encompassed more than free trade. The Treasury Department of Henry Morgenthau, Jr., promoted a worldwide financial order based on eventual free convertibility of currencies and movement of capital. Closed currency blocs, like closed trading blocs, were destined for elimination. Washington planners designed a set of multilateral structures to provide a legal framework for the new international order. The International Monetary Fund (IMF) and the International Trade Organization (ITO) would define and enforce the liberal rules of the road, while the capstone of the system, the United Nations Organization, would provide for collective security and collaboration among the "four policemen" of the postwar world – the United States, United Kingdom, USSR, and China.[16]

This internationalist vision was a harmonious marriage of interests and ideals. American leaders feared a postwar depression and believed that the health of the vastly expanded U.S. economy would depend on a world open to American exports and investment. Thus, American interests in free trade and convertibility coincided with those of the entire world. Early in the war, publisher Henry Luce had popularized the notion of an "American Century" based on the benevolent imperialism of large U.S. corporations. The new multilateral institutions would give free rein to the generous expansionism of the United States, the world's preeminent economic power in 1945.

This corporate idealism was perfectly embodied in Hull's chief disciple, Assistant Secretary of State for Economic Affairs, William L. Clayton. Clayton was co-founder and chief stockholder of Anderson, Clayton & Company, the world's largest cotton export firm. Originally opposed to FDR, he was converted, thanks to Hull's free trade policies, contained in the 1934 Reciprocal Trade Agreements program. In announcing he would vote for the president in 1936, Clayton told the press, "A vote for Roosevelt is a vote to keep Secretary Hull in office, where his work, just beginning to bear fruit, may go forward with infinite benefit to the nation and the world." As the State Department's senior official in economic affairs after November 1944, he became a tireless exponent of the liberal creed.[17]

Hull's department set up a vast network of committees to study postwar problems. An August 1944 report outlined a comprehensive approach to the Italian situation. The authors of "The Treatment of Italy" assumed that "the economic well-being of a country [was] a primary factor in its internal stability and peaceful relations with other states." Despite Italy's poverty and low war potential, it had "been a frequent threat to the stability and peace of Europe." U.S. policy must therefore promote "reconstruction designed to create an expanding economy which will offer the Italian people genuine opportunities for economic betterment." In accordance with Hullian doctrine, the statement repudiated the notion of spheres of influence. Italy should become a stable but independent member of the European community. The statement also called for the "elimination of uneconomic activities which have grown out of concentration for war, or out of the system of autarchy." Italy must be reintegrated into a system of "multilateral and non-discriminatory foreign trade" and guaranteed all benefits from international agreements on the free exchange of labor and goods. Department planners saw the need for interim trade and exchange controls, "not in harmony with the long-term objectives," but shared the hope of Italian liberal economists that the transition from autarchy to an open world economy would be rapid and complete.[18]

INTERVENTIONISM AND REFORM

The programs of the Italian liberal economists and their Roosevelt administration counterparts reflected a similar view of recent history. From their analysis of the causes of World War II arose a common diffidence towards state intervention and controls. Yet it seemed obvious to other observers that the transformation foreseen by Demaria and his colleagues was unlikely to occur. Even a cursory examination of Italian history suggested that Demaria's interpretation was a mystification of his country's economic past. Given its lack of raw materials and capital, as well as the advanced level of prevailing technology, Italy's industrial growth had depended from the beginning on the state. Using subsidies and tariffs, the state fostered the growth of a basic infrastructure as well as modern mining, metallurgical, and mechanical industries between 1878 and 1914. When the other great protagonists of industrial growth, the mixed banks, experienced their periodic crises, the state intervened to bail them out and in the thirties to relieve them of their untenable industrial properties. Demaria might regret that state intervention had often been irrational and politically motivated, but it was useless to deny that the formation of capital had always been a "public function."[19]

Demaria's critique of Fascism also discounted the role of an independent international business cycle, to which the Italian economy had always been especially vulnerable. Italy's growth before 1914 and in the twenties was indeed related to open markets for its products and manpower. The closing of those same markets after 1929 was sure to provoke a defensive readjustment by the domestic economy under the auspices of the state. Italian controls were imposed, after all, in reaction to British and American moves in 1930–33. Although unprecedented in scope, Fascist policies built on a long-standing tradition of state control.

Indeed, classical economic dogma would have relegated Italy to the status of such backward Mediterranean economies as Greece or Spain, based on subsistence agriculture and isolated labor-intensive industries. With the exception of the Lombard textile industry, Italian industrial development had not been the work of the individual entrepreneur exalted by the liberals. This is not to deny that dynamic figures like Agnelli, Donegani, or Pirelli played a vital role, but their activities were decisively aided by state protection, subsidies, and markets.

For people who held this view of Italian development, the ideas of Demaria and his colleagues bore little relevance to the short- and longer-term requirements of the economy in 1945. The possibilities for exports and emigration were bleak, and Italy at war's end cried out for public management of scarce raw materials and foreign exchange. The problem of inflation called for extraordinary measures to tax profiteers, pay for reconstruction, and restore price stability, while the advanced industrial sectors offering the best hope for future growth needed state help to survive and readapt. Indeed, why not use the techniques and instruments of intervention refined under Fascism for reconstruction and reform? In a bitter attack on the liberal Treasury Minister, Corbino, the Socialist Riccardo Lombardi would later observe, "People want to spread the idea that Nazism and Fascism were nothing more than controls and the negation of liberalism. Such judgements are blind and ignorant. Let us be clear. The instruments of public intervention . . . are not specific to Nazism and Fascism, but to every democracy and modern socialist regime."[20] Each of the major parties of the Italian resistance organization, the Comitato di Liberazione Nazionale (Committee of National Liberation), or CLN, held such views to varying degrees. Each party had its own ideological and political concerns, but each was determined to discipline private activity in pursuit of recovery and reform.[21]

The Socialist Party (PSIUP) leader, Pietro Nenni, called in 1944 for "all power to the CLNs," the local resistance committees. His colleague Rodolfo Morandi aimed to institutionalize worker's democracy in the factories as a stepping stone to a rationally managed socialist society. Their allies, the Communists (PCI), formed the heart of the armed resistance. The PCI favored special taxes, nationalization of selected industries, and basic land reform. The small Action Party of Ferruccio Parri and Ugo La Malfa bore aloft the radical liberal banner of Mazzini. The Actionists aimed to fulfill the promise of the first *risorgimento* by rooting

9

out once and for all the power of church and monarchy. They foresaw a modern mixed economy with ample powers for the state.

The Christian Democratic Party (DC), heir to the pre-Fascist Popular Party, emerged under the leadership of Alcide De Gasperi in 1943. Its wartime program called for a more progressive, egalitarian society, based on land reform, social services, and parliamentary democracy. De Gasperi's party represented a loose coalition of social and economic groups – small land owners, the urban middle classes, and conservative business. However, such influential spokesmen as Giovanni Gronchi, Giuseppe Dossetti, and the young Amintore Fanfani espoused Catholic socialist or corporatist ideas. Catholic economists like Pasquale Saraceno were committed and experienced economic planners.[22]

The resistance coalition was divided from the beginning along political and religious lines, and those fissures could only widen once the common enemy disappeared. Yet the "Vento del Nord," the wind of renewal from the North, seemed a force to be reckoned with in the spring of 1945. The Northern CLN's (CLNAI) Central Economic Commission drew up extensive plans for economic recovery while the CLNAI committees defended and operated most important northern industrial plants during the final stages of the war.

The division between classical liberals and interventionists in Italy corresponded to an ideological split within the American internationalist community. That loose alliance of government officials, academics, journalists, and businessmen agreed that a retreat from world power was unthinkable in 1945. However, there was less agreement as to the nature of the American dream at home or the American purpose abroad. The prospect of postwar renewal inspired Vice-President Henry Wallace's call for a world New Deal. The United States should not resist the radical and anticolonial forces released by war and Axis occupation but should aid and guide them toward universal social welfare and equality. In response to Henry Luce, Wallace and his followers espoused a "Century of the Common Man," fostered by American largesse and based on democratic planning and reform.

All internationalists shared a basic article of faith: The social pathologies of communism and fascism would disappear in an environment of economic well-being and liberal democracy. The world New Dealers also did not deny the potential benefits of free trade and convertibility. They remembered from the thirties, however, that the interests of the banker or large corporation in open markets and stable exchanges sometimes ran counter to those of the farmer and workingman. If democratically adopted controls were necessary to maintain employment and redistribute income, such measures became the instrument of the people's will. Although aiming to recast the international system, the liberalism of

Hull and Clayton was essentially negative. It called for new institutions whose purpose was essentially to remove barriers to the free exchange of goods, money, and labor. The evangelical "social liberalism" of the world New Deal, by contrast, was positive in content. It aimed to remake Europe and Asia by harnessing and directing the powerful impulse for social and political change.

The war gave birth to new organizations full of idealistic officials of New Deal inspiration. Wallace lost a crucial battle for control of foreign economic policy with the break-up of his agency, the Bureau of Economic Warfare (BEW) in 1943. But the BEW's successor, the Foreign Economic Administration (FEA), kept the New Deal fires burning. Its officials sought to use their control of wartime aid to promote democratic planning and reform. Wallace and others saw the United Nations Relief and Rehabilitation Administration (UNRRA), created in 1943, as the first concrete embodiment of the world New Deal. The reform spirit was shared by Treasury Secretary Morgenthau, confidant of FDR and outspoken antifascist. In late 1944, he dispatched the young economist Henry J. Tasca as personal representative to Rome. Tasca's duties included purging fascists from Italian financial institutions.

Progressive planners and relief specialists got first-hand experience in the FEA, UNRRA, and Allied Control Commission (ACC) in Italy, the Anglo-American body created to supervise the occupied areas. Those officials came to appreciate the need for systematic government intervention. An outstanding example was Harlan Cleveland, who, as acting vice-president of the Allied Control Commission Economic Section, and later UNRRA's deputy chief of Mission for Requirements and Distribution, became a key figure in the Allied economic bureaucracy. An article written by Cleveland in 1947 provides a sort of political manifesto in retrospect of the UNRRA mission.

Echoing Riccardo Lombardi, Cleveland noted that the "key was organization, planning and management of the country's resources in the interest of the country as a whole . . . . Too many people seem to believe that there are only two alternatives – either the totalitarian methods of a Hitler . . . or the wishful, day-to-day compromises with pressures as they arise combined with a tendency to confuse democracy and the wasteful use of resources. . . ." No, Cleveland countered, there was a "middle way: to control the vital points in the economy with the consent of the people and in their interest." Those "vital points" included fuel and raw materials, food supply, foreign exchange and the state budget. He concluded, "My thesis is that the necessary planning and control are not only compatible with political democracy, but are its very basis, for inflation and low living standards are the midwives of dictatorship."[23]

FORCES OF THE STATUS QUO

Despite their political and philosophical differences, classical liberals and reformists agreed that the world they intended to create, or, in the case of the nostalgic economists, to restore, would represent a clear departure from the recent past. Each of the postwar visions was sincerely anti-fascist, and the Fascist hierarchy was destined for destruction. But the regime had been based on a coalition of elites. The church, monarchy, armed forces, and high civil service had either made peace with or actively supported Mussolini. With a few exceptions, the Italian industrial leadership had not adopted fascism as its creed and had feared its radical social impulses. But industry's official representative, the Confindustria (General Confederation of Italian Industry), had assiduously cultivated a close relationship with the regime, to the considerable profit of its members.

Each of these groups had serious worries after 1943. The Vatican feared the anticlerical, materialistic forces of the left and looked with suspicion on the radicals within the Christian Democratic movement. King Victor Emmanuel III was discredited in the eyes of the majority of his subjects by his association with the Fascists and his abandonment of Rome to the Germans in September 1943. Important industrialists and bankers would face charges of collaboration with the Fascists and Nazis. Business as a whole felt menaced by socialist and communist plans and had decidedly mixed feelings about the transformation envisioned by Professor Demaria. Business had opposed Fascist taxes and controls, and the Confundustria was prepared to declare its conversion to classical liberal doctrine, at least for tactical purposes. Such arguments were useful in fighting radical proposals and also in disassociating business from the unpleasant Fascist past. But, with the exception of textiles and a few advanced firms like FIAT, who looked forward to open world markets, the end of protection was by no means welcome to Italian industry. Another essential ingredient in Demaria's recipe, the end of state subsidies, could only damage powerful established interests.

For these pillars of the old regime, survival meant forging new alliances. The monarchy lived out the war at the behest of Churchill and the British, and other threatened groups turned to their natural allies in the United States. The American Catholic hierarchy represented the Vatican in Washington, and Roosevelt maintained contact with Pope Pius XII through his personal emissary to the Holy See, Myron Taylor.[24] The wartime fears of Italy's elites were also well known at the Department of State. In early 1942, Assistant Secretary of State (and former ambassador to Rome) Breckinridge Long delivered a secret message to the departing

Italian ambassador, making clear that the United States regarded Italy "in an entirely different light from the German Reich." When the time came for Italy "to make her own decision the Italian people may count on a sympathetic hearing from this country insofar as it is warranted." The message was for the king, and "such others of the important circles in Italy as would presumably be in a position of authority under such circumstances."[25]

Long's message came in the aftermath of a fruitless campaign to keep Italy out of war in 1940. The department quietly pursued efforts to secure a separate peace, hoping to exploit the growing split between Mussolini and the royal circle. These attempts became meaningless after Roosevelt's call for Italy's unconditional surrender at Casablanca in January 1943, but Long and such colleagues as William Phillips (former under secretary of state and Long's successor at the Rome embassy) continued to fear that the Italian elites might face destruction after the war. Long had admired Mussolini and was deeply alarmed at the possibility of political anarchy and social unrest.

Long and Phillips were members of the tightly knit corps of professional foreign service officers who staffed the State Department's geographic desks in Washington and U.S. embassies abroad. The higher levels of the service had traditionally been the preserve of such well-born Republicans as Hugh Gibson, Joseph Grew, and Phillips himself. Those who gained acceptance from the outside, such as the Newark laborer's son James Clement Dunn (head of the Office of Western European Affairs after 1935 and later Ambassador to Italy) usually succeeded by adopting the outlook and manners of their socially superior colleagues.[26] The department's Eastern European Division (EE) formed a sort of corps within the corps and contained its intellectual elite. Many of these men, including Grew, Robert Kelley, Loy Henderson, and Elbridge Durbrow, served on the Bolshevik periphery before American recognition of the USSR. Most opposed dealing with the Russians and developed an implacable dislike for the Soviet regime. Those who staffed the new Moscow embassy after 1933 witnessed the awful spectacle of the great purge, an experience that profoundly marked George Kennan, Charles Bohlen, and Alexander Kirk. In 1937, EE merged with the Western European Division to form EUR, the Office of European Affairs. EE's anticommunist outlook prevailed within EUR. Its professional officers had no grand vision of the postwar world. For most of them, the world had been divided into two blocs since 1917. They were naturally sensitive to the interests of U.S. exporters and investors, but their concerns were primarily geopolitical. The purpose of diplomacy, as they saw it, was simply to maintain stability in areas of interest to the United States.

13

DIVISION AND ISOLATION

For Hull's dream of universal economic cooperation, Soviet expert George Kennan had a thinly veiled contempt. Kennan recalls, ". . . it seemed wildly unrealistic to expect that they [the Russians], with their jealously closed and controlled economy, and with a currency that had no status in world markets, with a wholly arbitrary and artificial price structure and a total monopoly of foreign trade, would be suitable part-ners for collaboration in the international monetary field, even if their purposes had been similar to ours, which they were not." During the Yalta Conference of February 1945, Kennan wrote his friend Charles Bohlen to urge that quixotic schemes for a United Nations Organization be scrapped "as quickly and quietly as possible," and that the division of Europe into U.S. and Russian spheres of influence be accepted as an accomplished fact. At least one study of the foreign service suggests that such opinions were not widely shared at the time. Views of the USSR and expectations for the future naturally varied with personal outlook and experience, as well as with the prevailing state of alliance relations. At times, the common wartime effort raised cautious hopes even among hardened EUR professionals for FDR's vision of postwar Allied collab-oration. Yet on the whole, an irreducible skepticism and hostility re-mained toward both the Soviet Union and "soft-headed" American pro-ponents of a universal liberal order. Those diplomats who had staked most on the possibility of postwar "ideological cooperation" were corre-spondingly embittered by Soviet behavior after 1944.[27]

The professional diplomatic corps was united on the other hand in its scorn for FDR's amateur diplomats and New Deal planners, and in the thirties the State Department had clashed frequently with such liberal Democrats and brain-trusters as Raymond Moley, Harry Hopkins, and Morgenthau. The liberal press in turn poured contempt on the Re-publican "white-spats boys," and Roosevelt infuriated the department by appointing his friend and financial backer Joseph Davies as ambas-sador to Moscow in the late thirties. Davies, a liberal Democrat and corporation lawyer, had orders to cultivate the Russians. To the profes-sionals, as Daniel Yergin observes, Davies was the "archtype of the fuzzy-minded American liberal who refused to see the truth as they saw it."[28]

However, each of the loose ideological-bureaucratic currents within the Roosevelt administration shared a common isolation from the real bases of power, the White House, the Congress, and the country at large. The declining influence of Wallace's social liberalism meant a gradual erosion of New Deal influence on foreign policy. Roosevelt dropped Wallace as his running mate in 1944 for the moderate conservative Harry

Truman. Wallace survived as Secretary of Commerce, but the New Deal was ebbing as FDR approached death in early 1945. *Fortune* magazine observed in March of that year, "The New Deal has lost its positive content. Its restless men have either deserted, or been purged or worn down by the war, or made cautious by being in office too long."[29] Even though the old idealism survived at the FEA and UNRRA, the New Deal establishment could not make good the loss of Hopkins and Morgenthau (and eventually of his powerful under secretary, Harry White) following the Truman transition. Morgenthau's successors, the Kentucky politician Fred Vinson and Truman's St. Louis crony, John Snyder, had less interest in foreign affairs. The treasury's international influence waned accordingly.

Hull's aspiring architects of liberal order were even more removed from political realities. The secretary's personal isolation from Roosevelt is well known. Even though the President had supported Hull's prized bilateral trade agreements program, Roosevelt himself had no deep personal commitment to free trade and acted as his own Secretary of State throughout the thirties. (He occasionally relied on Hull's bitter rival and – along with Phillips – one of his few friends in the Department, Under Secretary of State Sumner Welles.) At the outbreak of war, Roosevelt set up his own war cabinet, including Leahy, Marshall, Wallace, Morgenthau, and Hopkins, and his own team of personal diplomats, including Davies, Taylor, and Averell Harriman.[30] An acute first-hand observer recalled that Hull's isolation "led directly to the theoretical and unreal nature of the State Department's – and hence the Government's – thinking on postwar problems." Of Hull's planning committees, one of which produced the above-cited report, "The Treatment of Italy," Dean Acheson later noted, ". . . I cannot remember one of these meetings. Paging through the printed report, the whole effort, except for two results, seems to have been a singularly sterile one, uninspired by gifts either of insight or prophecy." The two positive results, in his view, were the writing of the UN Charter and the foreign policy re-education of the isolationist Republican Senator Arthur Vandenberg of Michigan, who was carefully cultivated by the State Department.[31]

Throughout the war, Hull's planners were isolated from the field. The occupation of Southern Italy in 1943 provided the first testing ground for State Department schemes, but a joint Anglo-American bureaucracy controlled day-to-day policy and subordinated economic rehabilitation to the imperative of "military necessity." Everyone in Washington backed department attempts to restore local autonomy and normal diplomatic relations with the Italians. The British, however, had no sympathy for their former enemy and blocked U.S. efforts at each stage. Although determined to win Italian-American votes in the November 1944 election, Roosevelt had more pressing concerns and turned to Italian matters only occasionally. As the military occupation regime was gradually dismantled after the war, the State Department came to assume chief responsibility for U.S. policy. Italian civil affairs had become a dreadful headache by 1945, and the military were more than happy to relinquish responsibilities to their respective governments. However, the transition proved fitful and confused. Anglo-American bickering and bureaucratic delays created a near vacuum of policy in Italy during the crucial summer of 1945.

Clayton and his colleagues soon faced other unwelcome developments, this time on the domestic front. Powerful segments of U.S. opinion had opposed the European war until Pearl Harbor and had no commitment to European recovery in 1945. Important sectors of the American political economy – labor, agriculture, and such traditional industries as textiles – were suspicious of free trade and foreign aid. The congressional elections of 1944 and 1946 reflected the strength of isolationism, protectionism, and fiscal conservatism, nor was it a simple matter to engage U.S. business in a common effort abroad. Hull's vision foresaw an ample role for private investment in postwar reconstruction, but such ventures were unlikely while political uncertainty prevailed. Moreover, because of its concern to extend free trade and equality of investment opportunity to Eastern Europe and elsewhere in the world, the department was bound to resist parochial corporate efforts to dominate areas under direct U.S. control. Clashes would occur in Italy where such potential U.S. investors as TWA and IT&T tried to evade the department's rules.

Without financial leverage, the State Department was poorly equipped to promote economic recovery and adherence to its liberal designs. Its only available source of funds during the immediate postwar months was the $3.5 billion lending authority of the U.S. Export–Import Bank. By January 1946, the bank had loaned or committed $1.6 billion to France, Belgium, and the Netherlands, leaving $1.9 billion to satisfy worldwide needs until the creation, anticipated for 1947, of the International Monetary Fund's Bank for Reconstruction and Development. In early 1946, $1 billion of the remainder was "set aside" for a possible loan to the USSR. Such was the situation when the Italian embassy in Washington asked for $940 million in February 1946. The problems involved in gaining new appropriations became clear during the congressional battle over the British loan. In the meantime, it fell to an interdepartmental committee, the National Advisory Council on International Monetary and Financial Affairs (NAC) to evaluate loan requests and make recommendations to the President. As State Department representative, Clayton had to contend with the conflicting views of his Treasury, Commerce, Federal Reserve, and Export–Import Bank colleagues.[32]

Clayton's colleagues, the foreign service professionals, had meanwhile been forced to conduct a bureaucratic holding action throughout the war. Using such allies as Admiral Leahy in the White House, they made occasional forays into the realm of high policy. James Dunn cultivated Hull's successor, the ineffectual Edward Stettinius. When the department was reorganized following Stettinius's arrival, Dunn became assistant secretary for political affairs, in charge of all geographic areas except Latin America. The archconservative Grew became under secretary of state, and the Soviet service veteran Alexander Kirk headed the new American embassy at Rome. Kirk, according to *Fortune* magazine, fitted the old school mold – "foppish, intelligent, and very rich."[33]

EUR's fortunes seemed on the rise as the war ended in Europe and power passed from FDR to Truman. The new president was unversed in European politics and inclined to listen to State Department advice.[34] However, the appointment of James Byrnes as secretary of state in July was a mixed blessing. Dunn became Byrnes's deputy and advisor for the work of the Council of Foreign Ministers.[35] As under secretary (and acting secretary in Byrnes's frequent absences), however, Byrnes appointed Assistant Secretary for Congressional Relations Dean Acheson to replace Grew. Acheson's Tory background suited EUR, but as a Democrat and protégé of Felix Frankfurter, he would never be a member of the trusted inner circle. In alliance with Clayton, Acheson soon clashed with the foreign service professionals when he tried to supplant the intelligence and research activities of their geographic branches. Byrnes himself was a more serious problem. As a senior figure in the Democratic Party, he considered himself independent of both the State Department and the president. Worse still, he seemed determined to pursue FDR's policy of accommodation with the Russians.[36]

INCHOATE ALLIANCES

It is clear that none of the loose currents who sought to define the American approach to postwar European problems possessed the necessary weight to prevail over its Washington rivals. None therefore could expect to have much effect on the events that rapidly unfolded in Italy after April 1945. Each sought public, congressional, and executive support for its line of approach. The success of those efforts depended in large part on domestic political trends beyond the influence of the Washington bureaucrats. In the meantime, each current naturally tended to promote those Italian forces whose outlook and approach seemed to correspond most closely to its own. Success there depended in large part on the inherent strengths and weaknesses of the Italian forces themselves. In traditional Italian fashion, moreover, those competing forces sought to

17

acquire from outside strength they lacked at home in order to consolidate their local positions. Thus, the story of U.S. policy in Italy on one hand is about competition for power and influence within both countries. On the other, it concerns mutual attempts to establish privileged relationships across the Atlantic.

Certain alliances were apparent. The Italian liberal economists shared Hull's enthusiasm for free trade and the release of market forces. Their views carried weight at a time when the recovery of production was almost universally seen as the first priority. Their dissent had been harmless to the regime, but their ideas became synonymous with anti-fascism in the minds of many and found new esteem in a moment of deep middle-class reaction against state interference. The liberal economists had no mass political base, and the Italian Liberal Party (PLI) to which most belonged had little electoral support. Yet the liberal approach to production and monetary stabilization suited the tactical purposes of private business who feared the interventionism of the left.

Aspiring New Deal reformers and would-be Italian planners, on the other hand, agreed that the state must play a central role in economic recovery and reform. The forces of *programmazione* also had great appeal because of their association with the resistance and hoped to exploit a widespread desire for social change engendered by fascism and the war. Critics have charged that the planners had little sense of technical problems, basic goals, or available instruments.[37] However, a series of practical measures (price, credit, and foreign exchange controls) were supported by experts of each of the major political parties.

The chief concern of the State Department's professional corps was to defeat the left and ensure a stable, prowestern Italy. Although badly discredited in 1945, the department's prewar interlocutors maneuvered to survive. Conservative forces were tacitly supported by the great mass of middle-class Italians, anxious for a return to normal rather than some radical solution to the postwar crisis. The basic advantage of conservative and middle-class groups derived, paradoxically, from Italy's prostrate and divided condition after 1943, from the remote but harrowing possibility of economic collapse and communist takeover in an area of strategic importance and U.S. domestic concern. Italy's historical experience suggested that relative weakness and isolation could be parlayed into political leverage and an external *punto d' appoggio,* or point of support vis-à-vis local enemies and vindictive European rivals.

POLITICAL STALEMATE

It was soon apparent that America's optimistic visions bore limited relevance to the practical tasks facing Italy during the early postwar period.

18

Few in the United States understood the Italian economy or the more immediate political-economic problems and possibilities in the aftermath of 1943. The Hullian and interventionist New Deal currents coexisted uneasily, producing tension and confusion during the crucial years, 1945–46. More important, their lack of domestic support denied them the political authority and financial leverage essential to their Italian plans. Their potential interlocutors in Italy, meanwhile, were also isolated or divided. The grand visions of both classical liberals and economic planners corresponded only temporarily and in part to the tactical requirements and broader strategies of the mass parties who dominated Italian politics after 1945. By late 1946, the problems of production and inflation threatened Italy with a serious financial and economic crisis. Problems of structural readjustment had been largely ignored. The reasons for this impasse were essentially political and psychological. They had to do with the incoherent policies of the major parties and the political stalemate that emerged in the wake of the Fascist regime.

The early postwar economic policy of the Italian Communist Party has been endlessly scrutinized and debated. The PCI controlled the Finance Ministry from December 1944 until February 1947. The party frequently called for special taxes combined with a currency conversion, public works, and nationalization of such key industries as electricity. At no point, however, did the PCI make specific economic reforms the price of collaboration. Through its power in the Italian General Confederation of Labor (CGIL), the party tended to suppress rather than encourage the desire for radical change within the working class. Economic reform was a secondary priority, as the party's leader Palmiro Togliatti said many times.[38] Instead, the party turned its attention and considerable energies to political and institutional questions, to defeating the monarchy, writing of a democratic constitution, and maintaining unity within the resistance coalition.

There were many reasons for this choice, and some have noted that the PCI should be blamed for not doing what it did not want to do.[39] The party emerged from a long period of clandestinity and resistance at a time when the country was occupied by American and British troops. Its leaders aimed to ensure the PCI's survival and growth in this hostile environment and to demonstrate the party's vocation and sense of responsibility as a governing force. The communists feared a resurgence of fascism and sought to cultivate those classes – small property owners and farmers – who had formed the mass base of the regime. However, even though they saw no alternative between an economic line that gave ample space to private initiative, and Soviet-style planning, which was clearly impossible, their strident lip service to a more radical program won them the profound mistrust of the groups they aimed to reassure.[40]

Introduction and overview

The economic policy of Christian Democracy was a similarly confusing and incoherent mixture of liberal and interventionist elements. Like Togliatti, De Gasperi sought to appeal to a wide spectrum of social groups and economic interests. When he became prime minister in December 1945, De Gasperi chose the orthodox liberal economist, Corbino, as his minister of the treasury. Dismantling controls and blocking special taxes served to cement the DC's ties to large industry, small land holders, and urban *commercianti*. The radical factions within DC meanwhile demanded state intervention and social investments.

Both parties sought broad social and political alliances. Neither had the electoral strength to govern alone. The resulting early postwar coalitions were a recipe for debilitating compromise and strife. Each party pressed home the claims of its constituencies for higher wages, political prices, and industrial subsidies. The much-vaunted private entrepreneurs, meanwhile, used the liberalization of trade and financial controls to make quick killings on the stock and commodity markets. Wary of the left, they funneled profits into safer havens abroad. By late 1946, Italy was in the throes of financial panic and open conflict in the streets. The political deadlock permitted no clear approach to the now urgent matter of monetary stabilization.

New Deal and Hullian-inspired U.S. officials were equipped neither intellectually nor politically to deal with the Italian stalemate and its financial-economic consequences. The world view of UNRRA planners drew its lessons from the Anglo-Saxon experience of the previous decade. Their well-intentioned middle way to economic reconstruction served only to reinforce the muddled approach of the Italian coalition. At a time of huge government deficits, mounting inflation, and severe foreign exchange constraints, UNRRA encouraged new welfare projects and controls on the dynamic export sectors. Liberal economics ministers and independent-minded businessmen quite naturally resisted. UNRRA found itself isolated and abandoned in Italy and at home. Hull's ambitions programs suffered a similar fate. Proposals for a return to free trade and convertibility bore little relevance to the needs of a bankrupt nation reeling from war and political disorder. Visions of a universal liberal order were clouded by British Empire resistance at the Geneva tariff conference in early 1947 and obscured altogether by the iron curtain that settled across Europe in the ensuing months.

THE POSTWAR SOLUTION

Both Hullian and social liberal idealism gradually gave way to a more hard-headed and compelling foreign policy whose basic concern with Italy was political and strategic. Conservative congressmen, the State

20

Department's Office of European Affairs, and other executive officials sobered by early postwar events recognized the utility of economic growth and modest social reform. They also grasped more readily than their economist colleagues the fundamentally political and psychological nature of the Italian crisis after 1945. No capitalist economic strategy could take hold until the stalemate had been broken by effective leadership. Such arguments not only corresponded to Italian facts, they also helped rally a skeptical American public behind an unprecedented financial commitment to European recovery. From the shambles of their original postwar program, American leaders fashioned a new policy based on anticommunism and massive U.S. aid. By mid-1947, the European continent was divided into Soviet and American blocs. With Prime Minister De Gasperi's expulsion of the socialists and communists from the coalition in May of that year, the Italian situation aptly mirrored the broader state of affairs. As the only major non-Marxist force uncompromised by Fascism, Christian Democracy (DC) gradually came to occupy the crucial terrain between a threatened and disunited bourgeoisie and its single source of outside aid. In the process, the DC became indispensable to both sides and achieved its remarkable internal influence and autonomy. De Gasperi committed his government to a passive, even servile, pro-American foreign policy, while guaranteeing the left's exile from the corridors of power. At the same time, the Christian Democrats capitalized on their privileged U.S. connection to deliver and distribute material resources, becoming the key mediators and administrators within the loosely constituted and politically diverse coalition.

The new departure did not mark an end to the misplaced hopes and self-deceptions of the early postwar years. To be sure, members of the victorious center-right coalition of April 1948 were more than ready to support those U.S. initiatives that served to consolidate their local position: monetary stabilization, European integration, and defense of Western interests in the Mediterranean. But once in power, they could afford to respond to outside advice and pressure in a calculated, selective way. The origins of this informal bargain can be traced to the earliest days of the postwar period. U.S. officials came to see the need for a more interventionist, coherent, and generous Italian policy thanks in part to a local political class that astutely emphasized the precariousness of its own position, while knowing in the end far better than its would-be American mentors how to manage the practical business of stabilization and recovery.

2

Wartime diplomacy

Three basic facts shaped the events from 1943 to 1945. First, the invasion of Italy was a joint Anglo-American affair. Second, the expectation that the battle would be brief proved a serious miscalculation. Third, the campaign that followed brought economic dislocation and misery with which the Allied military authorities were totally unprepared to deal. The U.S. military had opposed the Italian campaign as an unnecessary diversion of resources, and the decision to invade represented, in part, a compromise to win British agreement to the cross-channel invasion of 1944. Hopes that Rome could be captured quickly vanished almost immediately, and the Allies found themselves bogged down in a long and costly operation.

The progress of the war determined the phases of the occupation. The Allies occupied Sicily in July 1943 and attacked the mainland at Salerno in September. By October, the front had stabilized along the so-called Gustav line, running across the peninsula 200 kilometers south of Rome. This line defined the area under Allied control until the breakthrough at Cassino in May 1944 and the capture of Rome in June. The isolation of the southern third of the country had important long-term consequences. Because of its rapid liberation, the South remained outside the resistance experience, and the Gustav line established a separate economic unit in the poorest area of the country.

Allied political and economic policy was governed by the principle of military necessity. The Allied command thus imposed the Armistice of September 1943. Its terms reduced Italy to near total economic and political dependence, authorizing the Allies to exploit local resources without compensation according to the whim of the military authorities. Military necessity also dictated the decision to rule through the Italian authorities who had succeeded Mussolini in July 1943, rather than to

22

institute a direct administration. At the urging of Churchill and the American commander, General Eisenhower, Roosevelt agreed to recognize the king and his prime minister, Marshal Pietro Badoglio, for reasons of political and military expediency.

The political opposition in the South (embodied in the six-party CLN) was co-opted in early 1944. The six parties had pressed for the king's abdication and for creation of a new popular government. Following the Soviet recognition of Badoglio and the return of Togliatti from Moscow in March 1944, the six-party *giunta* accepted a basic compromise. Each party would be represented in a new cabinet, with Badoglio as premier. The king would cede his powers to a lord lieutenant (his son Umberto) after the capture of Rome. In return, the parties promised to shelve the so-called institutional question until the Italian people could decide the issue. (The understanding was that the decision would be made by a popularly elected constituent assembly. In the end, the Allies and Christian Democrats pressed successfully for a popular referendum.) The Allies obliged each successive government to renew the pledge not to discuss the fate of the monarchy. The new government also agreed to postpone basic social reform until the end of the hostilities. The Socialists and Action Party fought these arrangements, but they had little choice but to go along. The political settlement of March 1944 institutionalized a stalemate among the resistance forces that was to continue well after April 1945.[1]

A harsh armistice and indirect rule made obvious sense from a military standpoint. In accepting military necessity as the basic guideline however, the Roosevelt administration doomed earlier hopes for an anti-Fascist house-cleaning and social renewal. Both the president and Morgenthau had called for a serious purge in Italy after the embarrassing Darlan affair in North Africa, but circumstances permitted much of the old bureaucracy to survive. Fascist prefects were removed, but their lieutenants were usually the only available replacements. It was also clear that Washington officials would be effectively excluded from occupation policy. Even though civilians in the United States and Britain remained the final arbiters of high policy, day-to-day powers lay firmly in the hands of an Allied military bureaucracy. The chain of command extended from the Combined British and U.S. Chiefs of Staff (CCS) and their advisory body on nonmilitary matters, the Combined Civil Affairs Committee (CCAC), to the Supreme Allied Commander, Mediterranean Theatre, or SACMED (General Sir Harold Alexander) located at Allied Force Headquarters (AFHQ) at Caserta. The Supreme Commander was designated President of the Allied Control Commission (ACC), the vast, top-heavy bureaucracy created to enforce the Armistice. The deputy president, or chief commissioner (Admiral Ellery Stone, USNR), acted as executive officer of the

ACC. To complicate matters further, SACMED had his own advisory staff on occupation matters, known as the G–5 or Civil Affairs Section of AFHQ.

Both Hullian liberals at the State Department and New Deal interventionists concentrated in the Foreign Economic Administration (FEA) were hard put to influence Italian policy. The FEA administered the military's small aid program in the occupied areas, but its officials in Italy were under military command. The State Department was also isolated from the centers of power. A major U.S. objective was to revise the armistice and thus restore greater Italian autonomy. U.S. officials correctly saw such a revision as essential to any systematic approach to economic recovery by the Italians themselves and also as a way for civilians in Washington to make their wishes felt through traditional diplomatic channels. A second U.S. goal was to increase aid to the occupied areas, lest postwar rehabilitation be further complicated and delayed.

Due largely to the British, these efforts met with constant frustration. Roosevelt had rejected Churchill's suggestion that the British be "Senior Partner" in Italy, but early joint decisions tended to serve British rather than American purposes. The United States had neither long-standing political interests in the Mediterranean nor a clear Italian policy. Despite their longer-term weakness, the British had both in 1943. They aimed to keep Italy weak and dependent and to remove once and for all the Italian threat to their Mediterranean communications. The harsh armistice served these purposes admirably, and the British opposed revisions permitting greater Italian political autonomy or military participation during the war. The British also aimed, at least at first, to keep in power discredited forces who would be unable to resist British demands on the day of reckoning. Thus, indirect rule also suited British goals. Moreover, unlike the Americans, the British sent able and experienced people to serve in the joint Anglo-American bureaucracy. Harold MacMillan proved the outstanding example.

Finally, a complicated relationship emerged between the Allies and the Italian coalition. Without substantial aid, the Italian political authorities preferred to resist well-intentioned U.S. efforts to saddle them with the economic and financial powers surrendered in 1943. Such powers were essential to any prompt response to inflation and to the restoration of local sovereignty and control. However, the return of financial responsibilities also entailed Italian acknowledgement of liability for the vast amounts of paper currency introduced by the Allied armies and for other occupation costs. None of the local forces wished to do so, and the Allies were reluctant to press them for fear of undermining the feeble alliance. The first important Italian–American negotiations after 1943 concerned the questions of military currency and occupation costs. The episode provides a case study in the futility of U.S. economic diplomacy during the wartime period. The unhappy legacy of the occupation would plague U.S. policy throughout the long transition that began in April 1945.

OCCUPATION POLICY BEFORE HYDE PARK

According to guidelines hammered out before the invasion of Sicily, economic policy would promote local self-sufficiency and use normal commercial channels where possible. War materials were to be requisitioned, trade and prices controlled. An Allied Financial Agency (AFA) was created to control local banks and issue Allied military currency (AMlire). The AMlire served to pay troops, buy local goods and services, and make loans to local authorities. Under to the armistice, AMlire were an obligation of the Italian government. The AMlire exchange rate was set at 100 lire to the dollar, 400 to the pound sterling. The official prewar rate had been 19 lire to the dollar, and the Allies were well aware that the new rate substantially undervalued the Italian currency. (Comparing U.S. and Italian inflation rates, Pasquale Saraceno has calculated that the dollar was worth around 50 lire in 1944). However, this low rate represented a compromise with the British, who had sought an even more punitive exchange.[2]

The Allies quickly confronted problems with which they were totally unequipped to deal. The fighting had seriously dislocated agricultural and industrial distribution systems, and the occupied areas were completely cut off from their traditional sources of raw materials and remittances. A fundamental problem arose from Allied policy itself. According to the official historians, "The Army restricted its supply program to food, medical and sanitary items, and other classes of supplies *necessary to prevent disease and unrest from interfering with military operations.* Seriously needed supplies in other categories, it was presumed, would be obtained by civilian agencies, though as matters developed, it was difficult or impossible for such agencies to secure from supply and shipping authorities allocation over and above those certified as militarily necessary" (emphasis added).[3] Basic reconstruction policy was set out in a directive from Allied Force Headquarters (AFHQ) to the Allied Control Commission (ACC): ". . . No industrial rehabilitation will be undertaken in liberated Italy which is not:

(A) Absolutely essential to military needs whilst the war is going on, and
(B) Essential to minimum civilian needs of individual territories."[4]

The appalling consequences of these policies were reported to Washington by Adlai Stevenson in early 1944. Stevenson, a special assistant to the secretary of the navy, led a three-week fact-finding mission to Sicily and Southern Italy in late 1943. He found the Naples headquarters in a state of "organizational transition and confusion," a perhaps charitable assessment in view of the legendary chaos and corruption that characterized the Allied administration of the city. Food distribution was complicated by rampant hoarding and black marketeering so that the current ration of bread in Naples was 100 grams per day – well below the original allotment of 300 per day. Hospitals and flour mills had barely enough coal and petroleum. No coal had been distributed for industry or civilian homes. More than half of Stevenson's report was devoted to the sorry state of Southern industry. In Naples, the departing Germans had methodically destroyed machinery, power plants, and other utilities. Stevenson saw that the occupation authorities were totally unprepared for industrial rehabilitation. Even if agricultural self-sufficiency could be attained, large masses of industrial workers would remain unemployed.

The most urgent problem was inflation. Even though the expansion of the money supply had begun long before the invasion, the lion's share of increasing note circulation in the South after 1943 was Allied paper currency.[5] Although convenient for the average G.I., the rate of 100 lire to the dollar was a "surprise and a shock" to Italians and had "encouraged the buying of goods and the raising of prices." Stevenson's conclusion was pessimistic: "As long as the present rate of military expenditures continues in Italy . . . the lira has no future. There is no prospect and no plan for its stabilization."[6]

Reports from Stevenson and other American observers struck a responsive chord at the FEA, where New Deal–inspired officials were eager to promote recovery and reform on newly liberated soil.[7] The War Department was more than ready to transfer relief and rehabilitation to civilian departments (Secretary Stimson wrote Hull to that effect in June 1944), but the FEA had few funds at its disposal. Supply and shipping shortages prevented any immediate response to the plight of Southern Italy. The FEA was forced to hold up the transfer of responsibility until summer 1944, when it was hoped the newly created United Nations Relief and Rehabilitation Administration would do the job.[8]

In the meantime, FEA field officers assigned to the ACC's economic section bridled under the ironclad formula of military necessity. They clashed openly with their military colleagues in the ACC, who barraged the War Department with complaints of FEA disloyalty and political unreliability. The ACC's problems included the high turnover and simple incompetence among its top officials. Attempts to find a suitable and permanent vice president of the economic section (this position had been allotted to the United States by Anglo-American agreement) were frustrated by the White House, which made a series of short-term political appointments, such as William O'Dwyer of New York.[9]

The State Department was even more isolated than the FEA. It had no embassy in Italy and little leverage in Washington. As part of a so-called Combined Liberated Areas Committee (CLAC), the department began discussions with the FEA and treasury to formulate a concrete U.S. policy for occupied Italy. These discussions bore fruit only as the November 1944 presidential election approached. Roosevelt finally responded to public outcry over the state of Southern Italy by pressing the British to accept parts of a CLAC proposal for more aid and other concessions.

The new approach was contained in the joint Anglo-American declaration at Hyde Park, New York, of September 26, 1944. The "New Deal for Italy" promised more food, transport, and industrial rehabilitation.[10] The ACC personnel were to be completely civilian, then reduced to advisory status. Italy would receive official diplomatic recognition, and normal commercial relations would gradually be restored. To British dismay, FDR made several additional, unilateral announcements shortly before the elections, promising an increase in the bread ration and the extension of dollar credits to offset the net AMlire expenditures of U.S. troops in Italy.

The Hyde Park Declaration was an apparent victory for U.S. civilian officials, long preoccupied with the pro-British bias of occupation policy. The State Department promptly recognized the government of Ivanoe Bonomi and appointed Alexander Kirk to establish the new American embassy in Rome.[11] However, the continuing impotence of the State Department and FEA was clear during the prolonged Anglo-American squabbling and bureaucratic confusion that followed the September announcement. It was simple enough to drop the word *Control* from the ACC, but the British were offended and embarrassed by the American departure and delayed its implementation in the field. With some reason, they considered the New Deal an electoral ploy that only demonstrated the "contrast between American magnanimity and British austerity."[12] AC officers continued to interfere in the day-to-day activities of the Italian Government, and commodity and shipping shortages prevented any improvement in material conditions.

THE QUINTIERI–MATTIOLI MISSION

The Hyde Park Declaration nonetheless set the stage for the first attempt to resolve the tangled questions of financial autonomy and occupation costs. The troop pay credits gave the Italians a precious pool of foreign exchange for the first time, and Roosevelt's gesture seemed to suggest that

27

the entire cost of occupation might eventually be assumed by the Allies. According to the secret terms of the armistice (article 23), all currency issued by the Allies was an Italian government liability. Italy was also subject to the more comprehensive and punitive article 33, which authorized the Allies to requisition local goods and services at the Italian treasury's expense. The Italians refused to admit either obligation.[13]

The Hyde Park Declaration put the Italians in a delicate but not, they reckoned, altogether unpromising position. Financial experts were eager to consolidate AMlire with regular lire notes in order to bring the issue of all currency under a single Italian authority. At the same time, or so they reasoned, chances for an eventual reimbursement of occupation costs were probably better if the Allies continued to issue and spend a separate currency for the time being. Combining issue under Italian authority would be tantamount to accepting the terms of article 23. The Italian government feared the domestic political repercussions of such a step and preferred to conceal the armistice terms in order to avoid a possible flight from the lira. The Italians also realized that such political arguments were useful in sidetracking Allied attempts to force them to accept their obligations, pending the arrival of greater financial aid. Allied officials for the most part saw through the Italian tactics. Most, however, saw little choice but to concede the point for fear of provoking a financial panic. Thus, the armistice restrictions themselves became an instrument for extracting Allied concessions.

This became clear in mid-1944, when the Allies proposed to change the payment procedures for Italian goods and services. According to existing arrangements, the Allies took local resources without payment and the Italian government later reimbursed private suppliers. In August, G–5 (civil affairs section) AFHQ suggested setting up a lira account with the Italian government, which the Allies would use to pay local suppliers directly, but the Italian government violently objected. The AC reported that "the political effect of the proposed lira account would be 'disastrous' according to the Prime Minister. . . . Bonomi also fears the effect of additional deficit financing on public confidence."[14] In brief, the Italians wished to keep occupation costs an open question and resisted making direct payments to the Allies. The AC reluctantly accepted Bonomi's objections, and the plan was abandoned.

In the meantime, the Italians decided to test Roosevelt's apparently generous mood to obtain both more aid and vital changes in the occupation regime. If greater dollar credits were forthcoming, resuming control of their finances would not be the political disaster that Bonomi purported to fear. Seizing on a casual American suggestion that the two sides discuss economic issues, the Italian government dispatched its first high-level diplomatic mission to Washington in November 1944.

28

The Quintieri–Mattioli mission

The head of the delegation was Baron Quinto Quintieri, elderly president of the Banca di Calabria and a former finance minister. The real strategist and negotiator was Raffaele Mattioli, managing director of the Banca Commerciale and a leading figure in Milanese business and cultural circles. The choice of Mattioli was obvious from the Italian point of view. He had long matched wits with the best financial minds of his day and usually prevailed. Even though his Bank had been intimately involved in the regime's finances, Mattioli had kept his reputation as a political independent and was a current backer of the Action Party. He was accompanied by three young officials, all destined for prominence on the postwar Italian scene: Mario Morelli, later president of the Confindustria; Enrico Cuccia, future head of the parastatal Mediobanca and, like Mattioli, gray eminence of Lombard finance; and Egidio Ortona, eventual Italian ambassador to the United States. Ortona would become economic counselor and an indispensable fixture at the Washington embassy after the mission's departure in March 1945. The Italians were armed with full powers to negotiate loans, armistice revisions, and whatever other concessions they could obtain. They also intended to sound out U.S. private banks, where Mattioli was well-connected from the prewar days.

At the first meeting with State Department officials on November 10, 1944, Mattioli promptly asked for dollar credits for all AMlire, to be linked to centralization of all currency issue in the Bank of Italy. On November 14, the Italians presented a twenty-point agenda dealing mainly with AMlire offsets and credits for those goods and services provided by the Italian government as part of the war effort.[15] The Italians were quickly disabused of their initial hopes for more aid. The State Department realized at once that the mission sought far more than exploratory discussions and was somewhat taken aback. Meanwhile, Mattioli's brilliant reputation proved something of a liability. Harry White would chide him for the Commerciale's dealings with Nazi Germany. The U.S. embassy in Rome later described him as a "political opportunist," which he no doubt was.[16]

Mattioli's arrival in the United States had also been very badly timed. The mission coincided exactly with the Hull–Stettinius transition and reorganization of November–December, 1944. The newly appointed assistant secretary for economic affairs, William Clayton, was not briefed on the negotiations until January 2, 1945. According to an AC officer accompanying the Italians, the mission "encountered a profound disinterest" on the part of Assistant Secretary Acheson.[17] More seriously, the mission coincided with a major political crisis at home. During the fall of 1944, tensions within the six-party coalition erupted into a series of clashes on land reform, the anti-Fascist purge, and the relative powers of the CLN and the monarchy. Bonomi resigned in late November, stranding Quintieri and Mattioli in diplomatic limbo. The crisis also produced an open clash between the Allies themselves. The British vetoed the inclusion of Count Carlo Sforza, a noted antimonarchist, as foreign minister in the new cabinet. Sforza had spent the early years of the war in the United States. He had close ties to the State Department and was a political associate of Quintieri and Mattioli. The department publicly denounced the British, but the Italians were in no position to defy the veto. Bonomi formed a new cabinet in mid-December, but the Socialists and Action Party refused to participate. The impression of rife instability at home did little to bolster the credibility and bargaining power of Quintieri and Mattioli.

The Italians got more attention and apparent sympathy from the Treasury Department, where Morgenthau and Harry White appeared to greet them at the first meeting on November 16. It was clear, however, that the treasury was unable to meet the basic Italian demands for total AMlire and supply offsets, or for reconstruction loans. Treasury officials reminded the Italians that FDR had promised credits equal to net troop pay alone and that final responsibility for those credits would be determined by the eventual peace settlement.[18] In the meantime, state and treasury agreed that no real concessions were possible. "Nevertheless," Stettinius wrote Morgenthau, "I am sure you will appreciate the political importance, particularly at this stage of affairs, of our not allowing the mission to return to Italy without some accomplishment." The departments decided to give the Italians the information they desired and to support centralization of all currency issue under Italian authority. The State Department worried that even these modest steps would "cause trouble with the British," who would have to agree before anything could be done.[19]

For the Italians, such "concessions" were essentially useless without additional dollar credits. The Bank of Italy would not assume the AMlire or sole issuing authority without dollar backing. Allied procurement costs could not be assumed by the Italian budget without a dollar counterpart. The U.S. position represented a failure of the Italian ploy to link resumption of financial autonomy to more credits. An Italian Note Verbale of November 21 pointed out that available funds were "so scant that they will hardly suffice to meet the most urgent and essential requirements . . . , let alone actual rehabilitation needs."[20]

On January 9, 1945, a new figure on the diplomatic scene made the strongest denunciation yet heard of articles 23 and 33. Following the Sforza veto, Bonomi chose the Christian Democratic leader, Alcide De Gasperi, as foreign minister. In a message to the U.S. embassy in Rome, De

Gasperi warned the Americans that the financial situation contained "dangerous germs of distrust, which, should they develop due to unforseen circumstances, could make the slow but continual inflation degenerate into a monetary disaster which might produce incalculable consequences."[21]

Quintieri and Mattioli had arrived with wildly unrealistic expectations, in near total ignorance of the local scene. Thanks to new-found friends, they learned to maneuver with greater ease in the exotic world of official Washington. The mission established close ties with a group of Italian refugees, including Peter Treves, Bruno Luzzato, George Tesoro, and Bruno Foa. All had left Italy after the Fascist racial laws and become middle-level officials in the U.S. bureaucracy. Foa had both an expert knowledge of Italian finance and firm grasp of the local bureaucracy. He eventually became a consultant to the Italian technical delegation (Deltec), the Italian government purchasing agent in Washington. Another valuable connection was Oscar Cox, a Washington lawyer, insider, and deputy administrator of the FEA. Cox had written the lend-lease legislation before joining the agency that administered the program. After his resignation in late 1945, he would be retained practically full time by Deltec and the Italian embassy.[22]

After two fruitless months, the mission took Cox's advice to seek a lend-lease or reciprocal aid program of from $300 to 400 million. The FEA in turn tried to drum up support for the Italian request. Cox's boss, FEA Administrator Leo Crowley, told the State Department that the Hyde Park Declaration supply program would have "disastrous effects for the Italians and dangerous repercussions for the foreign policy of the United States."[23] Clayton had little love for the FEA, a rival agency that controlled millions in congressional appropriations. He also had his own good reasons for favoring an Italian lend-lease agreement. Since early in the war, American economic diplomacy had been based on lend-lease master agreements with allied countries. According to article VII of the standard agreement, the United States and the recipient government undertook "to cooperate in formulating a program designed to promote expanded worldwide production, exchange, and consumption of goods, the elimination of all forms of discriminatory treatment in international commerce, and the reduction of tariffs and other barriers."[24] Mattioli had long since grasped both the importance of article VII as well as Clayton's growing weight in the economic bureaucracy. Again and again, the Italians stressed their interest in United States–Italian trade and participation in the Bretton Woods Agreements. In its final memo to the mission, the department proposed an exchange of notes at some future date on the basic goals of article VII. But without lend-lease funds, this was meaningless talk. Whatever their interest in an open trading system,

31

the Italians would not bind themselves to article VII without material concessions.[25]

In the end, both sides abandoned the lend-lease request. On March 27, Clayton informed the newly arrived Italian ambassador, Alberto Tarchiani, that the plan had no future. Even though some people within the administration may have opposed it on basic principle – lend-lease was designed for Allied countries – the main reason for the decision was lack of congressional support. Clayton and the FEA were blocked by a parsimonious congress that had little sympathy for a country recently at war with the United States. Humanitarian arguments or appeals to Italy's effort on behalf of the Allies did not do much to change their minds, an early lesson for those who sought a more generous American financial commitment to European recovery.[26]

The Italians left Washington in mid-March, returning directly to Rome since the British had refused to see them. They carried paper concessions, the end of the Allied Financial Agency on Italian territory, return of control over external financial transactions, and promised steps to centralize the issue of all currency under the authority of the Bank of Italy. Each item was meaningless and unacceptable without more financial aid. Each item also required British approval in the meantime. U.S. officials were equally frustrated. Cox and Clayton had failed to deliver lend-lease. An agreement on mutual unconditional most-favored-nation status contained in the State Department's final memo to the mission was a dead issue at the time. Italy had neither goods to sell nor ships to transport them. Its external transactions remained under AC control, its pre-1943 assets in the United States and Britain frozen pending the final financial reckoning.[27]

THE IMPASSE CONTINUES

In January 1945, Democratic law professor Eugene Rostow called the situation in Italy "an object lesson in the inadequacy of our policy for dealing with the economic problems of the transition period. . . ." The United States had "arrived in Italy at a point of utter bankruptcy of policy."[28] The Quintieri–Mattioli mission's unhappy conclusion in March was a defeat for both the FEA and the State Department and confirmed the profound weakness of U.S. foreign economic policy as the end of the war approached. Following the failure to secure a lend-lease program, the FEA and War Department agreed on a stop-gap arrangement to extend aid beyond the strict disease and unrest formula. The FEA would ask Congress for a special additional $100 million as part of its 1946 lend-lease appropriation. The War Department agreed to support the request before congress and announced the end of its own limited program as of August 31, 1945. The FEA had little hope that this sum would satisfy Italian needs before the major UNRRA program began in 1946.[29]

Washington officials faced a two-front battle. In November 1944, the State Department had appointed Dean Acheson as assistant secretary for congressional relations. Acheson was a gifted lawyer with long political experience. His ability to manage public and congressional opinion would make him a formidable advocate during the spring of 1947. However, congress was by and large indifferent to the challenges of world leadership in early 1945. Despite Acheson's persistent lobbying, the department gained little sympathy on Capitol Hill. Dealing with the British was an equally thankless task. On January 31, 1945, the Combined Civil Affairs Committee (CCAC) of the Combined British and American Chiefs of Staff (CCS) issued a directive to the AC, designed to implement the Hyde Park concessions of September 1944.[30] However, the return of financial responsibilities was conspicuously absent, and British officials made it clear that they did not intend "to dig into the British pocket in order to assist the Italians." If credits were not possible, it was perfectly logical to oppose the return of financial powers, on the same grounds advanced by the Italians themselves at the time of the lira account proposal. Such a move, according to the British, would "affect public confidence in the lira, by disclosing the extent to which military currency has been issued and the burden which Italy has assumed under the armistice."[31] The British also sought to avoid demands for sterling offsets. They had provided no such credits and would not until 1947.

Both the AC and Rome embassy reluctantly accepted the British argument. Ambassador Kirk and Chief Commissioner Stone agreed that once the Italians had been denied more credits it made no sense to shoulder them with formal financial responsibilities. Kirk had served in Rome in the thirties and was an accurate reader of Italian thinking. He warned the department on February 13, "This control over the issue of currency . . . may well appear to the Italians far from a welcome concession. . . . Unless the two governments propose to accept this demand [for greater credits], they must face the question whether it is wise in the name of 'decontrol' to make the Italian Government and people resolutely undertake their financial obligations at this particular moment." Both Stone and Kirk favored more aid, but in the meantime they also feared the consequences of American "generosity."[32]

The Allied bureaucracy found itself at a typical impasse. The U.S. State and Treasury Departments favored transfer of control without additional credits. The AC and U.S. embassy officials on the scene advised delay until more credits were available. The British opposed both credits and decontrol. For the Italians themselves, return of financial responsibilities without additional aid was precisely what they had sought to avoid all along. Once the United States had turned down Mattioli, the Italians pursued other avenues but were in no hurry to accept the U.S. offer. Kirk, Stone, and the Foreign Office thought it politically unwise to press them.

Frustration bred anger in Washington. A State Department memo of February 17, 1945, observed, "British opposition to our Italian policy continues to be stiff all along the line with resultant deterioration in American prestige and the political-economic situation in Italy."[33] On February 22, Secretary Morgenthau called British officials on the carpet in Washington. The AC, he charged, was following "an exclusively British policy towards Italy." His representative in Rome, Henry J. Tasca, was present at the meeting. Tasca charged that the British head of the AC Financial Subcommission took his orders directly from the Foreign Office and was protecting well-known Fascists in important financial institutions. Shortly after the confrontation, Morgenthau confirmed Tasca as permanent U.S. treasury representative and troubleshooter at the Rome embassy. The British were furious about the meeting and dismayed by the appointment of the "famous Commander Tasca."[34]

The thirty-two-year-old Tasca was an economist and naval lieutenant commander at the time. In his letter of introduction (March 7, 1945) to Prime Minister Bonomi, Morgenthau observed, "I have instructed Dr. Tasca that he is to consider himself available for consultation on all matters of mutual concern." Tasca would fully exploit that ample mandate and become, over the next four years, the central protagonist of U.S. policy in the Italian capital. As an Italian-American of modest South Philadelphia origin and New Deal political inspiration, Tasca had little time for professional foreign service types (he was attached to the treasury throughout his tenure) or Italian favor-seekers compromised by the old regime. His direct, abrasive style served him well as a bureaucratic infighter and negotiator. He won few friends among his colleagues, but his political skills, wide powers, and knowledge of Italian gave him prompt access to the Rome political elite. A visiting U.S. official reported in November 1945 that Tasca had achieved "a unique status of influence both within the Embassy and with respect to the Italian Government." Tasca would be, at once, a shaper, vehicle, and bellwether of official U.S. attitudes toward early postwar Italy. Even though he never fully abandoned his initial hopes for postwar reform and remained ambivalent about America's conservative and Christian Democratic allies, he identified earlier than most people the political character of the Italian economic and financial crises and became a fierce opponent of the Socialist–Communist alliance.[35]

During his February 1945 visit to Washington, Tasca discussed the continuing wrangle over Italian financial powers. He was personally irritated by what he considered Italian stalling tactics. Both political outlook and temperament inclined him to force the issue, regardless of British, AC, and U.S. embassy reservations. In late February, Morgenthau revealed to a public session of the House Appropriations Committee that AMlire were an Italian responsibility according to the armistice. Tasca's role is not clear, but he may have advised his chief to make the announcement, thereby presenting a fait accompli to people who had feared such a disclosure. In any case, the embassy promptly changed its line, urging that in view of Morgenthau's remarks, power over the issue of currency be granted to the Italians immediately. Once the facts were in the open, it made no sense to maintain financial controls. The British were gradually persuaded by a similar argument. U.S. officials tried to soften the blow with the announcement that a net troop pay account had finally been created for the Italian government at the U.S. treasury. The treasury gambled, in effect, that the Italian political–financial situation was less precarious than conventional wisdom suggested. In fact, Bonomi's feared political disaster failed to materialize, and his argument to delay the return of financial responsibilities without substantial new aid accordingly lost force.[36]

Still, the story of the return of financial powers had barely begun in March 1945. Despite the setback, the Italian cabinet continued to temporize pending additional financial aid. Treasury Minister Soleri (PLI) denounced Morgenthau's disclosure and refused to admit that AMlire were an Italian liability.[37] Even though for the moment they could not use the political disaster argument to the old effect, the Italians could comfortably rely on the normal bickering and inertia within the occupation bureaucracy to slow the return of their formal financial responsibilities. The Italian government had no choice over the long run but to accept those responsibilities, but delay continued to suit the immediate political interests of the coalition partners. None of the parties was eager to admit Italian liability for the vast amounts of AMlire in circulation and other occupation costs. That common reluctance, combined with growing political tensions within the resistance alliance, prevented any prompt and systematic approach to the urgent task of monetary stabilization after April 1945. At the same time, the Italians gradually recognized that the party or individuals who, in return for appropriate U.S. concessions, were prepared at long last to accede to Allied pressure could thereby reap considerable political benefits both in Italy and the United States.

THE APPROACHING LIBERATION

The unsuccessful effort to restore financial autonomy was part of a broader campaign during early 1945 to secure an armistice revision and preliminary peace, designed, in the State Department's words, "to bring the legal relationship of the United Nations to Italy into line with the present practical working relationship that has developed in the last fifteen months."[38] All sectors of the bureaucracy supported this objective. FEA officials had long been troubled by the harsh economic consequences of the armistice. Clayton and his economists shared this concern and were eager to deal with a sovereign Italian government, through traditional diplomatic means.

Under Secretary of State Joseph Grew and the department professionals, meanwhile, looked forward with great apprehension to the approaching liberation of the North. The Greek uprising of late 1944 raised the possibility of similar unrest in Italy. Soviet moves in Poland and the Balkans could not fail to affect EUR's view of the Italian situation. The existing six-party coalition in Rome was not an acceptable arrangement over the long run, but it had to be supported and empowered in preparation for a showdown with its potential rival, the more radical and unpredictable Northern Resistance organization, the Comitato di Liberazione Nazionale Alta Italia (CLNAI).

The rapid collapse of German resistance in April 1945 lent new urgency to the search for a transition policy. However, U.S. efforts were stymied as the war ended in the North. At Potsdam in July, the Russians proved no more amenable than the British to American proposals for a preliminary peace, and the unresolved financial issue suggested that the Italians themselves did not welcome a prompt end to the Armistice regime.[39] In any event, it was clear that, like it or not, the United States would bear the main burden of economic recovery and political leadership in Italy and elsewhere in Western Europe. It was also likely that, as the British gradually withdrew from the scene, the splits within the American government – like those within the Italian coalition – would emerge in bolder relief.

3

Liberation and transition

Allied officials greeted the formation of the first postwar Italian government on June 21, 1945, with cautious optimism and relief. It contained prominent members of the Northern CLN (CLNAI), including Prime Minister Ferruccio Parri, a resistance hero and leader of the Action Party.[1] But the situation remained tense and potentially explosive. Armed partisans roamed the countryside, settling scores with Fascists and personal enemies. Communists and Socialists held key ministerial posts, and Parri's political abilities were at best an unknown quantity. Northern factories stood idle, and inflationary forces from the South threatened to penetrate the newly liberated areas.

Austere and incorruptible, Ferruccio Parri epitomized for many the nobility and promise of the anti-Fascist resistance. Novelist Carlo Levi called Parri a "chyrsanthemum in the dunghill" of early postwar politics. Another admirer, OSS Bern Chief Allen Dulles, was more prescient when he observed in June 1945, "As a politician he is probably a novice and I question whether he will be ruthless enough to grapple with the difficult situation facing him."[2] Parri was a compromise among the major political forces and lacked the political base and personal dynamism to impose his will on the likes of Nenni, Togliatti, and De Gasperi. Economic problems festered throughout his tenure, and Parri himself became a helpless bystander as wartime unity deteriorated into partisan strife. In addition the United States did not play an active role in Italy during the early stages of postwar recovery as the following chapter shows. The American foreign policy establishment found itself in the throes of transition and conflict after April 1945, its top officials preoccupied with the questions of Germany, Eastern Europe, and Japan.

The defeat of the Nazis and the early stages of the postwar European economic crisis coincided with a change of regime in Washington.

37

Truman became President in mid-April. James Byrnes replaced Stettinius in July. With the end of hostilities and gradual phasing out of the military occupation, the State Department emerged from its long isolation. The professional diplomats' main concern during the summer of 1945 was the rapid consolidation of Russian control in Eastern Europe and the Balkans. Russian intentions in their view were sinister and had direct implications for such war-torn areas as Italy. On June 18, Grew told Truman that "anarchy and political unrest" would follow unless immediate steps were taken to stabilize the situation. On June 23, AC Chief Commissioner Stone warned the Supreme Allied Commander, Mediterranean (SACMED), Field Marshall Sir Harold Alexander, "Italy is at the parting of the ways. . . . Like other European countries devastated by war, the ground in Italy is fertile for the growth of an anarchical movement fostered by Moscow to bring Italy within the sphere of Russian influence."[3]

Ambassador Alberto Tarchiani, the newly appointed envoy at Washington, painted a similar picture for his State Department listeners. Along with fellow exiles Carlo Sforza, Arturo Toscanini, and Gaetano Salvemini, Tarchiani had spent the early war years in the United States as a member of the liberal anti-fascist – and strongly anticommunist – Mazzini Society. When the State Department rejected the society's plans to play an active role in occupation politics, Tarchiani moved to London and then to Naples in late 1943. As a member of the Action Party, he served as minister of public works in the second Badoglio government (April–June, 1944). Salvemini, who came to despise him, called Tarchiani a "conservative, more anti-Mussolini than anti-Fascist." Whatever his original views, he had grasped the importance of close ties with the Americans.

Tarchiani arrived (he presented his credentials on March 8, 1945) just in time to witness the final stages of the ill-fated Quintieri–Mattioli mission. His immediate aim was material aid, and he realized that U.S. officials were unlikely to be moved by such vague phrases as "monetary disorder" or "political-economic unrest." Though not a Christian Democrat, he sought to bolster the position of his friend and foreign minister, De Gasperi, whom he correctly identified as the most able potential leader of the anticommunist forces. Salvemini wrote friends in Italy that Tarchiani would be "a poor fish out of water" in official Washington. The Harvard historian was wildly off the mark. As befitted the ambassador of a defeated enemy, Tarchiani's manner was modest but ingratiating, and he labored tirelessly to convince the Americans that their aid and guidance would make a crucial difference to Italy's fate. He had few scruples about tailoring the facts to suit his various listeners and alternated the image of an abject Italy with the bright prospect of future

Introduction

Italian–American partnership. Above all, he was persistent and single-minded in pursuit of his basic strategy: to exploit the communist threat to an area of vital interest to the United States in order to secure firm outside support for a nascent center–right alliance.[4]

Tarchiani promptly sought out Clayton and such sympathetic listeners as Assistant Secretary William Phillips.[5] On May 18, several weeks before the formation of the Parri government, Tarchiani wrote Phillips, warning of the "political consequences that may arise in Italy out of the present disruptive economic conditions." Two days later, Tarchiani observed that "the Italian people were beginning to feel that the Anglo-Saxon powers were no longer concerned with Italy's welfare. . . ." Referring to the imminent cabinet crisis in Italy and the possibility of a PCI–PSIUP government headed by Pietro Nenni, he noted that the socialist leader was "extremely excitable" and would "lean strongly to the left." The Allied attitude, Tarchiani argued, "would have considerable influence."[6] Grew, Phillips, and their professional colleagues realized that heavy-handed U.S. interference would be counterproductive and had not yet identified a reliable local interlocutor. At the same time, they wished to play an active role and shared Tarchiani's fears about the growth of communist power.

The April–June transition produced no consensus in Washington about Soviet intentions or their implications for Italy. In a June memo, the Allied Commission Economic Section's acting vice-president, Harlan Cleveland, told Chief Commissioner Stone, "Italy is possibly the most pro-American country in Europe today and can be kept that way. . . . We *should do everything possible* to ensure that the Government is genuinely representative of and responsible to the Italian people as a whole; that it expresses the economic and social forces and groups which will press for a rising standard of living and full employment at peaceful pursuits." Cleveland was not indifferent to U.S. strategic interests but made no mention of the communist threat.[7]

Even the June 23 message of Cleveland's superior, Admiral Stone, while alarmist in tone, was mild enough in substance. "Communistic growth," he noted, could not "be blocked by restrictive or repressive measures. . . ." Stone's attitude, like Cleveland's was that of aspiring patron: "We cannot expect nor should we try to impose Anglo-Saxon methods on a Latin country, but in the field of national and local government, of justice and public methods, of agriculture and labor, of electoral systems and social welfare, the Allies still have much to teach and the Italians much to learn."[8] FEA reformers in Washington agreed that prosperity and democracy were the solutions to Italy's problems. Like the State Department professionals, they sought to identify and support the local forces who would pursue their basic aims.

By May 1945, however, the New Deal forces in Washington were in serious disarray. Truman had kept Henry Wallace at commerce to placate left-wing democrats but ignored his advice. The FEA was abolished by executive order on September 27, 1945, and its functions transferred to state, commerce, and the Export–Import Bank. New Deal hopes rested largely with UNRRA, already in operation in Europe and Asia, and scheduled – pending congressional approval – to begin a major Italian program in January 1946.

EUR viewed these developments with satisfaction but was forced to contend with another formidable adversary in the person of Assistant Secretary William Clayton. On Clayton's arrival in late 1944, the department created several new divisions under the assistant secretary's control. The Offices of International Trade Policy and Foreign Development Policy and the Office of Transportation and Communications (reorganized in September 1945 to include aviation, shipping, and telecommunications divisions) all reported to the assistant secretary for economic affairs. Clayton and his staff remained strongly committed to Hull's goal of an open world economy. They therefore resisted the notion of Soviet, British, or American spheres of influence and advocated a patient, conciliatory approach to Soviet–American differences.

Clayton's office took up the problem of Italy shortly after the liberation. On July 10, 1945, Clayton cabled lengthy instructions to the Rome embassy. After noting with pleasure a recent article by Luigi Einaudi calling for the end of protection, the message continued, "In view of the strong influences which seem likely to impel Italy in the direction of restrictive trade practices, and in view of the background of autarchic policy in Italy, it is important that every encouragement be given the Italian Government to adopt liberal policies. . . . From the view point of Italo–American relations, the treatment accorded to American trade may have an important bearing on the extent to which financial assistance will be granted to Italy by the United States." Clayton listed a series of measures the Italians should be told to take, including the eventual elimination of bilateral trading, import monopolies, and trade barriers of all kinds. The exchange control system should provide for allocation on a "multilateral rather than bilateral, trade balancing basis. Such a policy would be in line, of course, with the objectives of the International Monetary Fund. . . ." As for internal reconstruction policy, the message called for the "liquidation of autarchic, comparatively high cost production by the refusal of the Italian Government to grant assistance for reconstruction of industries producing high cost articles" and for the end of trade barriers that protected those activities. The Italians should instead revive and expand those lines of production able to compete without special treatment in an open world economy.[9]

Clayton's vision of the Italian future emerges with great clarity from the July 10 instructions: a far reaching transformation brought about by the rapid return of private trade, tariff reduction, elimination of government intervention, and promotion of "natural" industry. An additional, complementary element in Clayton's prescription was the introduction of American capital in key sectors of the economy to permit modernization and rationalization without the need for state interference. Such ventures were unlikely as long as political uncertainty prevailed, but the department was prepared to support U.S. firms whose presence in Italy served to further its designs. At the same time, Clayton's staff was well aware that without financial leverage, the July 10 instructions would remain, in the words of one economist, "so much bilge." They added a small proviso to the message, ". . . in view of the inability of this Government to respond favorably to requests for economic assistance which have been addressed to it by the Italian Government, it may not now be timely to bring our suggestions formally to the attention of that Government."[10]

With Acheson's support, Clayton sought to gain control of lend-lease and continue the program as an instrument of postwar foreign economic policy. In May 1945, Acheson suggested to Treasury Secretary Vinson that Leo Crowley's duties as FEA administrator be transferred to Clayton. Clayton's assistant Willard Thorp could run the FEA, "while the elimination of friction by combining the offices and the additional powers would greatly strengthen Will's position within the government and abroad."[11]

The fate of lend-lease produced the first clash in what *Fortune* magazine described as "running warfare" between Clayton and the foreign service–dominated geographic branches.[12] Grew was determined to cut off lend-lease as a message to the Russians and formed an alliance with Leo Crowley, who resented Clayton and realized that the days of his own independent agency were numbered. Together, they convinced Truman, who announced the abrupt end of lend-lease aid to all countries on August 21. Acheson was on vacation, Clayton in London conducting talks on the British loan. Both were shocked and furious, but the decision stood.[13]

On August 27, Acheson replaced the retiring Grew as under secretary of state. With Clayton's support, he moved to set up an Office of Intelligence and Research to replace the information and policy recommendation functions of the geographic branches. Loy Henderson (chief of the Near East division), Spruille Braden (Latin American division), and Assistant Secretary for Administration Donald Russell led the fight against Acheson. They raised questions of loyalty among the new personnel and with allies on the House Appropriations Committee managed to stall the plan until April 1946, when Secretary Byrnes scrapped it altogether.[14]

The lesson was clear. Neither Acheson and Clayton could successfully challenge the professionals on their home territory; nor did they have much influence with Secretary Byrnes. During the fall of 1945, however, Byrnes shared Clayton's cautious hopes for cooperation with the Russians.[15]

The Truman transition and bureaucratic stalemate in Washington allowed no unambiguous American policy on Italian reconstruction. There was no consensus on the gravity of the Russian communist threat nor on how to secure long-term U.S. interests — whatever they might be — in the Mediterranean area. Since congress permitted only a trickle of funds during 1945, American officials in Washington and Italy faced the problem of economic recovery without internal unity or material resources. Against this background, the military occupation regime attempted to restore autonomy to the Italian government and transfer responsibility for policy to civilian authorities in Washington and London. Given the confusion and inertia inherent in such an operation, phasing out the occupation regime proceeded fitfully, at best. The British, facing a severe economic crisis, were now eager to place the financial and political burden of Italy on the shoulders of the United States. The weakness and isolation of the Washington bureaucracy itself resulted in a near vacuum of allied policy in Italy during the crucial early stages of postwar recovery.

This chapter explores the attempts of U.S. officials to promote industrial recovery and monetary stabilization between April and December 1945. Given the structural limits of U.S. policy, it was gradually clear that both the resolution of Italy's economic problems and the fate of America's longer-term plans rested primarily with the local Italian forces. It was equally evident that those same forces had no coherent answers to the economic questions of the day. The issues of financial policy and control over private economic activity produced bitter clashes within the coalition, but none of the major parties was willing to throw its weight behind a clear approach to the problems of inflation and production. Each supported the claims of its respective constituencies on a near-empty public purse while seeking to maneuver and compromise in order to widen its support.

GETTING THE FACTORIES GOING

Allied military government officers were under orders to restore maximum industrial production. The main bottleneck, they quickly ascertained, was not physical destruction but lack of coal and raw materials. They launched a series of appeals for a systematic intervention in the northern economic crisis. On May 24, the U.S. embassy proposed creating a "Tripartite Economic Advisory Board" to assist "the evolution from Italy's defective economic system, both past and present. . . ." Failing a basic agreement with the British on future economic policy, Harlan Cleveland favored creating an American economic mission to the Italian government. Chief Commissioner Stone's June 23 memo suggested an "Allied Economic organization (joint or separate) to assist Italy in correcting the basic defects of her former economy."[16] These recommendations evoked no clear response. In the meantime, officials on the spot had little choice but to try to mediate the intense political-economic contest that followed the liberation.

It is not the purpose of this chapter to describe relations between the Allies and Italian industry during the German occupation. The subject has been treated exhaustively by other students of the period.[17] Giovanni Agnelli and his managing director Vittorio Valletta of FIAT had funded the resistance and provided valuable information to Allied intelligence. This special relationship served them well during the postwar purge trials and industrial unrest. As the key to Northern industry, FIAT was bound to receive special attention in any case. Most businessmen had been unable to conduct such a double game, but the Italian *padronato* was strongly conscious of its indispensibility to the occupation authorities. After years of government interference, Italian businessmen were for the most part opposed to any kind of control and were determined to resist CLNAI proposals for higher wages and worker participation.

Under these inauspicious circumstances, Allied officials set about to stabilize industrial relations and impose some rationality on the course of economic recovery. In the event, the former task proved far simpler than the latter. The presence of large numbers of Allied troops was enough to prevent the armed uprising that many purported to fear. That presence, moreover, had much to do with the position of the communists and the newly created trade union federation they largely controlled, the CGIL. According to communist strategy, the CGIL promoted worker discipline and national solidarity in the interests of military victory and rapid economic recovery. The CGIL's economic aims were simple and straightforward: maintaining employment and defending the real wages of the industrial working class.[18]

The *padronato* resisted, but such demands were hardly very radical and could be satisfied within the framework of traditional industrial relations. The Allies limited their intervention to transferring authority for the purge from factory committees to the government. An appeal procedure was established that provided for the release of such prominent figures as Valletta. As for extraordinary measures taken to raise wages and protect employment, the Allies could do little more than accept a series of faits accomplis. In February 1945, the Fascist Social Republic banned the firing of industrial workers and agreed to pay 75 percent of the cost of maintaining surplus labor through an unemployment fund, the *Cassa Integrazione*. This arrangement, along with the payment of a contingency bonus, was reaffirmed by the CLNAI in April and accepted by the Italian government in July. The U.S. embassy labor attache called the measures "disheartening and disquieting," but the Allies declined to meddle in the delicate area of industrial relations.[19] The occupation authorities also could not impose schemes for Northern industrial recovery. The Central Economic Commission (CCE) of the CLNAI favored reorganizing an existing system of industrial councils set up by the Germans.[20] The AC had orders to vest authority for economic planning in the Italian government, but given its growing divisions, the cabinet was at a loss to carry out plans of its own.

It was soon clear that circumstances favored certain sectors more than others, especially the cotton textile industry. Textiles were an old but vital industry, concentrated in the North. A total of 3,000 firms had employed 14 percent of Italy's industrial work force in 1938, and textile exports had amounted to $3 billion – or nearly one-third of total exports – during the same year.[21] Even though the industry's future in an open world economy was uncertain, it enjoyed a unique position in 1945. Its machinery had emerged virtually unscathed, and thanks to hydroelectric power it did not rely on large amounts of coal. At a moment when the big mechanical and metallurgical firms were pleading with the government and reluctant private banks for credit, the textile industry found itself in relatively sound financial condition.[22] Two major competitors, the Germans and the Japanese, had disappeared from the scene, and war-ravaged Europe and Asia were in desperate need of textile products. The industry had one other important advantage in 1945: Its interests coincided closely with those of the Hullian economists at the U.S. Department of State.

For Clayton, promoting the textile industry made sense for immediate practical reasons. The United States had huge stocks of raw cotton, and the State Department wished to promote Italian private exports in order to move Italy toward the liberal commercial system outlined in Clayton's July instructions. The cotton textile industry was the only major potential exporter at the time. For Clayton, it was also an eminently natural industry whose efforts should not be bound by government restrictions. As chief stockholder in the world's largest cotton export firm, he understandably took a special interest in the affair. In mid-September 1945, Ambassador Kirk told the department that the cotton factories could produce, but the country was practically "denuded of cotton." Kirk enclosed a personal message to Clayton: "Here is a fine piece of business that will help us and the preservation of order in Italy but unless someone gets behind it, the whole project will go by the board on account of difficulties of financing and shipping."[23] Clayton, in fact, was already behind the project, but reviving the industry proved a long and frustrating enterprise. In late May, Clayton had directed William Phillips to cable the U.S. embassy in Moscow about the possibility of obtaining Polish coal for the North Italian cotton industry. That industry was "in fine shape and ready to go. . . . I do not need to stress the great importance of getting these mills going. . . ." Aside from small amounts of coal, the only problem was raw cotton, "of which," Clayton noted, "we have plenty."[24] But EUR opposed Italian contacts with the pro-Soviet Warsaw Government and tried to block Clayton. The assistant secretary prevailed, and the embassy was told in late July to authorize Italo-Polish trade discussions. The military bureaucracy then insisted on approving all goods the Italians planned to exchange in order to avoid the re-export of Allied supplies. On August 21, Clayton's office complained to Rome about AC delays in allowing an Italian trade mission to leave for Poland. The mission, headed by Enzo Storoni (PLI) and Eugenio Reale (PCI), left for Warsaw in early September. The talks dragged on until October 1946, when agreement was reached for the import of 750,000 tons of coal, worth $10 million, over a twelve-month period.[25]

The coal problem plagued Allied officials throughout the early postwar period.[26] But lack of fuel was only the first of many obstacles for Clayton and the local textile industry. Raw cotton had to be paid for in dollars, but foreign exchange resources were earmarked for more pressing imports, and little cotton could be shipped without new credits.[27] Repayment required Italian exports to the dollar area since sterling and other European currencies were not convertible. Yet the type, amount, price and destination of exports were still strictly controlled by the AC and Italian government. Finally, private exporters had to surrender their hard currency to the government's exchange control agency, the Ufficio Italiano di Cambio (UIC), at the by-now uninteresting official rate of 100 lire to the dollar. The UIC had been fostered by the Allies themselves. When the AC relinquished control over Italian external transactions in July 1945, it demanded that foreign exchange control continue.[28]

With the help of Clayton and the Rome embassy, the textile industrialists set out to dismantle this series of bureaucratic and political obstacles. Their first goal was to secure raw materials by whatever means available. According to "lavorazione per conto," or manufacture on commission arrangements, Italian firms imported and converted foreign raw materials into finished products for export by the foreign supplier. The local firm received a percentage of the raw material for its own use. No foreign exchange was involved, and the Italian firm could resume production and accumulate a stock of raw material. Another procedure was the so-called private compensation deal. Cinzano of Turin would export 20,000 cases of Vermouth to its U.S. agent, Canada Dry Company, at $5 per case. The $100,000 invoice would then be used to export raw cotton to the Milan textile firm, Fratelli Radici di Donato, who paid Cinzano the value of the Vermouth in lire. The embassy favored the transaction as "a practical procedure in an emergency."[29]

Such arrangements needed AC and Italian government approval, and local firms obviously preferred to obtain credit directly and export as they pleased for their own account. On July 31, 1945, Chief Commissioner Stone told Parri that the AC would end its involvement in Italian export activities. The Italian government was authorized to return the export trade to private channels. The AC, however, would retain a voice in the determination of Italy's "exportable surplus." Parri replied that his government would continue to control trade through a central agency (the Istituto per il Commercio con l'Estero, or ICE) but wished Allied approval of manufacture on commission deals. The AC ignored this request in a long response to Parri on the issue of Italian commercial autonomy.[30] The ICE, meanwhile, had no allocation plan for imported supplies and delayed paying private exporters who marketed their products through the government. The State Department, textile industry, and liberal members of the cabinet were eager to disband it, but AC policy continued to require some sort of export screening and import distribution agency.[31] The mill owners vented their frustration in shrill attacks on the Parri government. Their prospective U.S. suppliers were also unhappy. In late September, a representative of the Lamar Fleming Company, Anderson, Clayton, and Company's agent in Milan, complained to the U.S. embassy that the "Italian Government, or the agency procuring cotton in the United States had not consulted with the Italian cotton textile industry before purchasing." It also was not using normal trade channels in Genoa and Milan. "Delays and confusion" were the result.[32]

The situation called for a radical revision of the existing regime. On October 12, Clayton informed the Rome embassy that all trade with Italy should be returned to private channels. Kirk replied (October 15) that the department's decision was "most timely." Ministry of Industry and Commerce Undersecretary Enzo Storoni (PLI) had been "most anxious to resume private trading without ICE at the earliest possible moment." A plan presented by Storoni on October 16 permitted private traders to conclude deals abroad on the basis of "normal prewar licensing and related legislation." Storoni also asked that the Italian government be allowed to dispose of its dollar holdings without U.S. approval and that AC restrictions on Italian exports be progressively eliminated.[33]

The plan was a step forward, but there were other problems that only

Washington could resolve. The first was how to finance the export of raw cotton from the United States. Following his defeat on lend-lease, Clayton was forced to lobby within the interagency National Advisory Council (NAC) for the allocation of Export–Import Bank loans. His efforts bore fruit on October 8, 1945, when the bank announced a $100 million credit for the export of 600,000 bales of American cotton to Europe. In early November, Anderson, Clayton & Company's Italian representative confirmed to the U.S. embassy that a substantial portion – about $25 million – of the credit was earmarked for the Italian textile industry.[34]

A final hurdle remained. Repayment of the loan required the export of finished textile products for U.S. currency. Shortly after the war, the major Allied textile exporters, the United States, Britain, Canada, India, and France, had set up a Combined Textile Committee, to allocate textile exports on a worldwide basis. The Italians had no representation on any such international commodity boards, and whether Italian exports would be permitted to the dollar area was an open question in November 1945. As Storoni told the embassy, unless Italian exports earned dollars, the Export–Import loan was useless.[35] He no doubt realized that the American textile industry would oppose Italian exports to the United States and other Western Hemisphere markets. In early November, the Export–Import Bank officially authorized $25 million for the export of raw cotton to Italy. Until the repayment problem was resolved, however, the credits could not be made available.

The cotton mill owners and business press continued to denounce the Parri government, and the issue of trade and exchange controls added to growing political tensions. In this already poisoned atmosphere, A. P. Giannini, president of the Bank of America, concluded a six-week visit to Italy in mid-November. In a famous interview to the press on November 15, Giannini made no attempt to conceal his contempt for the Parri coalition. Italy needed "a new, strong government" headed by his pre-Fascist liberal friends. Giannini was equally outspoken on the question of credits: "Italy cannot expect anything from American private finance until it first establishes internal order and gives a clear impression of safety, order, and discipline." He immediately contradicted himself by adding, "We have financed a large shipment of cotton which after being turned into manufactured goods should be shipped to America." Until now, "neither the Allied Commission nor the Italian Government have permitted its exportation. Such obstacles and difficulties prevent an early restoration of commercial relations between Italy and the United States."[36] The Banca d'America e d'Italia confirmed that Giannini had offered a $1 million credit to Northern textile firms for the import of raw cotton, but foreign exchange regulations had blocked the deal. Clayton shared the frustration of Giannini and the local industry. The Export–Import loan negotiations had bogged down over the issues of exports and dollar repayments, and he would now have to contend with both the U.S. textile industry and the other members of the Combined Textile committee. In the meantime, Anderson, Clayton, and Company's own "fine piece of business" remained stymied by bureaucratic regulations on both sides of the Atlantic.[37]

Along with the restoration of industrial production and exports, the stabilization of the lira was a major economic battlefront after June 1945. Effective steps by the Italians themselves to halt inflation depended on the transfer of the issue of all currency to the local government. That transfer had proceeded tortuously since the end of the Quintieri–Mattioli mission. Nor did the Italian political forces show greater willingness to accept their responsibility for AMlire and other occupation costs after the end of the war. In late 1945, the restoration of financial autonomy became entangled with the explosive issues of monetary and fiscal policy and the underlying questions at stake: How should postwar economic recovery proceed, and who should pay for it? The Allied Commission, meanwhile, was unable either to impose its own anti-inflationary policy or to cede full powers to the Italians. Both the transfer and the Italian government monetary program remained unsettled six months after the liberation of the North.

The Italian controversy surrounded proposals for income and property taxes in combination with a currency conversion operation of the kind widely adopted in Europe during or shortly after the war.[38] Such operations cut the money supply directly by blocking a fraction of bank deposits and converting a proportion into government securities. At the same time, the old paper currency was called in and exchanged for new script at a preordained ratio. As production recovered, successive portions of the impounded money would be released. If effected properly, the operation would reduce inflation and increase state revenues. Depending on the design of the taxes, it could also serve to strike war profiteers and speculators and to redistribute income in favor of the victims of inflation. In any event, the operation required extensive preparation and an efficient administration to carry it out. Obviously, it required tight security and had to be timed properly to have the desired effect. If the operation were delayed too long or disclosed in advance, people would convert bank deposits and cash into real assets and thus escape the monetary purge.

Both Allied and Italian officials began to discuss a currency conversion (or *cambio della moneta*) well before the end of the war. During the summer of 1944, the Bank of Italy's head of research (and future governor), Paolo Baffi, recommended that a currency cutting or conversion operation be prepared for the following year. A high U.S. Treasury official with AC experience recommended to Morgenthau in December 1944 that "preparation be made for a currency conversion program combined with a heavy anti-inflationary tax." Such a program, "if combined with provisions for a confiscatory rate against fortunes made under 'fascist privilege,' from collaboration with the Germans, and from black market activities should substantially reduce the volume of purchasing power and eliminate the explosive inflationary pressures underlying the Italian economy." The AC studied the matter but decided to leave it to the Italian government on the grounds that it was politically too controversial to handle. In the meantime, inflation continued to ravage the liberated areas of the country. AC and Italian government anti-inflationary efforts were palliative at best.[39]

It was soon clear after the formation of the Parri government that the Italian political forces could not agree on fiscal and monetary policy. Parri's treasury minister, Marcello Soleri, was an old-fashioned Liberal who opposed extraordinary monetary-fiscal measures on the Belgian model. (The Belgians had converted their currency and imposed special taxes in the fall of 1944). The new finance minister, the Communist Mauro Scoccimarro, had other ideas. With the help of the PCI's chief economist, Antonio Pesenti, Scoccimarro made plans for a currency conversion to block 10 percent of liquid assets – cash, bank deposits, and short term securities – followed by special fiscal measures – a personal progressive property tax, and tax on increases in property values since the beginning of the war economy in 1935. Scoccimarro claimed the program would block one-third of existing purchasing power. A majority of the cabinet agreed, and the operation was scheduled for late September or early October.[40]

Then the troubles began. Most classical liberal economists claimed that the *cambio* and attendant fiscal measures served only to cut savings and destroy confidence.[41] The liberal vice-premier, Manlio Brosio, tried to sabotage the plan from within the cabinet, while his party colleague, Federico Ricci, the new minister of the treasury (Soleri had died on July 3), favored a conversion but not the special taxes. Even though Scoccimarro did not disclose the details of his plan, the business community reacted with great hostility. Their chief spokesman was Epicarmo Corbino, noted economist and polemicist, with a Neapolitan flair for rhetoric. Though not openly involved in the controversy, Luigi Einaudi, the venerable governor of the Bank of Italy, also made known his opposition to the Scoccimarro plan. (Following the cabinet's provisional approval of the plan, Einaudi dutifully prepared a technical memorandum to lay the groundwork for the operation.)[42] Those who favored the measure saw it as a vital shortcut to monetary stability as well as a source of revenue to direct reconstruction and reform. As Italian business was well aware, the proponents also intended to place the burden of reconstruction costs on those who had profited from fascism, war, and inflation. The Action Party and the PSIUP strongly supported the communist program, but the debate did not follow strictly ideological lines. Two prominent liberal economists, Costantino Bresciani Turroni and Giovanni Demaria himself, supported the *cambio*.[43] The Christian Democratic Party's radical wing favored the plan while De Gasperi maintained a typically ambiguous neutrality.

As in the case of trade and exchange controls, a bitter political battle developed over the *cambio* during the fall of 1945. Both sides later charged Allied interference. According to Enzo Piscitelli, author of the classic account of the *cambio* saga, the issue was the "direct and immediate cause" of the fall of Parri in November since the operation was about to be executed when the Liberal ministers resigned, precipitating a government crisis. Piscitelli also argues that ". . . it is a proven fact that, precisely on this line [that of the *cambio's* opponents] . . . and not on others such as the institutional question, the conservative opponents found open comfort and direct support from the Allied Control [*sic*] Commission."[44]

Such claims have little basis in fact. Neither the AC, military headquarters (AFHQ), nor the CCS tried to stop the conversion, and they remained neutral on the wider political questions. Rather, the story of the *cambio* serves to illustrate the AC's impotence during the dismantlement of the occupation regime. At the same time, it appears that factions within the State Department adopted partisan positions. Clayton's office supported the idea in principle, though it is not clear if they understood Scoccimarro's proposal. First-hand observers in the embassy were more sensitive to the political issues at stake. Both Ambassador Kirk and Henry Tasca were in contact with the *cambio's* opponents and may have tried to delay the operation.

It will be recalled that since late 1944, the State Department had aimed to return control of the issue of currency to the Italian government. Although unable to provide the credits to make the transfer palatable to the Italians themselves, by mid-summer 1945 the department had at least persuaded the British to agree. On July 3, the CCS in Washington issued a new financial directive to AFHQ. Control over external transactions was suspended. In return, the Italians were to maintain an effective exchange control agency and support Allied economic warfare objectives. Finally, AFHQ was authorized to enter into an agreement with the Italian government on the request first made by Quintieri and Mattioli in November 1944:

(1) The Italian Government or an Italian agency designated by it will be recognized as the issuing authority of Allied Military lire, including such lire now in circulation.

(2) Further currency needs of the Allied Forces in Italy will be met with currency issued by the Italian Government or its designated agency.

According to such a "currency agreement," the Italian Government would undertake:

(1) To supply such lire currency and credits as may be required by the Allied Military forces.

(2) . . . to establish a lira account upon which the Allied forces could draw for the purpose of making cash purchases for local supplies, services, and facilities . . .[45]

It was obvious that this "currency agreement" would have to precede the currency conversion. AMlire would have to be changed along with the other currency. They were legal tender, and 80 billion lire were in circulation by April 1945.[46] If control of all currency were not in Italian hands at the time of the conversion, the Allies would have to conduct a simultaneous call in and conversion of their own. This would further complicate an already complex operation. (The only exception was the Allied Zone A of disputed Venezia-Giulia province, where the Allies intended to maintain direct military control for an indefinite period. The CCS directive did not mention Venezia-Giulia specifically, but the orders made clear that the currency agreement would not apply to the area.) Soleri and Einaudi met with AC officials on June 27 to confirm that AMlire would naturally be included in the conversion and that the operation had been tentatively scheduled for September 15.[47]

Had the AC wanted for any reason to block the conversion, delaying the currency agreement was an obvious way to do so. In fact, Chief Commissioner Stone waited several weeks before transmitting the CCS financial directive to the Italian government. Moreover, when he did so on July 18, he confined himself almost exclusively to the new policy on external financial transactions. The letter did *not* propose the all-important "currency agreement." Stone told Parri that on the question of AMlire, "clarification of certain points is awaited and I shall communicate with you further as soon as possible."[48]

In the event, "as soon as possible" turned out to be November 1, 1945, nearly four months after the original orders from CCS to AFHQ. Were there political considerations behind the AC's delay? We shall never be absolutely sure, but there were at least two reasons of a procedural nature for delaying the currency agreement. First, the AC needed clarification from CCS as to whether the Italian government would have to continue to supply Allied currency in Venezia-Giulia, an area where the Italians would not be granted currency control. That the CCS reply was delayed for any reason other than bureaucratic inertia is unlikely since CCS had already spoken on the basic question of policy. The second reason for Stone's delay was explained in a July 23 memo from the AC Finance Subcommission (FCS) to the U.S. and British embassies in Rome. The FSC told the ambassadors that the currency agreement could not be concluded until both embassies had answered Foreign Minister De Gasperi's January 9, 1945, Note Verbale denying Italian responsibility for AMlire and goods and services procured by the Allies. The Italians had to be put on record officially that return of control over their finances in no way mitigated their liabilities under the armistice of 1943. The FSC urged that the official replies be sent immediately.[49]

Why the January 9 note had not been answered by late July is not clear. Despite AC pressure, however, the U.S. and British embassies delayed their replies for three more months. Only on October 29, 1945, did the embassies inform the Italian government that the question of AMlire and other occupation costs would be settled at the eventual peace conference. The reasons for the July–October delay are also unclear. Since the issue concerned Allied policy, the response had to be worked out with the British, but the question involved was simple. Both London and Washington had long held that occupation costs, including AMlire, would be determined at the peace conference.[50]

If the U.S. (or British) embassy had wished to block the currency conversion or buy time for its opponents, it could have done so by deliberately delaying its reply to the January 9 Note Verbale. That reply was a prerequisite to the currency agreement. The agreement, in turn, was a precondition for the conversion operation. Indeed, there is no question that the embassy was suspicious of attempts to tax Fascist and wartime profits and had close contacts with enemies of the Scoccimarro proposal. Clayton's office in Washington took a different view. In early September, the department cabled the embassy that the Italians should "mop up liquid assets" like the French, Belgians, and Dutch.[51] It is not clear whether the department was familiar with Scoccimarro's plan and its political implications, but the message was obviously an endorsement in principle of a fiscal currency conversion. It also is not known whether the embassy ignored Clayton's advice and dragged its feet until it was clear the *cambio's* opponents had successfully sidetracked the proposal. In any case, no evidence exists that Clayton's message in support of the conversion was made known to the Italians. Isolated and ill-informed, Clayton's economists were in a poor position to bring their views to bear.

In the meantime, awaiting CCS and embassy action, the AC proceeded

52

to make arrangements with the Italian authorities. Chiefs of Allied pay services met in late August and agreed that "one month's advance notice of the conversion was necessary" in order to prepare themselves to issue the new currency to the troops.[52] On August 27, FSC officers met with officials of the Bank of Italy to inform them of the time requirement. The Italians were now strangely noncommittal, saying that "neither the form nor the date of the conversion [was] firm." Still, the FSC informed AFHQ that there was a "strong possibility that the conversion may take place in October" and "negotiations for a currency agreement should begin by September 1. . . . It is obvious that the agreement must be in effect by the date of the conversion, in order that the Allied Forces may be assured of a steady supply of the new currency." The FSC urged AFHQ to press CCS on this point. If authorization were delayed after September 1, the AC wished to conclude an interim agreement on its own.[53] Clearly, the AC was eager to get on with both the agreement and the conversion. AFHQ agreed. On September 1, Kirk cabled Washington that AFHQ believed that the currency agreement talks with the Italians should begin immediately, "since it seems most probable [that the] currency conversion will be undertaken by [the] Italian Government in October. . . ."[54]

Allied officials soon realized, however, that the operation was in serious trouble. On September 14, Minister Ricci told Kirk that despite earlier reports, no "definite decision [had] yet [been] taken." The following day, Kirk told the State Department that "the possibility of conversion of Italian currency this fall appears to be fading rapidly." Bank of Italy and treasury officials had cited a series of technical obstacles: inadequate police protection, transport, and replacement currency. The Bank of Italy was legitimately concerned with such problems, but the issue dividing the government was obviously Scoccimarro's politically explosive tax plan. Henry Tasca's business contacts blamed recent speculation and inflationary pressures in part on "the complete reluctance of the Minister of Finance (Communist) to reveal the contents of his capital levy program."[55]

On October 23, the AC finally received clarification from CCS on the Venezia-Giulia issue. CCS accepted an AFHQ suggestion that the Allies conduct a separate conversion in Zone A. The Italian government would continue to supply Allied currency needs, and the ultimate liability for currency circulating in the disputed region would again be determined by the final peace treaty. On October 29, the U.S. and British embassies replied to the Italian Note Verbale of January 9. Its way cleared, the AC wrote Prime Minister Parri on November 1, proposing an agreement whereby the Bank of Italy:

> will be recognized as the issuing authority of Allied military lire currency, including all such lire now in circulation. . . . The future currency needs of

the Allied forces in Italy, *including* Venezia-Giulia, will be met with currency issued by the Italian Government or its designated agency. . . . (emphasis added)[56]

Clearly, had the Italian government been prepared to carry out the currency conversion in September or October, the Allied delay in proposing the currency agreement would indeed have prevented the operation. Equally clearly, the Italian cabinet had come to no agreement on the tax proposals and was unready to effect the operation at that time. The Allied delay was no doubt used by the *cambio's* opponents within the cabinet as an argument against the plan, but no evidence exists that proponents (Parri, La Malfa, or Scoccimarro, for example) pressured or even requested the AC to conclude a currency agreement before November 1. It is highly unlikely that they did not realize that the currency agreement had to come before the conversion. The Italian treasury reiterated precisely that connection in an urgent memo to other interested ministries on December 4. What is then to be made of Piscitelli's extraordinary claim that the fiscal conversion plan "was ready and about to be executed" in mid-November, thus constituting the "direct and immediate motive" for the resignation of the Liberal ministers on November 21? This was obviously not the case, since no currency agreement had been concluded. In fact, the situation was quite different from the one Piscitelli portrays.[57]

Stone received no answer to his November 1 proposal. At the AC's request, Ricci and Einaudi met with Lt. Colonel Timmons, acting director of the FSC, more than three weeks later, on November 23. Timmons reminded the Italians that the currency agreement was "an urgent matter . . . in view of the projected currency conversion." He repeated the need for at least one month's ("and preferably two") advance notice to the AC and asked about the *cambio's* status. To Timmons's surprise, Ricci replied that "no definite plans had been formulated." Main responsibility rested with the finance minister because of the fiscal questions involved. No firm date had been set, possibly the end of February or 15th of March. Timmons reported, "I received the definite impression that the entire matter of the currency agreement had, up to this moment, received only the most cursory attention." Ricci proceeded to quibble with the Stone letter, paragraph by paragraph. The Italian government declined to furnish Allied currency needs in Venezia-Giulia, where it would have no control of the financial situation. A second problem concerned the Yugoslav-controlled Zone B of the province. There, the Yugoslavs had issued their own occupation lire. Even though the AC had declared Zone B lire illegal, Timmons suspected the Italians feared they might eventually become responsible for the Yugoslav currency as well.[58]

But Venezia-Giulia was not the central issue. Einaudi and Ricci were probably aiming at the currency conversion itself. Holding up the agreement was an obvious way to stop the *cambio*. Their stalling, moreover, betrayed Italian ambivalence about the currency agreement per se and its wider implications. The basic Italian attitude toward the assumption of their financial responsibilities had not changed since Prime Minister Bonomi voiced his doubts about the lira account in October 1944. In a period of intense political maneuver and debate, no party or political leader was as yet willing to support the risky and unpopular step of placing Allied fiat currency on the books of the Bank of Italy. Like Mattioli a year before, the Italians still hoped to extract concessions in return for assuming their financial responsibilities. This was obvious, at least to Henry Tasca. In addition to the bureaucratic reasons for the currency agreement's delay, Tasca later cited "the still active question in the minds of the Italian authorities of the counterpart in dollars and sterling for all AMlire issued by Allied forces in Italy."[59]

It is also clear that Togliatti was impressed by the profoundly hostile reaction of business to the *cambio* proposal. Like his great rival De Gasperi, the communist leader had little interest in economic questions to begin with. (Giulio Andreotti recalls that Togliatti made a point of turning to his newspaper when Scoccimarro rose to speak to the party leadership on fiscal and monetary matters.) By November 1945, whatever enthusiasm he may have had for the Scoccimarro plan had subsided considerably, and Togliatti agreed without further ado to the operation's postponement in January. The fiscal-conversion plan not only required accepting onerous occupation costs, but it also ran counter to the PCI's strategy of alliance with the Italian middle classes. As De Gasperi understood at the time, the communists were unlikely to link their presence in the coalition to the adoption of specific economic reforms. Such considerations, rather than Allied interference, explain the lack of Italian political will, which Piscitelli correctly invokes as the ultimate cause of the *cambio's* failure.[60]

THE FALL OF PARRI

The failure to address the problems of industrial recovery and monetary stabilization was due in large part to the tension within the Italian government during the six months after June 1945. That same period saw a prolonged and confused transfer of responsibilities from the AC to civilian agencies. The local occupation authorities were caught in the middle, unable either to intervene directly in Italian affairs or promptly to remove the remaining obstacles to normal relations.

Factions within the State Department had different preoccupations at the time. Clayton sought to restore the private export trade and move Italy toward the liberal economic system foreseen by his July 10 instructions to the Rome embassy. EUR's main concern was political stability. The department was not of one mind on the gravity of the communist threat, a disagreement reflected in their divergent positions on Polish–Italian trade and the currency conversion. But neither Clayton nor EUR could bring much influence to bear on the immobile Italian government. Not surprisingly, there was a widespread and growing exasperation with the Italian political situation by the fall of 1945. A visiting U.S. Treasury official called the government "unwieldy and ineffective."[61] The observation was an understatement. The Parri coalition was hopelessly divided on almost every major issue – industrial, commercial, monetary, and fiscal policy, not to mention the explosive questions of public order and the anti–Fascist purge. On such questions as financial autonomy and occupation costs, the parties were in effect united against accepting responsibility. Neither the AC nor the Allied governments could force them to do so.

Ambassador Kirk told Washington that Parri's tasks would be simplified if direct military control were ended in the North and greater aid forthcoming from the United States, but the prime minister himself displayed no signs of "vitality and alertness . . . and certainly there was lacking any show of dynamic leadership." After communicating the U.S. view that local elections be held as soon as possible, Kirk cabled Washington, "I regret to say that due either to his physical fatigue or his constitutional indecision or the complicated political set-up which confronts him, his reactions are far from clear." The department found a more responsive interlocutor in the minister of foreign affairs. De Gasperi shared the U.S. view that local elections should come before national elections and attributed Parri's indecision to his fear that the Action Party would do poorly at the local level. Echoing Tarchiani in Washington, De Gasperi warned the embassy that, once elected, a National Constituent Assembly might "automatically put an end to all government in Italy," setting the stage "for a dictatorship with either Nenni or Togliatti as possible candidates."[62] By late October, Parri's cabinet was deadlocked on the local elections, the purge, and the fiscal-currency conversion. Pressure mounted from business and important visitors like Giannini to be done with the coalition. In mid-November, Leone Cattani, secretary of the Liberal Party, met secretly with De Gasperi to insure the DC leader's readiness to head a new government. The Liberal ministers resigned shortly thereafter, precipitating a cabinet crisis.[63]

According to resistance legend, Parri's fall on November 21, 1945, represented the betrayal and defeat of the radical, progressive forces. One need not deny the poignancy of the moment to point out that those forces, notably Parri's own party, had been on the defensive for some time and also that CLN unity was a not so-polite fiction after June 1945.

All of the big mass-based parties were eager to eliminate the ineffectual Parri and his isolated party from the scene. Even though they had done little or nothing to bolster his credibility, the Americans themselves were among Parri's few genuine supporters during the final agony of his government. U.S. officials faced an old dilemma, to be sure. As did nearly everybody, they had serious misgivings about Parri's leadership; but like the British Labour government, they were even more reluctant to see the country plunged into crisis at the time.

On November 10, Kirk had warned the Liberal Vice-Premier Brosio about "precipitating the country into political crisis." The following day, he expressed to De Gasperi "in no uncertain terms [his] personal feeling of disgust that at a time when foreigners were determining the measure of sacrifice which they would make in order to save the Italian people from starvation and anarchy, Italians themselves were thinking more of their personal and party ambitions than of the salvation of their country." In the midst of the crisis, Secretary Byrnes told Kirk to make it known that those responsible should be prepared "to accept the consequences of their actions both as regards the domestic situation and Italy's position abroad."[64] State Department aid planners were appalled by the spectacle of open political warfare while economic problems festered. An extended crisis might alienate congress, on whose good will any serious assistance program depended. (In the event, congress approved a $450 million UNRRA program following the resolution of the crisis in mid-December.) EUR's overriding concerns were political calm before the national elections for the Constituent Assembly and the resolution of the institutional question. Like Parri himself, U.S. officials were no more than helpless bystanders as the crisis took its course.

Yet thanks largely to the new prime minister, the fall of Parri was to usher in a more fruitful phase in Italian–American relations. In its first two months in office, the new government would prove a welcome contrast to the old six-party coalition. It rapidly tackled the political and technical problems that had poisoned the atmosphere after June 1945. For a brief moment, it raised new hopes among Clayton's economists, EUR professionals, and reformist planners alike.

4

The advent of De Gasperi

The brief period from December 1945 to March 1946 witnessed a series of initiatives that together produced a new phase in early postwar Italian–American relations and marked the beginning of the collaboration between Alcide De Gasperi and the United States. At its moment of origin, the relationship owed more to expediency and mutual dependence than to deeply shared convictions or mutual trust. American officials were struck by the cabinet's novel competence in dealing with financial, commercial, and political problems. The Italian government also addressed itself to other issues of interest to the United States, including the fate of the Fascist industrial sector and pending investment projects of major U.S. companies. De Gasperi himself was better equipped than his predecessor to manage the interparty conflicts that had bedeviled the previous coalition.

With the help of the Rome embassy, the State Department established closer relations with local Italian forces. The period also saw the birth of a major UNRRA aid program, considered by some the last best hope for U.S.-inspired reformism. During the first months of 1946, conflicts within the American government faded, albeit briefly, in the new atmosphere of cautious optimism. Parri's demise also brought a release of political tensions, and the parties turned their attention to the upcoming local and national elections. They also continued to prefer maneuver and compromise to clear choices of economic policy. This internal stalemate would continue for months. At the same time, the period from December 1945 to March 1946 saw a small but significant shift in the balance of political power, as De Gasperi subtly extended ties to the United States and the forces on his right.

DE GASPERI TAKES CHARGE

Alcide De Gasperi is undoubtedly the greatest yet perhaps most enigmatic of Italian postwar leaders. Pietro Nenni called him the "sphinx," a familiar but inscrutable character. Others saw him as a Machiavellian priest who beguiled and outmaneuvered the less cunning and alert.[1] De Gasperi's austere Trentino bearing reinforced that image, as did his great patience, tactical flexibility, and sense of political timing. In pursuit of the broadest possible alliance, he maintained a careful neutrality on the major political controversies of the day. At heart, De Gasperi was a man of simple passions and few concrete ends. He was devoutly Catholic and anticommunist, committed above all to the restoration of parlimentary democracy and close ties to the West. Beyond those principles, De Gasperi had neither an elaborate vision of Italian society nor preconceived strategy for political and economic reconstruction. This lack of specific aims proved his great advantage in the uncertain and fluid conditions after 1945. Pragmatism and mediation – to his enemies, cynicism and duplicity – were the hallmarks of De Gasperi's political approach.

His first government, formed December 10, 1945, reflected the dominance of the three mass-based parties, the DC, PCI, and PSIUP. De Gasperi retained the foreign affairs portfolio. His protégé Mario Scelba remained in the cabinet as minister of posts and telecommunications, as did the leading DC radical, Giovanni Gronchi, as minister of industry and commerce. Nenni became sole vice-premier. His fellow Socialist Giuseppe Romita became minister of the interior, a key position (held previously by Parri) in view of the upcoming elections. Togliatti and Scoccimarro stayed, respectively, at justice and finance. Communists, Socialists, and Christian Democrats alike welcomed the demise and imminent break-up of the radical Action Party. They also blocked the attempt of such aged Liberal politicians as Nitti and Orlando to play a role in the new cabinet. Politics henceforth would be the preserve of the mass-based popular forces born of the resistance era.

But "avvento di De Gasperi" and the emergence of three-party rule also marked the arrival of Epicarmo Corbino at the treasury ministry. In contrast to his Liberal party predecessors, Corbino was a tough, strident, and ambitious politician. He had led the Confindustria's public campaign against the tax-conversion plan and was implacably hostile to the left. Corbino's economic program reflected pristine classical ideas. "As you can see," he observed in January 1946, "we want no innovation in financial policy," only rapid liberalization that will "bring the country back to normal economic and financial life."[2]

De Gasperi shared Corbino's distrust of the left, but Corbino's plans were clearly incompatible with the prime minister's vague but nonetheless reformist program, not to mention the interventionism of Gronchi and the DC left. De Gasperi was also suspicious of potentially reactionary groups, including Northern industrialists, Southern landlords, monarchists, and high church officials. The presence of Corbino was designed to insure the neutrality, if not support, of those forces. Just as Togliatti did not hesitate to postpone the currency conversion, De Gasperi displayed his characteristic empiricism (*empirismo*) in downplaying reform.

De Gasperi's choice of Corbino also indicated his desire to establish closer ties to the United States. Greater American political and material support was seen as vital to avoid a punitive peace settlement, further economic reconstruction, and enhance the prestige of De Gasperi and his party. Corbino would prove a valuable asset in this respect. He also sought close relations with the United States and liked to portray himself as the champion of American interests. "Is it conceivable," he asked his fellow Liberals in May 1946, "that we can ask for aid from the United States when we want to set up an economy and political system that are diametrically opposed to the United States? We have the right to impose any kind of economic and political system that we want, but we must recognize the American right to lend a helping hand and send their aid to those countries who help themselves according to the American mentality."[3] De Gasperi and Corbino took the initiative in resolving the financial and commercial controversies pending from the Parri period. The United States gave its blessing by granting concessions in return.

THE CURRENCY AGREEMENT

The troubled U.S.–Italian financial relationship underwent a dramatic change within a few weeks of Parri's fall. Corbino took office on December 10 and shortly thereafter contacted Henry Tasca on the currency agreement question. According to Tasca, the minister considered the matter "of such importance" that he would handle negotiations personally. "We may therefore expect progress on this matter in the near future."[4] Colonel Timmons of the AC met with Corbino and Introna of the Bank of Italy the same day, and the Italians agreed to accept Stone's November 1 proposal without discussion. There was no mention of Venezia-Giulia nor of reimbursement in foreign exchange for lire issued to Allied forces. De Gasperi would simply write Stone, "accepting responsibility for all AMlire issued." The AC was astonished by the change in atmosphere. Corbino was "fully informed. . . . We encountered none of the disposition to haggle over small and unimportant points that had characterized our discussions with Ricci. . . ." De Gasperi wrote the AC on January 24, consummating the agreement.[5]

How can the sudden change of heart be explained? Italian opposition to the currency agreement was no doubt affected by the passage in late December of the 1946 UNRRA program. In that sweetened atmosphere, De Gasperi and Corbino were prepared to make concessions in order to establish their good faith. It is also clear that Tasca and Corbino worked well together. Tasca attended the January 3 meeting in order to expedite the agreement. Corbino asked him that "once the agreement becomes effective all lira currency supplied by the Italian Government to Allied Forces have a counterpart in dollars, sterling or other foreign exchange."[6] Tasca obviously could not deliver this long-sought concession himself, but he assured Corbino that he would lobby Washington to end the occupation regime. The embassy promptly urged Washington to support the AC proposal that all lira expenditures by Allied forces after January 1, 1946, "be compensated with current foreign exchange." Tasca noted that the communists were exploiting the issue, and the end of occupation cost repayment "would facilitate the maintenance of public order and the elimination of unrest in Italy."[7]

Finally, along with the coming of UNRRA and the prospect of future dollar credits, the indefinite postponement of the conversion program removed a last obstacle to the currency agreement. Corbino and other opponents of the *cambio* were fortunate to receive indirect Allied support in their efforts to sidetrack the proposal. In early January, Stone told De Gasperi that the Allies wanted at least sixty days' notice of any projected currency change. (The original request had been for thirty, but, again, it is doubtful that Allied policy was politically motivated. Timmons had asked Ricci for two months in November, and the new request came from AFHQ, who were concerned about the large amounts of AMlire that would be affected by the conversion.) Kirk reported De Gasperi was "delighted since he is suspicious of great haste in which his finance minister Scoccimarro is trying to put his reconversion plan into effect. Admiral Stone understood that Corbino would share De Gasperi's feeling since he wants more time to study draft." Corbino intended to scuttle the Scoccimarro program and made this plain to the embassy. With Togliatti's agreement, the operation was soon shelved on the grounds that the details were still unclear and all available security forces were needed for the local elections in March. Those who had sought to delay the currency agreement as a means of blocking the *cambio* therefore no longer had any reason to object.[8]

TRADE AND EXCHANGE

With some prodding from the embassy, the new government also took steps to restore normal trade relations. On December 24, the government established a new Ministry of Foreign Trade (Ministero del Commercio con l'Estero). Dispute arose over control of the allocation of private import licenses, but it was soon decided that the ministry would review recommendations from local chambers of commerce. On February 7, the

State Department announced that as of February 15, private trade between Italy and all countries except Germany and Japan would be resumed.[9]

Private exporters were naturally elated. They soon had additional reason to celebrate. In mid-January, the government set up an export premium arrangement that, in effect, devalued the lira by 125 percent. At 100 to the dollar, the lira was badly overvalued, but the Parri cabinet had been unable to take remedial action. Ricci had favored an immediate devaluation of 200 to 300 percent, while Einaudi had desired an export premium–import penalty arrangement. The U.S. embassy had opposed devaluation on the grounds that it might cause panic and "hasten the disintegration of Italy's financial structure."[10] Einaudi's views prevailed within the government, and Parri eventually wrote Stone proposing a system whereby "exporters would cash twice the official exchange in Italian value and all importers would pay the value granted to them on the same basis." The Italians were asking Allied permission for a 200 percent devaluation for commercial purposes. Stone forwarded the request to AFHQ, calling it "the adoption of a major financial policy by the Italian Government and as such should be referred to the CCS for their information and consideration by the interested Governments."[11]

Neither the CCS nor State Department had taken an official position on the question before the fall of the Parri Government. The department had obvious reasons to be opposed. Clayton's July 10 instructions had called for "reconstruction and expansion of those lines of production able to compete in export markets without subsidies," and the Bretton Woods agreement foresaw return to a single fixed exchange rate by all participants. When the De Gasperi government revived the issue in December 1945, however, the department agreed without hesitation. On January 18, 1946, the Italian government announced that henceforth the UIC would buy and sell U.S. dollars for commercial purposes at the rate of 225 lire. The Italian currency had been devalued by 125 percent. The U.S. Treasury was not pleased by the "apparent intention of establishing multiple rates of exchange for the lira." For the moment, however, the treasury insisted simply that U.S. military and other official transactions enjoy the most preferential rate. Corbino quickly agreed, and the matter was settled on February 2.[12]

Even though the January devaluation was only the first element in an elaborate multiple rate system that developed over the year, it appeared to make sense at the time as an export-promotion measure. The State Department cabled Rome on March 7 that total assistance of about $260 million in addition to UNRRA's $450 million would enable Italy to cover its minimum 1946 import requirements *"provided Italy pushes exports with greatest energy"* (emphasis added).[13] The additional $260 million included a possible $150 million Export–Import Loan and release of the $110 million treasury "suspense account" representing the dollar equivalent of lire furnished to the American army for its expenditures other than troop pay. Neither source would be available for an indefinite period. Exports for hard currency thus became an urgent matter in early 1946.

THE COTTON DEAL

The interrelated problems of export markets and raw material financing were still unresolved. In January 1946, the Italian embassy in Washington complained to Rome that the Combined Textile Committee would not permit Italian exports to Egypt (a British market) and the entire Western Hemisphere. The embassy pointed out that if Export–Import and other U.S. loans were to be repaid, Italy must be free to earn dollars. The U.S. embassy in Rome also condemned the arrangement. "It will," Tasca argued "unquestionably undermine our efforts to convince other countries that we seek to free trade and eliminate unnecessary restrictions."[14] The State Department agreed. On February 8, the embassy received word that if the Italians helped to supply the Far East, the department would press the Textile Committee to open the dollar area.

The cotton mill owners bitterly resented what they saw as an American attempt to limit their industry's "dynamic possibilities." At the same time, they were fortunate to have a pragmatic and effective diplomatic spokesman.[15] To plead its case to the Textile Committee, the Italian government chose the undersecretary of industry and commerce, Ivan Matteo Lombardo. Lombardo spoke colloquial English and had twenty years experience in the cotton textile business. In mid-March, the embassy reported that Lombardo would be leaving on a ten- to fifteen-day mission to the United States. Even though the Cotton Trade Association continued to reject U.S. allocation schemes, the embassy urged that Lombardo be well treated and that Italy receive full membership on the Textile Committee.[16]

Lombardo was also a prominent figure on the right wing of the Socialist Party and thus had a potential role in attempts to break up the PCI–PSIUP alliance. During his visit, Lombardo met with the Italian–American labor leader, Luigi Antonini, a character involved in efforts to sabotage Nenni and create an anticommunist, pro-American Socialist party.[17] The cotton mission coincided with the twentieth Congress of the PSIUP in Florence, where Lombardo was elected party general secretary. American intelligence reports attributed the choice, in part, to threats by Antonini to withdraw financial support unless the party shifted to the right. Lombardo refused to join Giuseppe Saragat's Social Democrats following the PSIUP split-up in January 1947. Because of his anticommunism and special ties to the United States, Lombardo nevertheless played an important role in future economic negotiations.[18]

From the industry's viewpoint, Lombardo's American mission was only a partial success, but it was undoubtedly the best obtainable deal. Lombardo was satisfied with the committee's allotment of Italian exports for the period ending July 31, 1946, – 75 million yards of cotton, including a minimum of 27 million to the Far East, 5 to Egypt, and 9 to the Western Hemisphere. Lombardo estimated that Italian exports would reach $190 million in 1946 and that textiles alone would account for $150 million of the total. According to the State Department, Lombardo had been "exceptionally well informed and possessed good judgement and tact." Overall, he had made "an excellent impression." Once the dollar area had been opened, negotiations for the Export–Import Bank cotton credit were rapidly concluded. On April 1, 1946, the bank announced a $25 million credit to Italian commercial banks for the purchase of 200,000 bales of American cotton.[19]

WHAT TO DO WITH IRI

The revival of the textile trade was an important step in Clayton's July 1945 scenario. Along with the reintegration of Italy's natural industries into the world economy, Clayton foresaw a basic transformation of the domestic political economy through the elimination of state aid to inappropriate, high-cost activities. But such changes required much more political and financial leverage than was available to the department in 1945. Even though such influential figures as Einaudi, Corbino, and Demaria had similar hopes, labor, left-wing planners, as well as vested business and bureaucratic interests, were ranged against the liberal design.

The State Department also foresaw a role for private American capital in the rehabilitation and modernization of the Italian economy. Here, again, they faced serious obstacles. U.S. business was unlikely to venture into an unstable political situation, and unless outside investment were carefully controlled, it might end up subverting rather than advancing the department's program by strengthening the monopoly position of local and foreign firms. During the early postwar months, Clayton's economists – in particular, the Investment and Economic Development (ED) and International Resources (IR) Divisions – were concerned less with promoting the penetration of U.S. corporations into the local economy than with enforcing the rules of free competition and equal access. Important developments concerning the fate of IRI, the Fascist state sector, offered additional evidence that the new De Gasperi government was ready to collaborate with State Department plans.

The future of IRI's heavy industrial empire was very much in doubt in 1945. Its metallurgical and mechanical sectors had suffered heavily from sabotage and bombardment. IRI's already grave financial woes were badly aggravated by the ban on firing industrial workers extended to the entire country in August 1945. By 1946, billions of lire had been invested to maintain inflated payrolls. Along with the PCI, PSIUP, and the CGIL, IRI's first postwar commissioner, Leopoldo Piccardi, favored IRI's expansion and reorganization as an instrument of central industrial planning. Given the virtually total uncertainty about future economic conditions, no basic decisions could be made about which activities to promote.[20]

Even if IRI had never threatened the principle of private ownership, most classical liberal economists favored its prompt and total liquidation. Italian business was divided. Angelo Costa, the Genovese shipbuilder and first postwar president of the Confindustria, was gradually convinced that IRI was a necessary evil but that its scope and function should be strictly limited. Other businessmen, such as Oscar Sinigaglia, president of IRI's Finsider steel holding, had ambitious plans that required state support. Business as a whole agreed that IRI must not become a tool of the left and opposed any basic change in its role and structure.[21]

Despite widespread suspicions, neither the United States nor Britain had made any effort to control specific IRI holdings during the war. In July 1945, however, Clayton called for the "liquidation of autarchic, comparatively high cost production." Thenceforth the problem was how to reconcile this long term goal with the need to maintain employment and provide financial aid to beleaguered private and public industry. Many feared that the left would use IRI to gain control of private industry, but as a source of emergency funds IRI could not be eliminated without disastrous consequences.[22]

A case in point was reported to the U.S. consul in Genoa in mid-October 1945 by the local shipbuilder (and future motorscooter magnate) Rocco Piaggio. Piaggio was a major stockholder of the failing San Giorgio Company, whose management had asked the government for a 500 million lire loan. In return, Commissioner Piccardi demanded that IRI's share in San Giorgio be increased from the actual 23 percent to more than 50 percent. Piaggo claimed that his company was a "marked target" of communist nationalization plans and proposed that the "abolition of IRI and the participation of American and British firms in some of its organizations would eliminate one of the greatest menaces which today threatens the future of our country."[23]

Such a notion was, in fact, already under discussion between the U.S. embassy and minister of reconstruction, Meuccio Ruini. In September 1945, Ruini proposed to Henry Tasca that IRI be liquidated through an influx of American capital. On September 21, Tasca cabled Washington that IRI's dissolution "would deal a severe blow to future hopes of totalitarian elements in Italy . . . [and] would be a key step in the realization of policies envisaged in the Department's confidential instructions of July 10."[24] Clayton's Investment and Economic Development (ED) and International Resources Divisions (IR) endorsed the idea in principle but had several reservations. To guarantee a fair price to the Italian government, the sale would have to await general industrial recovery. The department was also determined to have a say in the location and extent of private foreign investment. It requested detailed information on IRI's holdings and assured the embassy that the matter would receive close attention.[25]

In the meantime, Tasca had learned "in extreme confidence" that a group of Italians (including a high ranking but unnamed IRI official) was "drawing up in secret section-by-section specific plans for introducing into the IRI network of United States capital." Washington continued to have second thoughts. ED argued that IRI's sale must await the Parri government's tax measures against war profits and speculation, obviously in doubt at the time. Otherwise, the liquidated properties would "fall in the hands of the same undesirable elements, [former Fascists and collaborators] as now control a large part of the Italian economy."[26]

The department's International Resources Division was concerned that existing industrial concentrations "not be augmented by the purchase of Italian holdings." Prospective investors would undoubtedly already have substantial control over their particular industry and "the long term benefit of the Italian economy might not be served by foreign investors whose main concern was in 'protective ownership' (control for the purpose of disciplining production . . .)." IR recommended further study of the matter.[27]

In the meantime, pressure for an inflow of U.S. capital was coming chiefly from IRI member firms themselves. A high official of the Ansaldo Company (75 percent IRI-controlled) reported that many IRI firms would prefer American participation up to 50 percent to Italian government loans with political strings attached. On November 15, 1945, the embassy transmitted a memo from Edoardo Adler, a Milan businessman who claimed to represent an IRI-sponsored corporation set up to extend the foreign connections of member firms. Soon after, an unnamed American businessman delivered a memo from another IRI official, Dr. Gabrio Permuda, to the Embassy. Permuda proposed a combination United States–IRI "Technical Commercial Organization" to secure exclusive use of U.S. patents for IRI firms. The memo listed eighteen areas of interest, including marine diesel engines, boilers, machine tools, cranes, pumps, mining equipment, and electronics. Permuda was no doubt aware that FIAT had already begun to look for licenses for diesel engines and other products. Unlike FIAT, however, IRI's mechanical sector lacked longstanding relations with U.S. private industry. No evidence exists that Permuda's memo was received with any particular interest by either the State Department or, if they ever saw it, by American business circles.[28]

The most detailed and intriguing proposal for help came from Oscar Sinigaglia, whose Finsider holding company controlled 45 percent of Italian steel production. Sinigaglia envisioned a modern, complete-cycle steel industry to replace the traditional industry based on the conversion of imported scrap. Sinigaglia held that an expanded and efficient steel industry was vital to the growth of the Italian mechanical sector. That sector, he observed prophetically at the time, offered the only hope for a "really radical change in the production and reserve situation." The potential of textiles and agriculture were limited, but the mechanical industry would have "practically unlimited export possibilities" in the postwar world economy.

Sinigaglia outlined his program to the U.S. embassy in November 1945. Finsider needed U.S. coal, iron ore, and technical advice to rationalize and expand. An up-to-date Italian steel industry would not threaten the United States. Rather help from the United States would allow U.S. industry to establish a local *pied à terre*. Sinigaglia would be happy to see IRI resold to private industry but assured the Americans that the Italian government had never used IRI to meddle with private business. As for IRI's future, there was "little to worry about, even with a Socialist Government." A communist government was another matter, but "if any covert plan [was] being developed to institute more direct government control, [Sinigaglia] was unaware of it."

The State Department had no specific plans for the Italian steel industry, but Clayton's economists obviously did not share Sinigaglia's vision in 1945. Finsider was a deviant outgrowth of the Fascist war economy. Clayton's instructions stated that "autarchic, comparatively high cost production" should be eliminated, and department policy aimed to promote a radically different industry, cotton textiles, at the time.[29]

By the time of Parri's fall on November 21, plans for a U.S. intervention in IRI had been stalled indefinitely. The State Department feared the operation might strengthen "undesirable elements," both foreign and domestic. In contrast to Tasca, Clayton's economists did not view the operation as an urgent measure to forestall a left-wing take-over, nor did they identify American interests with the likes of Piaggio, who had grown rich under the previous regime. The task for the moment was to contain IRI's role and size until an improvement in economic conditions would permit its gradual liquidation.

In this, as in other respects, the new De Gasperi government provided quick satisfaction. IRI increased its share of the San Giorgio Company from 23 percent to a controlling 43 percent in return for a major loan, but the takeover was to be the only such operation in the early postwar period. In March 1946, the cabinet approved a law increasing IRI's endowment from 2 to 12 billion lire, but the use of the funds was strictly limited to emergency aid to firms already under IRI control.[30]

Commissioner Piccardi resigned in early 1946, and his replacement became a test of strength within the government. In March, the cabinet appointed Giuseppe Paratore, whom Tasca called "an outstanding Liberal Party man." Paratore told Tasca that he desired IRI's liquidation "at the earliest possible date," but not before production was resumed and "essential conditions for such liquidation established." That view coincided closely with the State Department's, and U.S. officials had reason to be pleased. The March law was followed by a basic modification of IRI's statute. According to a decree law of April 19, 1946, IRI's budget and basic policy were subordinated to the cabinet's Interministerial Committee for Reconstruction. Any effort to expand IRI's role could henceforth be blocked by the conservative members of the committee.[31]

TWA AND IT&T

The early postwar history of IRI shows that the United States made no attempt to intervene in state-controlled heavy industry. Speculation has always been rampant about the alleged plans of the Allies to carve out spheres of influence elsewhere in the Italian economy. In May 1945, Kirk reported that high British officials were preparing to "castrate" Italian industry and eliminate future competition in British markets. The British ambassador in Rome reported that Americans in the AC were laying the groundwork for future U.S. economic penetration. Such reports were largely fantasy. The only serious American concern was a British attempt to exploit prewar connections with the Italian chemical industry. In 1945–46, the British chemical giant, ICI, attempted to gain control of ANCA, a Montecatini subsidiary that controlled the local market in aniline dyestuffs. ANCA had been owned fifty-fifty by Montecatini and I. G. Farben. After the Farben share was sequestered by the Italian government, ICI tried to control it and succeeded in obtaining certain secret formulas from ANCA officials without compensation. Tasca investigated and protested to Corbino. When Clayton discussed the issue with the British in June 1946, he was told that ICI had no designs on Montecatini.

In February 1947, the general manager of Montecatini assured the Americans that even though ICI "had expressed an interest in a close rapprochement . . . it was the policy of the Montecatini Company to stay out of the sterling bloc and to attempt to establish its main industrial relationship with firms in the United States."[32]

The British, for their part, were worried about the ties between FIAT and private U.S. capital. FIAT's management realized that the firm's growth depended on a close relation with the Americans, and FIAT needed raw materials and financial aid in 1945. Over the longer run, FIAT sought U.S. technology and international marketing agreements. Shortly after the liberation, a senior FIAT executive, Aurelio Peccei, ordered the firm's representative in New York to open discussions with a variety of U.S. companies. Peccei was one of four commissioners who ran FIAT pending investigation into the regular management's wartime activities. These discussions aimed to secure new patents and to market FIAT diesels in the United States. The company's chameleon-like managing director, Vittorio Valletta, was cleared of all charges in late 1945. Like Oscar Sinigaglia, Valletta had an ambitious vision of expansion and modernization using U.S. loans and technical knowledge. In March 1946, he publicly affirmed FIAT's desire to cooperate with the Americans ("with whom we have always had magnificent relations") and was a frequent visitor to the United States in the late 1940s. Rumors at the time suggested that FIAT might be bought by General Motors. GM and FIAT were indeed in close contact, but a take over was not at issue. Such a move would have been opposed by the U.S. and British governments, and it seems unlikely that Valletta and the Agnelli family would have sold out to a foreign company after their skillful defense of the firm's independence during the war. The GM–FIAT contacts concerned raw materials, licenses, and other technical aid. Negotiations persisted until 1947, then broke off completely when GM decided to restore its prewar European connection with Opel of Germany.[33]

The full story of private U.S. capital and early postwar Italy cannot be written until the archives are opened on both sides. The evidence now available makes clear that there were indeed two major U.S. projects pending when De Gasperi took power in December 1945. Both Transcontinental and Western Airways (TWA) and the International Telephone and Telegraph Company (IT&T) had begun discussions with the Parri government in mid-1945. The State Department's Office of Transportation and Communications (TRC), through its telecommunications (TD) and aviation (AV) divisions had kept track of both firms in order to enforce armistice regulations and to insure equal access for and among U.S. interests. De Gasperi, in turn, rapidly consummated agreements that appeared, at least at the time, to satisfy American requirements.

IT&T had proposed that the prewar network of five telephone companies be consolidated into a single entity under the joint control of public and private capital. The system was largely in ruins in 1945, and IT&T would undertake to modernize, manage, and service the entire business in return for a percentage of its gross annual income. The Italians wanted direct participation by IT&T, but given political and economic conditions, the Americans preferred to hedge their bets and proposed instead an Export–Import Bank loan to the Italian government. The telecommunications division was sympathetic to American participation, but Export–Import Bank loans were usually limited to the dollars required for commodities and services exported from the United States. The bank's lending capacity was practically exhausted in late 1945, with no immediate prospect of new appropriations.[34]

The presence of IT&T's American competitor, the Automated Electric Company of Chicago, also worried the department. Like IT&T, Automated Electric already controlled an Italian switchboard equipment and construction company. Together with OLAP, owned by Siemens-Halske of Berlin, Automated Electric's subsidiary, SATAP, had controlled 75 percent of the prewar market. IT&T-owned FACE, and FATME, a subsidiary of L. M. Ericsson of Sweden, controlled the rest. (IT&T, in turn, effectively controlled Ericsson with 35.2 percent of its stock.) SIRTI–Pirelli had enjoyed a virtual monopoly in long-distance cables. The State Department was unaware that both IT&T and Automated Electric had designs on the German-owned OLAP Company, under Italian sequestration at the time.[35] In late August 1945, Automated Electric lodged a strong protest with the telecommunications division, citing rumors that IT&T-inspired consolidation plans would include SIRTI–Pirelli and FACE–IT&T. "If the proposed union of telephone operating companies materializes," Automated observed, "our efforts in Italy would be neutralized. . . . Italian manufacture would be substituted for U.S. manufacture and we would for all practical purposes, be forced out of the market."[36]

Department officials shared the view of such Italian liberal economists as Einaudi that consolidation of existing units of production made sense in the case of natural monopolies, but Automated Electric had raised the issue of fairness and equal access among U.S. firms. TD Chief Francis Colt de Wolf told Clair Wilcox of the International Trade Division, "It seems to me obvious that we cannot object to any proposal of the Italian Government to merge Italian telephone companies. However, we cannot give the appearance of favoring the IT&T vs. the Automated Electric Company." IT&T pursued its talks with the Italian government, but differences developed over the fee and the five-company consolidation. IT&T seemed willing to compromise on the former issue, but TD in

Washington continued to have misgivings. Automated protested again, and the rehabilitation project was stalemated by late November.[37]

On December 12, 1945, two days after the formation of the new government, Mario Scelba, a De Gasperi protégé and now minister of posts and telecommunications, formally invited IT&T "to undertake the studies necessary to elaborate a complete financial and technical reconstruction plan. . . ." The premise of the plan would be "the merger of the five concessionary telephone companies and the long distance telephone and telegraphic systems in a single entity. . . ." The deal was made contingent on the Export–Import Bank loan. IT&T would receive a tax-exempt fee of 2.5 percent of the gross receipts of the Italian entity (one half payable in dollars) and would be compensated tax-free for the salaries and expenses of its personnel. The contract was to last for twenty years, with provision for either side to withdraw after an initial ten-year period. The agreement contained several additional clauses designed to maximize the benefits to the local economy and of special interest to the Sicilian Scelba and Southern Christian Democrats: "The plan of reconstruction should contemplate an extension of the services adequate to the social requirements of the various regions and in particular of southern Italy and the islands. . . ."[38]

The gist of the deal had obviously been worked out with the previous government, but the speed with which De Gasperi's lieutenant moved to formalize arrangements indicated an eagerness to cement ties to U.S. private industry. Later reports revealed that De Gasperi believed that the U.S. government strongly favored IT&T control of Italian telecommunications, an impression fostered in part by AC Chief Commissioner Ellery Stone, a high IT&T executive before the war.[39]

TD remained doubtful about Export–Import financing but was satisfied with the December agreement. Department pressure brought about the inclusion of a final clause designed to protect Automated Electric: "The *status quo* of foreign interests already existing in the telephone field shall be safe-guarded." The consolidation issue also remained unsettled. On January 23, TD told the embassy to express its pleasure with the deal to Italian officials and also to "impress upon them the necessity . . . of a plan for an overall rehabilitation program, in which rehabilitation of the telecommunications system is obviously an important factor."[40]

The De Gasperi government simultaneously completed negotiations for the creation of a new Italian airline company. Discussion between TWA and the Italian air minister, Mario Cevelotto (of the small Democracy of Labor Party), had begun in the summer of 1945, when the Civil Aeronautics Board awarded United States-to-Rome air service to TWA. On November 5, TWA Chairman General Tom Wilson met Stanley Morgan of the department's aviation division in Washington. Both the

British and the Russians had their own plans for Italy, but, according to Wilson, the Italians preferred a U.S. company: "The proposal would be that TWA undertake to operate a commercial service in Italy, or that TWA accept a management contract to operate in Italy, if the Allied Control [sic] Commission will permit operation by an Italian company at this time."[41]

As part of the department's campaign to liberalize international civil aviation, AV had already convinced the Italian government to grant nonreciprocal landing rights to U.S. aircraft. The Italians had at first resisted but then agreed, probably because they wished American support for the revival of their own industry. According to a policy laid down by Roosevelt himself and incorporated in the armistice of 1943, the Germans, Italians, and the Japanese would not be allowed "to fly anything larger than one of those toy planes that you wind up with an elastic band." AV supported a revision of the armistice to permit an Italian airline, but as of November 1945, the matter was unresolved with the British and the CCS.[42]

Morgan passed the TWA proposal to EUR's Southern Europe Division with the request that it consider:

> whether the Armistice terms permitted the operation of domestic aviation by an Italian company; whether, if the answer were yes the U.S. should like to see TWA undertake the management of such a company, and finally if the answer were no, whether TWA should undertake the operations in its own name.

Assuming there were no objections, AV was ready to handle the details with TWA, "if and when the formal proposal is received." Pending approval by the State Department and the Anglo-American military authorities (CCAC), TWA and Minister Cevelotto drew up plans for a joint Italian–American company, "Linee Aeree Italiane" (LAI). On December 26, 1945, the embassy reported that Cevelotto had discussed the proposal with De Gasperi. The prime minister was very pleased, and a copy of the final agreement creating LAI (60 percent Italian owned, 40 percent TWA, with voting control in TWA through two-thirds rule) was cabled to Washington on February 8, 1946. The contract was executed pending final CCAC approval three days later in Rome.[43]

THE NEW UNRRA

The Rome embassy paid tribute to De Gasperi in mid-January 1946. The new government had addressed itself "with energy to the solution of both immediate and longer term problems." The Tasca–Corbino collaboration had proved particularly fruitful, and Tasca's cables were henceforth laced with excerpts from the minister's speeches and pro-Corbino citations from business journals.[44] The young Tasca had arrived in Rome with a mandate to purge Fascists from Italian financial institutions. His political priorities had shifted considerably by early 1946 as both the departure of Morgenthau and his day-to-day contact with Italian businessmen and liberal economists contributed to a growing preoccupation with communist subversion. With the retirement of Alexander Kirk in February 1946 (his duties were assumed until early 1947 by the lackluster charge d'affaires, David Key), Tasca emerged as the dominant force within the Rome embassy.

But despite the promising debut, neither Tasca nor the State Department was by any means convinced that De Gasperi could lead an anti–Communist alliance. Both the prime minister's position and general political conditions remained highly precarious. During the first six months of 1946, however, De Gasperi continued his adroit performance in conducting the country through a series of delicate appointments: local elections, the resolution of the institutional question, and the formation of the constituent assembly. In late March, the ticklish question of the assembly's powers was resolved. The Italian cabinet, in accordance with EUR's legal opinion, decided that the assembly's function would be limited to preparing a new national constitution. This represented a major concession by the PCI and PSIUP, who had originally pressed for a sovereign body with full legislative powers. It was another impressive victory for De Gasperi, who had warned the State Department that the assembly might "set the stage for dictatorship with Nenni or Togliatti as candidates." Once more in accordance with the views of De Gasperi and the State Department, it was decided that the monarchy's fate would be determined by a popular referendum rather than a vote by the assembly, as was favored by the left. The decision for a referendum was a classic illustration of De Gasperi's practical approach to politics. He realized that a vote in the assembly would reveal a clear pro-republican majority among the DC party leadership. Regardless of his personal view (which was characteristically unclear), the decision for monarchy or republic was less important to De Gasperi than keeping the party attractive to the large promonarchist electorate, especially in the South.[45]

Henry Tasca's increasing identification of U.S. interests with Italy's propertied and anticommunist classes prefigured the evolution of the American foreign policy establishment at large. In early 1946, however, some people in the State Department still hoped for an open economic system, embracing the European continent as a whole. In a February 8 memo, Clayton's investment and economic development division argued that American interests in Italy were best guaranteed by "a stable and progressive government, inclined to follow the Anglo-American lead in international economic policy . . . [(but)] which is not hostile to the USSR."[46] Even though Clayton's influence in Italy was slight, on the issues of IRI, U.S. private investment, and export trade promotion, the new De Gasperi government had displayed an apparent willingness to go along with the department design.

The first months of the De Gasperi government also offered encouragement to a set of American officials who favored democratic planning and social change. On January 19, 1946, De Gasperi signed an agreement with Spurgeon M. Keeny inaugurating a $450 million UNRRA aid program for 1946. Keeny was a New Deal Democrat and relief expert with several years of Italian experience. Approximately 70 percent of the Italian program would be paid for by the United States as part of congress's $750 million UNRRA appropriation of December 1945. The agreement represented a dramatic expansion of the small existing UNRRA program (in operation under Keeny since March 1945) and was designed to provide free-of-charge to the Italian government 70 percent of Italian food, 40 percent of fuel, 82 percent of agricultural, 22 percent of industrial, and 100 percent of medical import requirements for 1946.[47]

Even though they were dependent on congress for future appropriations, Keeny and his staff were international civil servants responsible to UNRRA's European Regional Office (ERO) in London rather than to the Rome embassy or to Clayton's divisions in Washington. The majority were Americans with AC or FEA backgrounds, the mission staff also included many British and a scattering of Russian officials. Keeny knew that UNRRA's ambiguous, semi-independent status might lead to friction with the State Department and the Italian government and also that the mission lacked the political and financial leverage to impose any overall reconstruction plan. (In December, 1945 Harlan Cleveland estimated that UNRRA would provide at most 50 percent of the approximately $1 billion in foreign exchange needed by Italy in 1946.)[48] Nonetheless, UNRRA possessed substantial resources. According to the January (so-called Supplemental) agreement, the Italian government would also create a special lira account to receive the proceeds of sale of UNRRA-supplied goods on the local market. The receipts would then be used to finance relief and rehabilitation projects agreed on by the two sides. UNRRA hoped thereby to help guide the formation of Italian government policy and favored strict price and foreign exchange controls during the reconstruction period.

CONCLUSION

The UNRRA mission began its 1946 operations in a brief interlude of political calm and cautious optimism about the future of the local econ-

Conclusion

omy. Inflation had subsided as imported supplies became available in greater abundance. Thanks to joint United States–Italian efforts, the key textile sector showed signs of sustained recovery. But the honeymoon atmosphere of early 1946 tended to obscure the serious conflicts within both the Italian government and the American foreign policy apparatus. Indeed, the advent of De Gasperi served eventually to clarify and rein-force the basic contradictions at the heart of the Italian coalition. Tensions mounted in April and May as the constituent assembly elections and institutional referendum approached. In Epicarmo Corbino, more-over, De Gasperi had introduced a dynamic and potentially explosive element into the political equation. His stubbornly orthodox policies soon laid bare the political obstacles to a coherent liberal strategy and threatened to provoke an open confrontation with the left.

The experience of March to September would belie the promise of De Gasperi's arrival for UNRRA and Clayton alike. They pursued their respective programs with great energy and conviction, but both faced a series of unsurmountable barriers. Clayton's campaign to extend the foothold gained in early 1946 became bogged down almost immediately. It is to Clayton's growing troubles that one now must turn, for they reveal the emerging domestic as well as external challenge to the State Department's design.

5

Clayton at bay

INTRODUCTION

Historian John Lewis Gaddis has argued that ". . . the convergence of external and internal trends in late February and early March 1946, produced a fundamental reorientation of United States policy toward the Soviet Union." That brief period thus marked a turning point in American policy, the end of hopes for a satisfactory accommodation between the wartime Allies.[1] Gaddis offers impressive supporting evidence. Following Byrnes's conciliatory approach to the Russians at Moscow in December 1945, the secretary of state came under heavy fire from White House Chief of Staff Admiral William Leahy and Republican leader Arthur Vandenberg. The president himself rebuked Byrnes, and the secretary's subsequent statements indicated a new inclination to hold the line against Russia.

On February 9, Stalin made a speech predicting another world war unless the capitalist system were transformed. Opinion polls in the United States reflected a growing distrust of Russia, and the Iran crisis and Soviet spy scandal in Canada reinforced the emerging anticommunist consensus. On February 23, George Kennan's 8,000-word analysis of Soviet behavior arrived at the State Department in Washington. The effect of the "long telegram," as its author later noted, "was nothing less than sensational." Kennan's missive was seized on by Secretary of the Navy James Forrestal as a brilliant statement of his own visceral anti-Soviet feelings and made required reading in the military and foreign affairs bureaucracy. Churchill captured the new mood in his famous Iron Curtain speech delivered at Fulton, Missouri, on March 5.[2]

The events of February–March 1946 doubtless strengthened the hand of Forrestal and his fellow hard-liners, but Gaddis's assertion that those developments produced a new consensus and departure in Washington is harder to accept. It is clear now – indeed it was obvious at the time – that the rhetorical offensive on both sides was aimed primarily at domestic political objectives. Stalin's speech was designed to rally the Soviet people behind the massive reconstruction effort, Churchill's to drum up support for the pending British loan. Truman, Byrnes, and Acheson realized that public displeasure with the Russians was a political fact of life, but they were neither ready nor able to launch a new policy designed to secure American interests against the Soviet Union. Truman did not associate himself with the view of the world propounded in the Churchill speech.

The hopes of both New Deal and Hullian liberals were still alive in March 1946. Though isolated within the Democratic Party, Wallace and Morgenthau attacked the revival of British and French colonialism in Asia and called for the recognition of legitimate Soviet interests in Eastern Europe. State and treasury began preliminary talks on an international trade organization in early 1946 and held a major organizational meeting of the International Monetary Fund at Savannah in March. Many officials hoped that the USSR would play a role in both institutions. Indeed, it was such hopes that Kennan sought, in part, to disabuse in his famous February telegram. In his memoirs, Kennan recalls that he "reached for his pen" in exasperation after yet another inquiry from Washington about Russian reluctance to join the IMF and International Bank for Reconstruction and Development.[3] But the National Advisory Council (NAC) continued to set aside $1 billion of the Export–Import Bank's limited funds for a possible loan to the Soviet Union. Despite rising domestic anticommunism, Byrnes continued his pragmatic horse-trading approach to the Russians.

A "convergence of external and internal trends" would indeed produce a deep crisis, broad consensus, and new departure in American foreign policy. Throughout 1946, however, the paramount domestic fact of life was not the ground swell of anti-Russian feeling, but that such sentiment did not readily translate itself into new foreign aid to promote American interests abroad. The dominant domestic trend – dramatically confirmed by the November Congressional elections – was mounting pressure for demobilization, protectionism, and budgetary cutbacks.[4]

Rising isolationism at home coincided with the worsening of Europe's political and balance-of-payments situations. The Russian blackout of the East, combined with the spread of exchange controls and bilateral trading in the West, raised doubts about America's liberal commercial and financial order. The inadequacy of U.S. aid programs became painfully apparent as the European economies were beset by material shortages and inflation. The focus of concern was naturally Germany. It was obvious that German recovery was essential for sustained growth in Europe as a whole. Yet, U.S. occupation officials were forced to contend with both French and Russian demands for reparations and dismemberment and with the strictures of official U.S. policy inherited from Roosevelt, which demanded denazification of German industry and finances and permitted only limited economic recovery.

Italy's role in the revival of Europe was trivial by comparison. Yet as the strategic linchpin of the Mediterranean and as proving ground for the Hullian and UNRRA programs, Italy received close attention from the Truman Administration. For Clayton, in particular, the Italian situation presented a series of challenges in 1946. It was a year of endless lobbying in Washington for additional economic aid. Meanwhile, the investment projects that had promised private help for Italian recovery became entangled in a controversy that questioned the basic principles of department policy. Congressional and public reluctance to pay the cost of department policy was a tiresome and familiar reality. It now proved equally difficult to engage U.S. international business in pursuit of the department's liberal plans.

Clayton's response to the crisis of Hullian policy showed his determination to resist the logic of anticommunism and spheres of influence. But domestic and European trends brought about a gradual meeting of minds among high department officials. The British loan debate convinced Acheson of the domestic political uses of anticommunism.[5] At the same time, the left's threat to the recovery of business confidence became more and more apparent, at least in the case of Italy, where Corbino's liberal experiment foundered during the summer of 1946.

STALEMATE IN WASHINGTON

Clayton's problem was neatly summed up by Harlan Cleveland in December 1945. He noted that UNRRA would provide $450 million, at best half of Italy's 1946 foreign exchange requirements. Where, he wondered, were they going to find the rest?[6] In January 1946, $1.9 billion of the Export–Import Bank's original $3.5 billion remained to satisfy a global foreign economic policy. On February 6, the NAC earmarked $1 billion of that amount for a possible Russian loan.

On February 14, Ambassador Alberto Tarchiani presented a request to Clayton for a $940 million Export–Import loan. According to Tarchiani, total Italian aid requirements for 1946 amounted to $1.7 billion. Italy expected $760 million from UNRRA, remittances, exports, and other sources, leaving $940 million to be made up by the bank. This proposal had been prepared by the Italian purchasing mission in Washington with the help of Oscar Cox. Their figures were a far cry from Allied Commission and Minister of Industry Gronchi's estimates of approximately $1 billion, and the episode illustrated an utter lack of coordination among the Italians themselves. An official of the Interministerial Committee for

Reconstruction in Rome told the AC that the loan request had been prepared by Cesare Sacerdoti, head of the purchasing mission, so as "not to lose Italy's place in the queue."

Minister of Trade La Malfa "had vaguely heard of the request" and thought it was based on old instructions from Reconstruction Minister Ruini. When the AC told La Malfa that the request had come from Tarchiani, the minister appeared stunned and immediately called the Foreign Ministry. The Foreign Ministry confirmed that the ambassador was involved and promised a full report. The Foreign Ministry told the AC independently that Tarchiani had been authorized to negotiate but that Rome had "no idea as to the form the loan was to have." State Department officials were also taken aback and immediately told Tarchiani to forget about "a loan anywhere near the size requested." Meanwhile, they made quick work of Cleveland's smaller estimate. On March 7, the department informed the Rome embassy that $260 million would satisfy Italy's additional requirement in 1946. That figure represented the $110 million treasury suspense account, or dollar equivalent of lira expenditures by U.S. forces in Italy for supplies and services (so-called nontroop pay dollars), plus a possible Export–Import Loan of $150 million.[7]

Obtaining $260 million alone involved Clayton in a complicated political-diplomatic campaign. Everyone agreed, as Byrnes told the Council of Foreign Ministers (CFM), that "The United States was not going to pour millions of dollars into any country in order to permit it to pay reparations to others." Accordingly, Clayton informed Tarchiani on February 14 that it would be impossible to consider a substantial Export–Import loan until the reparations question had been settled. The matter would be taken up during the Paris session of the CFM, scheduled to begin in April. In early March, the National Advisory Council postponed discussion of an Italian loan but agreed to seek prompt release of the nontroop pay dollars. However, release of those funds involved another set of problems. The NAC recommended to Truman that the money be made available, but congressional approval was required. Clayton and Treasury Secretary Vinson undertook to lobby the house and senate appropriations committees.[8]

In the meantime, Clayton himself was the object of an intense effort by the Italian embassy in Washington and its U.S. counterpart in Rome. Both embassies pointed to the national elections, tentatively scheduled for late May. Tasca argued that immediate release of the suspense account would make Italians vote "more objectively" in the upcoming elections. The department agreed and had already embarked on a final, ultimately fruitless effort to revise the 1943 armistice before the final peace treaty took effect.[9] Clayton's basic objective in early 1946 was the integration of Europe into the IMF and ITO. But he was increasingly preoccupied with the political consequences of economic distress. In early March, Clayton and Harry White agreed that the NAC should consider "political loans" (i.e., where "there is not a reasonable expectation that they will be repaid with interest") in such cases as Italy. They were immediately opposed by Bank President William McChesney Martin, who, mindful of his congressional masters, insisted that the bank be run on a "strictly business basis."[10]

On April 19, Clayton urged the NAC to reconsider an Italian loan: "The country's economic situation was desperate. There were elections scheduled in May, and it was important that we take action before then. . . . Almost anything could happen unless we gave financial assistance for the purchase of supplies." But the NAC had no choice but to postpone the Italian request anew. One billion dollars were earmarked for the Soviet Union, and the NAC soon agreed to set aside another $500 million for China, where General Marshall was conducting delicate negotiations.[11]

By early May, Clayton was engaged on three fronts: the Paris session of the CFM, Congress, and the NAC itself. When the CFM convened on April 25 to discuss peace settlements with the smaller Axis powers, the Russians immediately claimed $100 million in Italian reparations, including current industrial production. On May 2, Byrnes announced that the United States was prepared to examine such sources of reparation as external assets "but was not going to do as it had done after the last war, and that was pay out hundreds of millions of dollars for reparations accounts of others." The same day he cabled the department to order that the Italian loan be given prompt consideration. Approval of the loan would bolster the U.S. argument in Paris against payments from current industrial production. On May 7, Clayton told the NAC of the Byrnes message: "Nothing had happened which would make him want to postpone consideration of the [Italian] loan."[12] Two days later, however, the Federal Reserve representative Marriner Eccles raised the question of possible French and British claims on Italy. In spite of Clayton's pleas, the banker's argument prevailed. The NAC voted to delay the loan again until the situation was clarified.

By mid-May, the CFM had adjourned, still deadlocked on the issue of Italian reparations. Molotov had insisted that Italian external assets were not adequate to satisfy Russia's $100 million claim and insisted on payments to the smaller victims of Fascist aggression – Greece, Yugoslavia, and Albania.[13] Clayton was obviously powerless to affect events in Paris. The situation in Washington was scarcely more encouraging. The bank was stretched to the limit following the allocation for China, and Clayton and his treasury allies faced more opposition on the question of political loans. On May 2, Commerce Secretary Wallace made a rare appearance at the NAC to discuss a loan to France, where national elections were imminent. Rumors of a communist coup had excited EUR, and former prime minister Leon Blum was in town seeking major American credits. To Clayton's great annoyance, Wallace asked whether there was a general policy "of making loans to influence foreign elections." Clayton discounted news of a PCF uprising but pointed out that economic stagnation might lead to "serious political and social disturbances in countries such as France."[14] When the NAC discussed the matter again on May 6, Eccles took Wallace's side, arguing that he did not want the U.S. government accused of buying foreign elections.[15] The NAC voted nonetheless to approve $650 million in new credits to France. The decision was an important victory for Clayton, but it effectively eliminated the already slim chance of a similar pre-election loan to Italy.

On May 10, Clayton and Vinson approached the house appropriations committee to secure the other potential source of aid, the treasury suspense account. They received the polite but firm suggestion that instead of making a gift of dollars to Italy, "we lend them the money that they would be under obligation to repay . . . ; they did not think that the cost of occupation was in the same category." Clayton's predicament deepened when he met Tarchiani on May 16. The Italian elections were now scheduled for June 2, and the ambassador appealed for an increase in the proposed Export–Import loan to compensate for congressional rejection of the suspense account release. Clayton replied that a $100 million loan would probably be approved eventually, but the amount could not be increased because the bank had now exhausted its lending authority. Tarchiani was desperate for a pre-election gesture. If the bank got more money, he suggested, the United States could announce an increase in the loan. Moreover, the "psychological effect of any statement would be such that it might be worthwhile to exaggerate a little to influence the elections." Clayton would offer nothing of the kind. "When the loan is ready to be announced we would have to weigh our words most carefully in order to obtain as much advantage as possible from the announcement, but it seemed a little doubtful whether we could promptly say much about funds which we would not actually have at that time." The ambassador departed empty-handed.[16]

Despite his manifest problems, Clayton did not resort to the anti-Soviet geopolitical arguments that had become common currency in Washington since the Kennan telegram. He was obviously sensitive to the broader implications of Europe's balance-of-payments crisis, and the French loan was clearly political in its timing. It was also an instrument of classic Hullian policy and included explicitly economic rather than political strings: a pledge to limit state trading and import controls, endorsement of the ITO charter, and the immediate importation of American motion pictures into France.[17] Although Clayton planned to do away with UNRRA and bring all aid funds under State Department control, he defended a controversial relief program operating in the Ukraine. When Capitol Hill Republicans tried to ban the use of United States–appropriated UNRRA funds in countries that censored American news dispatches, Clayton made a personal appeal, arguing that the move would "seriously complicate our relations with the Soviet Union." When the NAC decided to seek an additional $1.25 billion for the Export–Import Bank in June, Clayton secured agreement that $1 billion in existing funds would continue to be set aside for the Russians.[18] Clayton, in short, was deeply reluctant to abandon the foreign economic policy inherited from Hull in 1944.

But that policy had no future without congressional support. Acheson later noted that the "burden of bureaucratic infighting" weighed heavily on his friend Clayton in mid-1946. Clayton was persuaded not to resign, in part through his elevation to a new position designed to enhance his prestige in Washington: under secretary of state for economic affairs. Meanwhile, the more pragmatic Acheson had begun to demonstrate his own keen sense of domestic realities. The passage of the $3.5 billion loan to Britain in July was a major success for the under secretary of state. In contrast to Clayton, Acheson freely exploited the anticommunist susceptibilities of such Anglophobe congressmen as John McCormick and managed to sell an essentially Hullian economic package as an anti-Soviet design. Skeptical congressmen were converted for reasons similar to those expressed by House Speaker Sam Rayburn: "I do not want Western Europe, England, and all the rest pushed towards an ideology that I despise."[19]

The same logic would become less and less escapable to other administration officials. In July, Rayburn and Senate Majority Leader Alben Barkley told the State Department that the Export–Import Bank's new appropriation stood no chance as long as $1 billion remained set aside for the Russians. Neither Clayton nor Truman was prepared to foreclose the possibility of a Russian loan, and the president decided to delay the appropriation request. Thus, the bank ceased to function as an instrument of foreign economic policy. In September, Bank President Martin began to refer all new loan requests to the International Bank for Reconstruction and Development. But the IBRD also depended on congress and could not begin operations until sometime in 1947.[20]

Italian lobbying efforts were sidetracked following the pre-election meeting with Clayton. The $940 million request had proved to be a tactical blunder, and the embassy was later rebuked for "blowing up the Italian problem with totals of millions." In a letter to the Italian technical delegation (DELTEC) in October, Mario Einaudi, professor of economics at Cornell and son of Luigi Einaudi, warned that U.S. officials were "hardboiled and practical" and unlikely to give money to people who "can't put their house in order." Therefore, the Italians had better "give the impression that U.S. dollars are not being thrown into a bottomless pit."[21] Tarchiani would take the lesson to heart. It was constantly repeated by bank and congressional officials. At the same time, the ambassador surmised that broader political, strategic, and ideological considerations would compel the United States to become lender of last resort regardless of Italy's immediate ability to repay, and he would endeavor to reap maximum material and diplomatic advantages from Italy's rapidly deteriorating internal situation in late 1946.

THE PRIVATE INVESTMENT CONTROVERSY

"The Summer of 1946," Acheson recalled, "was a time of almost uninterrupted troubles both in Washington and abroad."[22] While wrestling with the congress and bureaucracy, Clayton faced another less expected challenge to his basic policy. Once again, Clayton's response is testimony to his commitment to Hull's program, even as political and economic events moved rapidly beyond control. The test involved the two American firms that had shown an interest in Italy – TWA and IT&T. Their projects were of some importance to the State Department at a time when official aid programs could provide little more than half of Italy's foreign aid requirements. However, things began to go awry before the ink was dry on preliminary agreements between the companies and the new De Gasperi Government.

The creation of LAI, the joint company foreseen by the February contract between TWA and the Italian air minister, Mario Cevolotto, had awaited review by the Anglo-American occupation authorities. On March 16, 1946, the combined chiefs of staff gave unconditional approval to the revival of the Italian airline industry. Four days later, the AC formally notified the Italian government that an Italian civil aviation service could be reestablished. TWA held that the CCS directive satisfied the conditions of the contract. Thus, according to their view, the February contract became operative on March 20, 1946. By mid-March, the details had begun to filter out in Washington, London, and Rome. The deal established an Italian company (LAI), 60 percent Italian owned, 40 percent TWA owned, with voting control in TWA through a two-thirds rule. A department memo cited the contract's most important clause: "The Italian Government shall grant exclusively for a period of ten years to LAI the right to operate the following airlines, also shown on the attached map. . . ." The map included every practicable civil air route in

Italy, Sicily, and Sardinia. The contract was "to all intents and purposes an exclusive one."[23]

This news provoked storms of protest from all directions. The British immediately sent top BOAC officials to talk to Cevolotto. The minister referred them to TWA, but the U.S. company was in no mood to bargain with the British. According to TWA Chairman Wilson, BOAC had "absolutely nothing to offer." The British then demanded that the Italian government delay passage of legislation implementing the TWA contract and asked for a 20 percent share of any local company. There was some mystery surrounding the decision of the British members of the CCS to authorize an Italian airline company in the first place. Gerald Norton, chief of TRC, observed to Clayton, "There is no doubt British liaison in this matter has been poor. . . ." Perhaps the British generals had been "asleep at the switch."[24]

Although irritated and embarrassed, the Foreign Office believed it had a solid case. The TWA–Italian deal coincided with the Anglo-American civil aviation conference at Bermuda (January–February 1946). Although Italy was a peripheral concern, both the Foreign Office and the State Department later noted that the British had expressed a desire to participate in the revival of Italian civil aviation. On April 13, the British reminded the State Department that the United States government had been on record of the British position since Bermuda. The Foreign Office insisted that the department intervene with the Italians and TWA to insure BOAC participation in the contract. The U.S. embassy in London reported that the Foreign Office had not warned the military (CCS) in time and was now "trying to cover up by saying they relied on the understanding with the State Department."[25]

Cevolotto and others involved on the Italian side appear to have had a substantial personal stake in the affair.[26] Evidence also exists that both the U.S. embassy in Rome and the aviation division (AV) in Washington had presumed the British might accede to the TWA plan in consideration of the pending $3.5 billion loan. Both the embassy and AV had known of the contract's terms since February 8, if not before. The embassy had supported it, and AV had taken no action to revise it, explaining later that they assumed the British would have a say through the CCS. Circumstantial evidence suggests that AV hoped for British concessions on the matter. On January 3, 1946, the British Ambassador Lord Halifax called on Acheson to suggest that talks on a bilateral aviation agreement begin at once. With the loan debate looming, London seemed to be in a conciliatory mood. The same day AV cabled Rome: "Department . . . would prefer to see TWA plan accepted and believes that such a step would be in best interests of Italy and U.S." Once the CCS had acted on

March 16, AV told the embassy to "give appropriate support to this legitimate U.S. enterprise in its efforts to implement such contract."[27]

Liaison within the department was also poor, and few people had been apprised of the contract's monopolistic nature. When the details came to light, Clayton's divisions joined in a resounding condemnation of the deal. TRC chief Norton sent a long memo to Clayton calling for "a prompt decision . . . at a high level in the Department." Norton noted that the Russians were organizing companies in the Balkans "with the same features of monopoly and exclusivity as are involved in the TWA contract although on paper they do not appear as objectionable as the TWA contract." According to the international trade policy division, the contract would be "extremely embarrassing, in our opposition to Soviet arrangements in Eastern Europe. . . . The proposed deal should not be approved unless the exclusive feature is eliminated. . . ." The international resources division recalled that it had urged the department all along to "discourage monopolistic penetration from abroad." Emilio Collado, a top assistant to Clayton, called the contract "a flagrant case of restrictive agreement. . . . Such a precedent would give any country an appropriate reply to an American protest about a restrictive agreement to the detriment of American interests in any part of the world." Elbridge Durbrow of EUR's Eastern Europe division agreed that "The proposed TWA–Italian deal stands on all fours with the Soviet practice of setting up exclusive joint companies and is open to precisely the same objections. . . ."[28]

In early May, the department told TWA that it would oppose any contract providing exclusive rights to the subsidiary of a U.S. company. TWA had little choice but to renegotiate the contract. At the same time, both TWA and the department rejected British suggestions for a joint Anglo-American monopoly. BOAC promptly attempted to create its own Italian subsidiary. Those decisions set off a laborious round of new negotiations designed to secure equal treatment for TWA with the British company. The revival of the Italian airline industry was delayed for months as the parties squabbled over market shares and route agreements.[29]

The TWA imbroglio had direct implications for IT&T's plan to modernize the national telecommunications network. In mid-April, the embassy warned Washington to expect problems with the IT&T agreement as a result of the aviation dispute. The embassy confirmed an earlier report from IT&T that the British had offered De Gasperi their own deal (no details were reported) in lieu of sterling troop pay credits and had advised the Italians not to proceed with IT&T unless British interests were represented on an equal footing. Shortly after its veto of the TWA

85

contract, the department told the Rome embassy that it would be "most hesitant to approve" the deal outlined in the December 1945 Scelba letter if monopoly control of equipment and supply were implied. The Export–Import Bank loan for the project was also very much in doubt. In any event, a loan did not exclude the possibility of British participation in the project.[30]

In July, the telecommunications division produced a telecommunications policy and information statement with special reference to Italy. The basic guidelines laid down reflected the lessons of the aviation case, and the prevailing view that the U.S. interest in global access to markets would be jeopardized by allowing U.S. companies to establish an exclusive hold in areas under strong American influence and where local groups were ready to grant exclusive rights to U.S. firms. The statement observed:

> No arrangements shall be made which might expressly or implicitly limit the freedom of action of the United States with respect to future developments in the telecommunications field in any region of the world. . . . The policy of the United States should be to favor the development and conduct within foreign countries of communications services controlled by their own nationals. The United States should not adopt a general policy of aiding United States companies to develop or participate in internal communication within foreign countries.

At the same time:

> The United States in individual meritorious cases may properly assist United States companies diplomatically and financially – if adequate funds are not available from other sources on reasonable terms – provided that in making arrangements between the United States and foreign enterprises, nothing shall be done by the United States company to discourage equal opportunity to all competing companies on a non-exclusive basis either to supply equipment or to bid for the provision of services.[31]

IT&T obviously constituted a "meritorious case" in the view of TD. But the TWA episode dealt a severe blow to IT&T's effort to secure substantial control of the Italian market. Continued pressure from the British and IT&T's American competitor, Automated Electric, insured that the July guidelines were more than empty rhetoric. Despite help from the Rome embassy – the embassy was inclined to give the phrase *may properly assist . . .* a liberal interpretation – it became increasingly hard for IT&T to maintain the fiction with the Italians that it enjoyed categorical U.S. government support. That impression was probably dispelled entirely when the Export–Import Bank rejected an Italian request for $50 million to finance the IT&T project. The bank was obviously pressed for funds. A May 1947 memo also noted that "in view of IT&T control of potential competitive manufacturing groups, such approval in

Conclusion

principle might carry with it approval of commercial practices that the Department would not in fact care to approve."[32]

In September 1946, the department asked for and received a general pledge from the Italian government forbidding "rights of exclusivity" for any foreign investor, American or otherwise. The following summer, IT&T launched an intensive lobbying campaign to sell a more limited scheme to the Italian cabinet. Despite embassy support, IT&T's proposal encountered waning enthusiasm within Italian government and industry circles. Automated Electric continued to press an alternative plan. The matter dragged on until 1949, when De Gasperi finally rejected all foreign offers and decided to undertake the modernization project using local resources.[33]

CONCLUSION

The resolution of the TWA and IT&T controversies reflected the department's determination to uphold a basic tenet of Hull's wartime policy: the repudiation of economic and political spheres of influence, whether British, Russian, or American. Clayton and his divisions were clearly prepared to enforce the principle of open and equal access at the expense of parochial American interests in order to preserve the integrity of Hullian policy in Eastern Europe and elsewhere in the world. However, this small victory for principle came at a time when the tide of battle was turning against Clayton elsewhere on the European front. The Russians showed little inclination to accept Secretary Byrnes's proposals for equality of commercial and investment opportunity in the Danube region. The secretary's speech at Stuttgart on September 6 signalled the U.S. intention to set up a separate economic unit in the British- and American-controlled areas of western Germany.

Other economic and political developments in Italy, meanwhile, posed a more serious challenge to Clayton and the Hullian program. The orthodox liberal policies of Epicarmo Corbino had encountered serious obstacles by mid-1946 and served mainly to aggravate the political divisions within the Italian coalition. UNRRA, meanwhile, pursued an independent course, sometimes in conflict with both Corbino and the State Department. Clayton had neither the financial leverage nor diplomatic influence to affect the all-important political situation in Italy. By fall 1946, his plans for the swift recovery, structural readjustment, and external reintegration of the Italian economy were in serious disarray.

6

Corbino, UNRRA, and the crisis of the liberal line

INTRODUCTION

During the first eight months of 1946, Italian economic policy bore the stamp of Professor Epicarmo Corbino, the dogmatic and combative treasury minister who took office in December 1945. Behind Corbino stood the prestige and support of Luigi Einaudi, famed economist and governor of the Bank of Italy. Together, they sought to remove the state from the economic arena and to bring market forces to bear on the problems of production, inflation, and structural disequilibrium. Few would deny that the *linea* Corbino produced disappointing results when measured against its stated objectives: the restoration of price stability, business confidence, and sustained investment. Yet few people played a more decisive role in early postwar events. Corbino's policies acted as a razor's edge that cut away the Italian coalition's facade of unity and exposed the weakness and internal contradictions of American policy in the process.

Even though the dismantling of controls in reaction to fascism had begun early in the occupation period, Paolo Baffi notes that Corbino undertook "with real zest" to complete the process. The war profits tax, surtax on stock transactions, and dividend limitations were eliminated and depreciation allowances increased. The currency conversion program had been postponed in January with communist agreement. Corbino also delayed an issue of government securities scheduled for February. These measures were designed to restore confidence and activate the moribund financial markets.[1]

The measures succeeded, but with ironic side effects. Corbino took office at a moment when both banks and private individuals held large hoards of cash and the loosening of stock market and tax regulations produced a wave of speculation. Between May and December 1946, the index of Milan stock prices shot from 480 to 1,353 (1938 = 100). The

88

bull market was fueled by the rapid and uncontrolled expansion of private credit. Throughout 1946, Einaudi declined to use the credit control authority at his disposal. According to liberal doctrine, the private banks should have free rein to finance the incipient recovery.[2]

The liberalization of exchange controls in March (this measure is discussed later in this chapter) was designed to spur exports, increase imported supplies, and achieve equilibrium between local and international prices. In practice, it served largely to encourage private speculation. Large amounts of export earnings were invested abroad or sold at high profits on the black market. During a year of severe foreign exchange shortages and dependence on foreign supplies, only 5 percent of total imports were bought with the hard currency placed in private hands by the March measure. As the lira fell on the free market, exporters reaped large gains while import prices rose to record levels.[3]

The centerpiece of Corbino's strategy to restore investor confidence was a balanced budget. Here, again, his policies brought ironic results. He had fought the currency conversion and delayed an ordinary bond issue for fear of crowding out the private markets. In a period of unsuppressed demands for government spending, the treasury was thus forced to rely increasingly on indirect taxes and the Bank of Italy. The combination of borrowing from the Central Bank and credit expansion in the private sector produced an average monthly increase in the money supply of 5.6 percent between June 1946 and September 1947.[4] By late summer 1946, the boom in private shares had crowded out the government's own short-term securities, and Corbino was obliged to take emergency steps before his sudden fall from power in September.

The attempt of Corbino and Einaudi to unleash the constructive forces of the market was certainly not without its internal logic and popular appeal. However, the approach also had several basic flaws. First, its authors were unable to affect the underlying political and psychological conditions essential to the success of their economic and financial policies. Second, their ideological purpose was shared only in part by the business forces who were the necessary protagonists of the liberal reconstruction strategy. The presence of the left at the highest levels of government was a fundamental obstacle to any attempt to balance the budget and divert resources away from wages and consumption into savings and investment. Corbino's problem was not that the communists and socialists pushed for concrete, radically different economic policies. However, the left parties were determined to defend the standard of living of the working classes. They used their political clout to defend wage indexation and the ban on firings and pressed claims for subsidized political prices and public works expenditures.

While blaming increasing deficits and inflation on the left, Corbino and Einaudi miscalculated the reaction of their business allies to the liberalization measures. Observers have noted the liberal economists' childlike faith in the creative genius and initiative of the entrepreneur. Businessmen themselves, however, showed less than boundless confidence in the future of the economy. In a moment of deep political uncertainty, the policies of Corbino and Einaudi resulted in hedging, capital export, and the rush for quick profits through nonproductive speculation. Concentrated heavy industry meanwhile saw little interest in the free market and the end of state support. Big business demanded and received its own subsidies for reconstruction and conversion. The combination of private credit expansion, stock and commodity speculation, and government deficits created a serious inflation by midsummer 1946. The communists blamed Corbino and clamored for his resignation. Their provocations reinforced middle-class anxiety and mistrust and heightened tensions within the coalition.

Corbino saw that the fundamental obstacle to renewed confidence and sustained productive investment was the power of the left in the government, backed by the organized working class. His policies depended on the creation of a psychological climate favorable to private investors, both foreign and domestic. The liberal strategy, therefore, could be coherent and effective only if carried to its logical conclusion: the defeat of the left. This is precisely what Corbino hoped to accomplish, and he viewed the growing polarization as an inevitable and not unwelcome development.

It was obvious to De Gasperi that Corbino had the backing of influential economic and social groups. Even though the national elections of June 2 confirmed the power of the three mass parties, the DC (35.2 percent), the PSIUP (20.7 percent), and PCI (18.9 percent), De Gasperi insisted on retaining Corbino as an "apolitical technician" in the three-party coalition formed in July.[5] However, De Gasperi was not yet ready for a confrontation with the left. The DC leader saw no choice but to manage the political strife generated in part by Corbino's policies until the inevitable confrontation could be engineered with greater probability of success.

U.S. officials viewed these developments with growing dismay. The most immediate and telling impact of Corbino's policy fell on Keeny, Cleveland, and the local UNRRA mission. UNRRA sought to foster a middle way based on control of the economy's "vital points" and Keynesian spending programs. Such efforts clashed with official financial and foreign exchange policy and met open resistance from Corbino. Economic developments also revealed the practical contradiction between the export-led recovery strategy encouraged by Clayton and the UNRRA attempt to discipline exporters – particularly textiles – and divert a share of production for domestic use. State Department officials in Rome grew tired of UNRRA interference in Italian affairs, and Clayton prepared to eliminate UNRRA and bring all aid appropriations under the control of his planners and economists.

But the Corbino line had serious implications for the department's own economic program. By the time Clayton announced to the United Nations in August that the United States would not fund UNRRA after 1946, the Italian government was on the verge of a serious financial and political crisis. Both Clayton and his UNRRA counterparts were reluctant to conclude that a showdown with the left was necessary and inevitable, but that conclusion was inescapable. Both the New Deal and Hullian programs were stalemated by September 1946.

Henry Tasca, by contrast, was quick to identify the essentially political obstacle to Italian economic recovery. Like De Gasperi and Corbino, Tasca was convinced of communist duplicity and interpreted the party's attacks on government policy as a ploy to create economic chaos and disorder. Tasca's analysis, moreover, struck an increasingly responsive chord within the Truman administration. The fear of collapse in Italy and elsewhere in Western Europe in late 1946 combined with the pressure of domestic isolationism to push American foreign policy toward the single-minded anticommunism of the early Cold War years.

UNRRA: EARLY TRIALS

UNRRA inaugurated its $450 million 1946 program in the atmosphere of cautious optimism surrounding the formation of the first De Gasperi government. In addition to relief, the mission hoped to play a role in formulating special projects financed by the proceeds of sale of the original supplies, to be deposited in a so-called lira fund at the Italian treasury. In Spurgeon M. Keeny, Sr., UNRRA had found a tough, shrewd, and compassionate chief of mission with vast experience in the field of wartime relief and supply. Keeny had served in Mesopotamia and with Hoover's famous Russian relief mission after World War I. He was a Democrat of New Deal persuasion, handpicked by UNRRA's first Administrator, Governor Lehman of New York. Keeny in turn chose Harlan Cleveland, a fellow Rhodes Scholar twenty years his junior, as chief economist and collaborator.

From the beginning, however, the UNRRA mission was hamstrung by its ambiguous relationship to both the Italian government and the U.S. foreign policy apparatus. According to the supplementary agreement (signed by Keeny and De Gasperi on January 19, 1946) governing the 1946 program, UNRRA was a joint enterprise and Italian government decisions were influenced by a variety of competing interests. The mission was not without its natural allies – left-wing Christian Democrats, Republicans, and Socialists – within the Italian coalition. However, these potential interlocutors were themselves divided along political, bureaucratic, and religious lines. Moreover, very little communication, not to speak of collaboration, existed between UNRRA and the Rome embassy or State Department in Washington. As an embassy official later observed, UNRRA insisted that as an international organization it "could not accept the direct and active cooperation of one or even several Embassies in its work."[6] The embassy, in turn, tended to view Keeny and company as far to the left and liable to pursue misguided policies. Understandably, perhaps, embassy personnel resented the enormous aid resources congress had placed in UNRRA's hands. The embassy had advanced it own tutelary schemes such as the so-called Tripartite Economic Advisory Council, but the State Department had rejected direct interference in the Italian economy as impractical and contrary to U.S. policy. Embassy interest in the council was rekindled in early 1946, in part by the desire to counterbalance UNRRA.

An embassy economic counselor noted on March 15 that reconstruction planning and the disposal of future aid "should not be left by default, as it now is, largely in the hands of a small number of UNRRA officials who have developed good working liaison with Italian Ministers on supply and related problems and are in a position to foster programs which, it may be, neither the Italian Government nor the U.S. Government would approve." Some Italian officials shared the fears expressed in a Foreign Ministry memo of January 5, 1946, that the UNRRA program, in particular, the operation of the lira fund, would "limit significantly the Italian Government's freedom of action in the area of financial policy and foreign trade." The embassy listened sympathetically when important DC figures such as Pietro Campilli (trade minister after July 1946) complained that ". . . UNRRA frequently encroaches on the authority of the Italian Government." The Italians soon realized that the mission enjoyed less than categorical U.S. government support and were thus in a position to resist or ignore unwelcome pressure and advice. They also did not hesitate to go over Keeny's head to UNRRA's European Regional Office in London. Following complaints by Italian visitors to London in July, Keeny was told to rein in staff members who meddled "overmuch in Italian Government affairs."[7]

Under these unpropitious circumstances, the mission attempted to hammer out price and lira fund policies with the Italian government. The January agreement provided that the government "consult with the Administration" but set up no machinery. The Italian government had no coherent approach of its own. An interministerial committee on prices laid down general guidelines but had no enforcement powers. Prices were determined by individual ministries or, in the case of key items, after debate and compromise within the cabinet.[8]

This mission was soon engaged in complicated discussions about the sale prices of UNRRA-supplied goods. The minutes of these meetings offer a clear insight into UNRRA's political difficulties. They also reveal immediate and fundamental differences over the basic purpose of the lira fund. On February 1, Keeny and Cleveland met with undersecretary of industry and commerce, Enzo Storoni (who had moved from the Trade Ministry in January), to set the price of UNRRA seed potatoes. Storoni noted that it was well and good to sell the potatoes at low prices, but the wholesaler was beyond control and would reap a windfall profit. The alternative was to charge a high price to the middleman. The government would take the profit, but with no immediate effect on the price level. Keeny suggested that a proportion of the potatoes be distributed free in needy areas. Storoni hastened to point out that they would simply appear the next day on the black market.[9]

Keeny and Cleveland met the following day with Storoni, Trade Minister Ugo La Malfa, and Ivan Matteo Lombardo (Storoni's fellow undersecretary at industry and commerce) to discuss the price of imported coal. Cleveland emphasized that UNRRA goods offered the possibility of a "stable and lower price level," in the case of coal, where virtually the entire stock would be UNRRA-supplied. The Italian government should therefore set a low initial price in order to avoid an immediate shock to the domestic price level. La Malfa, on the other hand, reported that industry would be charged 4,500 lire per ton, whereas direct consumers – utilities, and hospitals, for example – should enjoy the existing price of 2,600 lire. In short, the government preferred "to fix an adequate price now in order to avoid that the present price advantage should go to private firms and individuals, and [would] rather diminish the price of coal as time goes by." Moreover, the Italians argued, a higher price would help fill up the lira fund and remove money from circulation to the treasury's benefit.

Keeny was irritated that the government had decided on this policy without UNRRA approval, but he agreed that the basic dilemma was "whether it is better to have a large lira receipt for . . . rehabilitation or reconstruction, or keep the prices low and thus give whatever benefits we can directly in that way." The two sides wrangled over the relative deflationary effects of immediate lower prices versus cutting monetary circulation through higher prices. UNRRA pointed out that the lira fund was not a stabilization instrument and that the money would eventually be pumped back into the economy through rehabilitation projects. The basic purpose of the lira fund would become a serious bone of contention between UNRRA and the Italian treasury.[10]

It was soon clear that comprehensive price controls were politically and administratively impossible. In the meantime, the mission tried to set up formal joint committees to determine price and lira fund policy. In April, Cleveland told Keeny that the government was "stalling" on the committees. In mid-May, he lamented that "the whole business of setting prices . . . seems to be in a state of utter confusion."[11] Later in the month, Cleveland left for Washington to negotiate the mission's requirements for the second half of 1946. The first six months had scarcely been encouraging. Roughly half the coal and wheat originally allotted for January to June 1946 had not arrived. The Italian government had a serious image problem, and Keeny feared that the failure to control prices, the black market, and luxury restaurants would undermine Cleveland, who was in the United States at the time, "fighting very hard for Italy." There had been serious distribution problems, especially in the area of medical supplies. As of March 1946, only 6 percent of the medical supplies received from abroad since September 1, 1945, had been distributed. Much of the rest had found its way onto the black market. Admiral Stone wrote De Gasperi that the situation created "a deplorable impression on Allied Relief organizations and UNRRA. . . ."[12]

By late May, Keeny's patience was nearly exhausted. During a discussion on the price of wheat, he warned Italian officials that the government must decide "whether it is going to run the country or not. . . . Words must be followed by action." With difficult talks in progress in Washington, this sort of pressure prevailed.[13] In June, De Gasperi agreed to the long-sought special committees – the so-called Lira Fund Control Committee and the Joint Price Committee. Under Cleveland's chairmanship, the Price Committee worked out a series of compromises on the sale cost of UNRRA commodities. According to the official historian, the committee's work was based on the agreement that there would be "a single price policy for all commodities regardless of provenance. . . . In the result, and despite the constantly changing situation, a generally coherent price structure was evolved that helped to effect a smooth transition for Italy's economy from UNRRA to the post-UNRRA period."[14]

UNRRA VERSUS CORBINO

The post-UNRRA transition was much more tumultuous than the official account implies. The creation of the Joint Price Committee coincided with the renewal of an inflation arrested only by the draconian measures of late 1947. Inflation quickly overwhelmed UNRRA efforts to stabilize prices and, in so doing, revealed a fundamental problem of the 1946 program: Mission officials had to swim against the prevailing tide of official foreign exchange and financial policy.

The launching of the UNRRA program coincided with the campaign of Corbino and his business allies to dismantle existing restrictions. At its national convention in January, the cotton textile industry had called for an end to the government's foreign exchange monopoly, a demand echoed at the first National Convention of Foreign Traders, held at Bocconi University in Milan, March 11–14. The issue sparked a heated debate. Guido Carli, acting head of the government's foreign exchange control agency, the UIC, and former Finance Minister Guido Jung argued for complete control. Most cabinet ministers supported some degree of liberalization as an export promotion measure. Almost all, including the Communist Finance Minister Scoccimarro, tended to assume that the confused state of the bureaucracy made effective controls extremely difficult in any case. During his brief tenure as minister of trade, La Malfa argued that exporters should be able to hold one-quarter of their hard currency earnings; others called for 100 percent.[15] The result was compromise:

> As of March 23, 1946, 50% of the foreign exchange proceeds of exports to non-clearing countries (in practice the United States and most countries of the sterling area) were left at the disposal of exporters, in special bank accounts, subject to the limitation that the foreign currency had to be sold to importers or in default to the Foreign Exchange control within sixty days, or be used to import directly commodities included in two approved lists. . . . By a single stroke [the measure] created a limited but very substantial free foreign exchange market.

List A, which included raw wool and cotton, was for goods to be imported against a permit from the customs authorities, against production of a certificate from a bank to the effect that the foreign exchange required for payment had already been surrendered by the importer. List B contained less essential items whose importation required a license from the Ministry of Trade.[16]

The measure created two new exchange rates in addition to the existing official (100 to the dollar, for tourists, remittances, and capital transfers), commercial (225 to the dollar, established in January), and various black market and bilateral clearing rates. The first was the freely fluctuating export rate, at which the exporter sold 50 percent of his hard currency; second was the effective rate received by the exporter, or the average of the commercial and export rates. Between May and October 1946, the export rate (monthly average) fell from 364 to 600 lire to the dollar; the effective rate, from 294 to 412.[17]

The 50 percent measure was a major turning point in early postwar economic policy. Along with the failure to carry out a currency conversion, both contemporary and latter-day critics have considered it one of the gravest mistakes of the liberal economic managers. Whether continued exchange control would have contributed to balanced, planned recovery or simply tended to strangle the country's dynamic export sectors has been a moot question since 1946. There is no doubt, however, that the falling lira fueled domestic inflation (a danger that Einaudi and Corbini discounted during preliminary discussion of the measure) nor is there doubt, as De Cecco notes, that the exchange system helped to build "very strong privileged positions," in particular for the cotton textile industry.[18] Indeed, the new policy was made to order for that industry. Merchants could now deal directly with foreign banks and immediately began to build up their inventories. As the lira fell and domestic prices rose, the textile industry realized increased exports overseas and, by holding back stocks, handsome profits on the local market. Exporters were also free to invest foreign exchange abroad and to speculate at will against the lira.[19]

UNRRA was understandably dismayed. The 50 percent measure struck at the heart of its planning philosophy and wrought havoc with attempts to control prices and speculation. In a January 1946 speech, Cleveland had warned that Italy "must husband carefully its precious pool of foreign exchange." In late August, Cleveland called the 50 percent measure "a major error on the part of the Italian Government, since it knocks a gaping hole in their foreign exchange control. . . . We should do nothing that strengthens the position of those inside the Government or outside of it who believe that the Government should not maintain an effective exchange control, and that individuals, as exporters should be free to do what they like with the proceeds of exports. . . ." After several months in Italy, State Department official Peter Treves called for new, tough controls on current Italian use of dollars and for tight strings on future U.S. aid. He noted that the 50 percent measure had led to widespread hoarding of imported supplies and emphasized "*It should be required of the Italian Government that it also exercise the right of recapture if the goods have been imported by private interests and not distributed in a reasonable time.*"[20]

Corbino's financial policies, meanwhile, produced a serious conflict over the lira fund. The notion of the fund as a source of finance for rehabilitation projects was resisted from early on by the Italian treasury. Corbino was determined to control spending and opposed on principle to a central plan to allocate the fund. Instead, the treasury sought to use the sale of UNRRA supplies as a deflationary instrument rather than a source of social relief or productive investment. In a period of politically backed claims from all sides (including Corbino – he secretly asked De Gasperi for a large pay raise in April) on its slender resources, moreover, the treasury began to use the UNRRA proceeds of sale to meet its current expenses. The official historian observes, "In actual fact, the Fund did not exist . . . since the proceeds of sale were largely used by the Treasury to finance current operations, leaving what amounted to a paper obligation by the Government to find money for Lira Fund projects when needed."[21] This reliance became all the more acute in the summer of 1946, when the share and commodity booms – stimulated by Cordino's liberalization measures – began to undermine the government securities market and reduce the treasury's cash reserves.

When the Lira Fund Control Committee was set up in June, government ministries and private interests promptly fell over one another in pursuit of a stake in the eventual 85 billion lire (estimated) kitty from UNRRA sales. The money was available only in theory, however, and Corbino tended to see the projects as additional, unacceptable demands on the public purse. UNRRA officials, on the other hand, were legally bound to wrest the funds from the treasury and remained stubbornly committed to the fund as a device not of monetary stabilization but of stimulation and relief.

No episode reveals more about UNRRA's difficult Italian experience than that of UNRRA–Tessile and the mission's long battle with the local textile industry. The story also illustrates the conflict between the export-led recovery strategy of Corbino and the State Department and UNRRA's attempt to favor local consumption. Large amounts of UNRRA cotton had begun to arrive at Genoa by March 1946. The mission intended that it be quickly manufactured and distributed to the needy local population at low prices. Inevitably, however, UNRRA came face-to-face with a well-organized and politically powerful industry that had no intention of satisfying the local market.

An article in the American industry's *Cotton Trade Journal* described the situation in which the industry "concentrated its efforts on exportation to such a point that orders for the domestic market were accepted only at very high prices. Of the production of spun cotton, at least 70 percent was sold abroad, directly through wholesalers or through foreign weavers."[22] Given the volume of exports, increased imports of cotton and wool had little effect on either the local price or availability of finished textile products. By July 1946, the situation had become a serious political controversy, and the Socialist Party tied its participation in the government formed after the June elections to the enactment of a law forcing textile firms to produce for the local market.

The issue became something of a personal crusade for Rodolfo Morandi, one of the party's most forceful leaders. With the formation of the new coalition on July 13, Morandi replaced Gronchi as minister of industry and commerce. Using the threat of requisition powers and financial sanctions, Morandi negotiated with the cotton trade association for the production of low-cost cotton goods at government expense. The parties reached an agreement on prices to be paid the mills at the end of July. In August, the government created a special committee known as UNRRA–Tessile (textile) to administer the manufacture and distribution of 31,000 tons of UNRRA-supplied cotton (as well as lesser amounts of raw wool and hides) for domestic needs. The program called for the sale of two-thirds of the goods at special low prices. The remaining third was to be distributed free of charge. The Lira Fund Control Committee agreed to allot 14.5 billion lire to subsidize the manufacture.[23]

Needless to say, the private firms were not enthusiastic. Production for the local market consumed raw materials and plant capacity more profitably employed for export orders, and the diversion of resources raised export costs and depressed domestic prices. In October, the cotton and wool associations declared that the July agreement was unfair and clearly aimed to delay or sabotage the program. UNRRA mission officials hesitated to interfere since, according to the original agreement, they had no formal powers in the areas of manufacture and distribution.[24] By the end of 1946, conversion of the UNRRA raw materials had yet to begin. A mission textile division report cited the "utter failure" of the cotton association to cooperate, as well as the "absolute lack of cooperation of the Associazione Laniera [the wool trade association] . . . [and] the strong opposition of the manufacturers themselves."[25]

Mission officials in Rome were furious, yet they were powerless to deal with the situation. Keeny threatened to reveal the story to the international press, implying that such a move would destroy Italian chances for future American aid. He did not follow through, however, perhaps because UNRRA was by then a lame duck agency enjoying little sympathy with Congress or the public. UNRRA and Morandi continued to badger the mill owners during the spring of 1947. That pressure, along with the fading of the textile export boom, eventually led the industry to fulfill its original commitments. The broader controversy over the lira fund dragged on until November 1947, when, thanks to Keeny's persistence, the two sides reached agreement. The Italian government would allocate 55 billion lire for projects. The remaining proceeds of sale were placed in reserve, in effect, at the disposal of the Italian treasury. UNRRA agreed to extend the time limit for spending the fund from three to six years.[26]

By the time UNRRA–Tessile and other fund projects were completed, the Rome mission had long since disappeared as an independent agency. By early fall 1946, the embassy was planning to take control of future aid and liaison with the Italian government. The embassy shared the desire, expressed by Trade Minister Campilli in September, "to wipe the old slate clear [he referred specifically to UNRRA] in order to prepare the way for relations on a government to government basis through traditional channels. . . ."[27]

Any account of postwar recovery must pay tribute to the dedication and concrete achievements of the Italian UNRRA mission, especially in relieving the abject human conditions that prevailed in 1946. Faced with those conditions, Keeny recalled years later, "We never thought much in terms of long term policy. We spent most of our time just trying to stay afloat." It also seems clear in retrospect that the program was not designed to address the emerging economic problems of 1946: rising government deficits and inflation. UNRRA's experience did not bode well, moreover, for future attempts to dictate the spending priorities of the Italian government. The UNRRA–treasury conflict presaged that of 1948–50, when UNRRA's Marshall Plan successors would make a similar attempt to impose expansionary policies on the country's orthodox financial managers.[28]

THE FALL OF CORBINO

UNRRA's increasing isolation in Italy mirrored the fortunes of the New Deal foreign policy establishment. Clayton's August announcement that UNRRA would be terminated was followed in September by the dismissal of Henry Wallace, the administration's last New Deal spokesman, after his Madison Square Garden attack on U.S. policy toward the Soviet Union. With congressional elections upcoming in November, Wallace had become a liability that neither Truman nor Byrnes was prepared to tolerate.

But the purge of Wallace did little to help the administration. At home, Truman faced a Republican Party both fiscally conservative and fervently anticommunist. Abroad, the hoped-for transition to multilateralism had been stalled by the Russian challenge in Eastern Europe and by political-economic uncertainty in the West. In Italy, September 1946 saw the climax of a bitter dispute between Corbino and the Communists. It was resolved without a break-down of the three-party formula, but henceforth the battle lines were clearly drawn. Economic recovery was hostage to the political struggle. American policy in Italy faced an urgent challenge after September 1946: how to help resolve that struggle and permit the economic recovery on which longer-term political stability depended.

Thanks to Togliatti's caution and De Gasperi's finesse, an early showdown was avoided after the June elections. The elections confirmed the PCI as a working class formation but showed little appeal to other social groups. The workers demanded wage increases to offset inflation, but the Communists could ill afford to antagonize the middle classes. In the negotiations leading to the first postelection government, they saw little choice but compromise on economic issues in order to stay in the political contest.

The elections confirmed the DC's wide appeal, but De Gasperi's position was also difficult. The peace treaty discussions had resumed in Paris on June 15, and the four powers soon agreed to internationalize Trieste and grant reparations from current production to the USSR. These decisions were a major defeat for De Gasperi, who had tried to bargain payment of reparations for the return of the city. The USSR also supported large reparations for Greece, Albania, and Yugoslavia. Those claims were unsettled when the CFM adjourned on July 12.[29]

The Italian public was outraged. The Communists charged that De Gasperi had antagonized the Russians while delivering nothing from his American friends. Combined with labor protests and the defeat of the monarchy, the events in Paris also raised the possibility of a serious backlash from the right. The neofascist Uomo Qualunque Party had won thirty seats in the Constituent Assembly and the Confindustria pressed for a crackdown on the workers, including the resumption of dismissals and a freeze on wages.

Amid deliberately planted rumors that he might resign, De Gasperi labored to fashion the DC–PSIUP–PCI coalition dictated by the election results.[30] He thought it prudent to retain Corbino, a monarchist and champion of the middle classes. Corbino agreed to leave the PLI and enter the government as an independent technician, but he demanded that the government remove a series of impediments to his liberal line. His personal program included the definitive cancellation of the currency conversion, a freeze on wages, increase in bread prices, resumption of firings of industrial workers, and an end to government subsidies to private industry. De Gasperi agreed but had to convince the left to go along. The currency conversion was not a serious issue. Togliatti had agreed to its postponement in January. Wages and food prices were more important, and *l'Unità* attacked Corbino for trying to shoulder the working class with the burden of reconstruction.[31]

After several weeks of intense negotiations, De Gasperi arranged a compromise between Corbino and the left. The PSIUP and PCI accepted a version of Corbino's program, including postponement of the conversion, resumption of some dismissals on August 1, and the rejection of new wage demands. In return, they obtained a *una tantum* bonus, the so called "premio della repubblica," for industrial and agricultural workers. The measure struck at the heart of Corbino's program (it was to cost the treasury 30 billion lire) but cleared the way for a tripartite government on July 13.[32] The embassy called the program "a series of compromises adding up to a moderate right of center position." Specific measures were "so mild, and in some cases so obscure" that no one was satisfied. Still, a trend to the right was discernable, and the embassy saw trouble on the horizon.[33]

Corbino's program was badly compromised by the salary bonus, and he sought an early showdown with the Socialist–Communist alliance. De Gasperi agreed that a confrontation was inevitable and was angered by PCI attacks on the treaty while the Communists delivered nothing from Moscow. The economic program, meanwhile, was bound to increase social unrest. De Gasperi assumed personal control of the Ministry of the Interior in July and enlisted U.S. help to strengthen the police and military forces.[34] However, a basic difference of opinion developed between De Gasperi and Corbino on how and when to deal with the left. Corbino was a fighter and schemer, intent on pushing events toward their logical conclusion. De Gasperi's more global view endowed him with greater patience and caution. He was determined to have the signatures of left-wing ministers on the peace treaty and did not wish to break with the PCI and PSIUP until he was more confident of U.S. backing. Byrnes had displayed sympathy for De Gasperi at the peace conference and later intervened with the House Appropriations Committee to obtain release of the treasury suspense account. But the United States had compromised at De Gasperi's expense on vital treaty issues. It was obvious that the Americans were unready and unable to provide the support needed to weather a confrontation with the left.[35]

In the meantime, the forces released by Corbino's policies pushed the country toward a major financial crisis. The free-floating export rate fell from 364 to 515 lire to the dollar between May and late August. Stock market speculation drove the government securities market toward collapse. The crisis was aggravated by a vitriolic campaign launched by the Communists in early August. The embattled Corbino was forced to take emergency measures on August 30, imposing a 25 percent tax on the revaluation of industrial properties. In order to stem the expenditure of foreign exchange by the textile industry, cotton and wool were shifted from list A to list B, the latter requiring a special import license from the Ministry of Trade. As a final measure to halt the flight from government bonds into the stock market, the treasury imposed a 25 percent deposit on all new stock purchases.[36]

On September 2, the Central Committee of the PCI called for a "*nuovo corso*" (new course) in economic policy in which "private initiative is left wide liberty, but the State intervenes to prevent any means of speculation that threaten to provoke a collapse of the currency and the starvation of the people." The resolution reiterated a program announced in June, but quickly shelved. It called for a capital levy and bond issue; nationalization of the Bank of Italy, electrical utilities, and other key industries; land reform; and major public works expenditures.[37] Corbino announced his resignation the same day. He remained in office, pending its acceptance by De Gasperi, who was in Paris at the time. Tasca cabled an analysis of the situation on September 5. Echoing Corbino, he placed the blame squarely on the shoulders of the Communist Party:

> Immediate cause of present crisis is attributable to the policy of the Communist Party to agree in Cabinet meeting on Government economic program and subsequently in party press to attack such program agreed to through personal attacks on the present Minister of the Treasury. As a result of organized agitation on part of Communist Party, instability and uncertainty in Italy has been greatly accentuated with consequent impossibility of permitting Ministry of Treasury to carry through Government's financial program of stabilizing the lira.

According to Corbino, "there must be a showdown in Italy between the forces who sincerely desire reconstruction and those who desire to keep the country in a state of disorder and confusion for political reasons. He [Corbino] believes that the time for such showdown is present."[38] Several days later, Corbino told Tasca in great secrecy that an attempt might now be made to form a government without the PCI. Corbino "strongly preferred" excluding the Socialists as well and claimed the Christian Democrats agreed. However, such a move might precipitate communist-inspired violence, even Yugoslav or Russian intervention. According to Corbino, De Gasperi's decision to exclude the left depended finally on what the Allies would do in the case of such foreign intervention.[39]

Corbino's motives were clear, but his attempt to force De Gasperi's hand did not succeed. The prime minister made a lucid statement of his position to Tasca on September 13. De Gasperi "sympathized wholeheartedly with Corbino's desire to have a showdown with the Communists," but it was not possible now "owing to the Peace Conference and the effect a whip hand exclusion of the Communists might have on the Russians with respect to the final peace terms to be imposed on Italy." Once the treaty was signed, there would "be a showdown out of which would develop a general crisis, the main purpose of which would be to defeat definitively the Communists." According to Tasca, De Gasperi left "the impression of great bitterness towards the Communists and a desire to make a real effort at the appropriate moment to eliminate them from Italian political life."[40]

In avoiding a confrontation in September 1946, De Gasperi showed himself a far more pragmatic and self-disciplined operator than the impetuous Corbino. He was aware that the economic risks involved in an open battle with the left were best not taken without greater American support. That such support was unavailable was clear from his latest conversation with Byrnes in Paris, shortly before Corbino's resignation. On August 24, De Gasperi had vented his anxiety about "violent attacks" in the Communist press and appealed for changes in the draft treaty, such as the enlargement of the Free Territory of Trieste. Byrnes

Conclusion

had listened sympathetically but promised nothing to bolster De Gasperi's position.[41]

If a general crisis was inopportune, it remained to restore some semblance of calm following the *crisetta Corbino*. De Gasperi feared that the strident Neapolitan might now become leader of a right-wing opposition bloc including Liberals and neo-Fascists. Moreover, as De Gasperi told Tasca, anyone taking Corbino's job "was almost certain to fail and would be sacrificed to the interests of the big parties." Campilli, the DC minister of trade, refused, as did the able and experienced Donato Menichella, former IRI manager, currently Einaudi's lieutenant as managing director of the Bank of Italy. De Gasperi presumed Communist attacks would continue in any event, but he hoped for a joint DC–PCI–PSIUP declaration on economic policy. Although such an agreement would be violated, it "would serve a useful purpose later" in the open showdown with the left.[42]

CONCLUSION

On September 18, De Gasperi settled on Giovanni Battista Bertone, a moderate Christian Democrat, who had been finance minister before 1922. But subsequent attempts to defend the lira confirmed Corbino's judgment that no coherent policy was possible as long as the basic political contradiction remained at the heart of the coalition. Corbino's strategy had foundered on PCI–PSIUP and union opposition and the speculative behavior of private capital. With local elections scheduled for mid-November, De Gasperi was now caught between growing pressure from his own party, the Church, and private business to break with the left, and increasing public agitation by the Communists. He saw no choice but to ride out the storm until circumstances permitted a more definitive solution. The shape of that solution was clear to Tasca and also to another first-hand observer, UNRRA's Spurgeon Keeny. Keeny and the mission had received news of UNRRA's termination with shock, followed by resignation. In late October, he made the depressing observation to the *Economist's* Barbara Ward that "the only way they can save the situation is to cut out the emergency jobs and abolish social services – save the lira at the expense of the people."[43] In practical terms, such a course meant drastically reducing the political power of the left and organized labor.

A similar analysis gained converts in Washington, where EUR officials viewed the PCI offensive not as a response to pressure on real wages and living conditions but as part of a Soviet design to thwart Western economic recovery. For the moment, however, the Truman administration was powerless to help De Gasperi or to salvage its battered foreign

103

economic policy on the wider European front. Its aid funds were virtually exhausted. More money would depend on the results of the U.S. congressional elections, scheduled for November 5. Those elections consumed the attention of observers on both sides of the Atlantic during the early fall of 1946.

7

The emergency response

INTRODUCTION

The elections of November 1946 in both Italy and the United States marked the convergence of trends that had threatened to undermine the foundations of American foreign economic policy throughout the early postwar period. The clouds of domestic discontent burst forth on November 5, producing a landslide victory for the Republican Party. On November 10, economic distress and political paralysis in Italy produced an equally dramatic defeat for the Christian Democratic Party at the hands of right- and left-wing forces. The elections left De Gasperi more vulnerable than ever, but the simultaneous political shift in the United States raised doubts about post-UNRRA aid to Italy and other foreign nations. Indeed, the arrival of a Republican Congress in Washington posed a serious challenge to the Hullian initiatives pursued by Democratic administrations since the days of the Atlantic Charter.

The period between the November elections and the convening of the Eightieth Congress in January 1947 was thus one of deep uncertainty. Pressure from all sides threatened to topple De Gasperi and bring general political chaos. Even though the State Department was in no position to respond to De Gasperi's urgent calls for aid, his predicament helped to reinforce a growing consensus within the department based on the long-standing view of EUR and Henry Tasca that communist subversion was the primary threat to economic recovery. For the first time, EUR professionals and Hullian economists joined in a common response to the Italian crisis.

The centerpiece of their impromptu strategy was De Gasperi's January visit to the United States. The visit provided a unique occasion for De Gasperi to enhance his prestige in the United States and among the anticommunist forces at home, and his presence in Washington helped to break the bureaucratic deadlock that had delayed the Export–Import

105

loan since early 1946. As for new aid, however, the mission produced scant results. The trip coincided with the launching of a Republican offensive against Truman's budget and foreign economic policies, and the department's emergency response did little to resolve the longer-term problems of either De Gasperi or the U.S. administration.

Moreover, even though the visit consolidated the ties of mutual aid and dependence that had developed during the previous year, it did not improve U.S. control over the internal situation. The United States could threaten and cajole, but the fate of American policy remained very much in the hands of the Italians themselves. De Gasperi, in turn, would seek more support, but he found himself essentially alone in the face of the most serious challenge of his career. Obviously, the State Department consensus achieved in late 1946 also did not suffice to rescue its endangered programs on a European scale. The success of U.S. policy required an unprecedented political consensus in support of massive foreign aid.

ELECTORAL SHOCKS

Few people saw the return of Republican majorities to the House and Senate for the first time since 1932 as a mandate to abandon the nation's postwar responsibilities.[1] The Roosevelt administration's prodigious wartime campaign had generated broad support for the United Nations and other internationalist programs. Naturally, the campaign had stressed the benefits rather than the costs to the American taxpayer. In November 1946, the electorate expressed its dissatisfaction with what were, in part, the domestic consequences of the Truman foreign policy: continued price controls, high taxes, and budget deficits, as well as the prospect of sharply lower tariffs on farm and industrial products. The Republicans ran their successful campaign on a platform of protectionism, fiscal restraint, and the rollback of union power. Declaring the "official end of the New Deal," a New York *Times* editorial observed sarcastically, ". . . the Congressional Republicans, after fourteen years of eloquent promises 'to eliminate useless activities,' and 'cut down extravagant expenditures' will now find the center of the stage all set for them to redeem their fervent pledges."[2]

The scenario seemed all too plausible to administration officials. Senate leader Vandenberg had been converted to the main lines of Truman's foreign aid and commercial policies, but his powerful colleague, Robert Taft of Ohio, was lukewarm on new loans and tariff reductions. Taft had opposed the IMF and British loan (although he had been willing to approve an outright gift of $1 billion) and was committed to major tax and budget cuts. Republican back-benchers, meanwhile, were openly hostile. Three days after the election, *Times* Washington correspondent James Reston wondered pointedly if the Republicans intended to "take the nation back to the Smoot–Hawley tariff days."[3]

The November 5 results cast an ominous shadow in the path of William Clayton. On October 15, 1946, representatives of eighteen UN member countries had met in London to prepare a charter for Clayton's prized International Trade Organization. On November 10, Clayton told the press that multilateral tariff reduction negotiations would begin in Geneva in April 1947. Even though the Russians had not accepted an invitation (nor had they been present in London), he hoped for Soviet cooperation. Clayton was deeply worried about the new political climate and admitted that the November 10 announcement had been delayed in order to avoid a pre-election debate on the Geneva conference. A post-London report observed that the success of the ITO would depend in part on the Russian attitude but more importantly on domestic political support: "The other nations on the Committee have their fingers crossed. They will go along with our program if we give evidence that we are prepared to practice what we preach. They will abandon it if we don't. . . ."[4]

In the meantime, the department had other urgent matters on its mind. The adherence of Italy and other European nations to the IMF and ITO obviously depended on the recovery of economic growth and political stability. However, conditions in Italy had only deteriorated following Corbino's resignation. In an atmosphere of growing tension, the Italian cabinet attempted to patch together an emergency program to stem inflation and raise revenues. As the UNRRA program neared completion, urban food stocks fell to dangerous levels. De Gasperi's enemies fully exploited the situation, and voters registered their feelings in the November 10 municipal elections. Both Uomo Qualunque and the left made large gains at De Gasperi's expense. Compared to the June totals, the DC lost 100,000 votes in Rome and 40,000 in Naples, where the PCI and PSIUP presented a common list. Where the two parties ran separately, the PCI made clear advances vis-à-vis the Socialists, a result that in part reflected unhappiness among right-wing Socialists with Nenni's alliance with the PCI.

De Gasperi was severely castigated by his own party in the atmosphere of despair and near panic that followed the elections. The attacks were joined by business and the right-wing press, who feared that continued cohabitation with the left would lead to higher taxes and other punitive measures. Evidence released years later shows that at this point De Gasperi only narrowly avoided an open break with the Vatican. Under the shock of the Rome defeat, Pope Pius XII sent Substitute Secretary of State Giovanni Montini, friend and confidant of De Gasperi, to inform the prime minister that the Holy See could no longer tolerate the DC's ties to the anticlerical parties. De Gasperi apparently persuaded the Pope to withdraw his ultimatum by pointing out that completion of the new constitution required a minimum of cooperation with the left.[5]

On November 15, the U.S. embassy reported that De Gasperi would appeal for 240,000 tons of wheat by mid-January 1947. The alternative was an immediate reduction of the daily bread ration.[6] The same day, the Italian treasury floated its first major public loan since early 1945. Interest on the thirty-year bonds was set at 3.5 percent – instead of the usual 5 or 6 percent – on the grounds that subscribers would escape the future capital levy. These conditions, combined with the election results, offered little incentive to investors, and the loan raised a disappointing 231 billion lire. As an anti-inflationary measure, it was an utter failure. Bruno Foa noted that cash subscriptions to the loan brought a withdrawal of 35 billion lire from the reserves of the banking system held with the Bank of Italy and a large increase in the Central Bank's advances against the collateral of the loan. "In a single month, note circulation went up by 4.4 billion lire. Thus, far from relieving the inflationary pressure, the loan added heavily to it, and its ultimate effects were not very much different from those which would have been obtained if instead of floating the loan the Treasury had proceeded with the direct printing of notes."[7]

Embassy analysts expressed frustration with the government's financial program in the wake of Corbino's fall. They estimated the foreign aid requirement for 1947 at $300 million and were angered by De Gasperi's public assertion that Italy would need at least $4 billion in outside aid between 1947 and 1950. Given the impossibility of enforcing a serious financial policy, they concluded, De Gasperi had decided instead to rely on heavy external borrowing.[8]

THE OUTLOOK FROM WASHINGTON, NOVEMBER–DECEMBER 1946

Needless to say, De Gasperi's appeals arrived at a rather inopportune moment for Washington officials. Even though resolution of the reparations question (at the New York session of the CFM, November 4 to December 12) prompted the National Advisory Council staff to recommend a $100 million Export–Import loan, final approval was by no means a foregone conclusion. The bank was now dependent on conservative Republican masters, and President Martin and his staff would scrutinize the proposal with more than their usual special care. The department had informed De Gasperi on October 12 that $50 million in non-troop pay credits would be transferred, but the funds were still tied up for technical reasons. Italy was ineligible for IBRD or IMF funds since it was not a member of either institution, and post-UNRRA aid requests awaited the verdict of Congress.[9]

State Department officials pondered the now inextricably connected Italian and American political situations. The November elections in Italy seemed to lend new credibility to the old EUR line that the Communists threatened economic chaos and a dramatic shift to the left. In a November 21 letter to EUR Director H. Freeman (Doc) Matthews EUR's Southern Europe Division Italian desk officer, Walter (Red) Dowling mused at length on the Italian situation. The letter merits lengthy citation not so much for the probably typical attitudes it revealed as for the practical suggestions it contained. Dowling observed that the elections were "hardly a surprise to any of us," nor was the situation beyond salvation:

> . . . pro-American sentiment in Italy has suffered remarkably little from the bitterness and disappointment over the Treaty or from ruthless Communist propaganda against us. What has been shaken is their faith in our pro-Italian sentiment; the wops do feel that we have let them down, and that they cannot again count on the degree of support which they had led themselves to expect from us. . . .

If the United States decided it was "in the national interest . . . to make the great effort which will be necessary to prevent Italy going Communist," Dowling saw two possible lines of action:

> The first, which I would prefer as the easiest and most sensible, is to say to the Italians, Now lookahere, we've done more for you than anyone else and will probably continue to do so. It's about time you started behaving like adults if you want us to help you help yourselves. But remember that it's up to you. The fault with this line, I fear, is that it may be too practical to stand up against the party propaganda being used so adroitly by Togliatti and his friends. Besides, the Italians are still too hungry and too defeated for us to place much reliance on their common sense.
> The alternative is a policy so damned pro-Italian that even the dumbest wop would sense the drift, and even the cleverest Italian comrade would have trouble denouncing it. It would have to be a judicious mixture of flattery, moral encouragement and considerable material aid. . . . This policy would of course require a sustained program for a considerable period. It could not be a one-shot cure, but should consist of a kind word, a loaf of bread, a public tribute to Italian civilization, then another kind word, and so on, with an occasional plug from the sponsors advertising the virtues of democracy American style. Naturally it would not be anti-communist, nor would it need to be, just pro-Italian. Also, it would cost a lot of money and mean a lot of bother, but if I know anything about Italians, it would pay off handsomely.

Dowling's program included a $150 million Export–Import Bank loan, "now, not next week or month," a "fulsome speech" in support of Italian membership in UNESCO, abolition of the AC, and the withdrawal of U.S. troops. These steps should be followed by an invitation to De Gasperi to visit the United States in January 1947, using "trade discussions or any other subject we wish as an excuse." Finally, the administration should present a relief program for Italy and other countries to Congress "with plenty of publicity." Dowling acknowledged the difficulties on the right, but the real menace lay at the other end of the spectrum: "I am not yet particularly disturbed about Uomo Qualunque; it will disappear if the threat of Communism can be eliminated. It seems fairly obvious, however, that without some strenuous show of interest on our part, a Communist–Socialist regime will result from the national elections in the Spring." It is impossible to document discussion of the Dowling proposals, but the letter acquired a significant marginal notation, probably from Matthews. EUR's director checked off Dowling's suggestions in approval. The Export–Import loan, however, was "probably not possible now."[10]

In late November, EUR officials set out to mobilize the support of Clayton and mount a concerted response to the Italian crisis. In a November 26 memo, EUR Deputy Director John Hickerson praised the under secretary's earlier efforts while urging prompt action on the Export–Import loan.[11] Several days later, the Office of the Assistant Secretary for Economic Affairs asked the International Resources Division for quick action on requests for more wheat: "Dowling told me this morning that there is a coming cabinet crisis during the next few weeks, at which time there will be an effort to put in Nenni, Communist [*sic*] leader, as Prime Minister. Our people believe that food crisis may well mean the difference between forestalling this move and not." Rumors of a cabinet crisis were premature and probably originated with Tarchiani, who wished to discredit Nenni in the eyes of the department. Dowling, in any case, put the rumors to good use in lobbying his department colleagues.[12]

In a long memo to Acheson and Clayton the same day (December 2), Hickerson elaborated the EUR scenario. "As we see it, the Communist strategy is to discredit De Gasperi and thus force his resignation as Premier; to form a new government more to the left; and then to hold national elections which would be expected to return the Communists as the strongest party. . . ." To achieve this, the Communists needed a "few more failures by De Gasperi." The treaty had been the theme thus far, but a "good domestic issue" was now needed, and the food crisis was tailor-made. Clayton promptly replied in the margin of Hickerson's memo: "I agree and we are doing every thing possible to get more wheat going to Italy."[13]

It would be a mistake to assume that Clayton's agreement with Hickerson represented his conversion to the EUR conception of the world. His politically risky statements at the time indicate that he still hoped for

110

basic agreement with the Soviet Union on economic matters, and as late as May 1947 he was unwilling to blame the USSR for Europe's economic plight. Europe's difficulties, he argued then, arose from the massive dislocation wrought by the war, a problem, he admitted, that he had failed to understand. Clayton had always had his own reasons for wanting to help Italy, reasons distinct from the geopolitical concerns of the professional diplomats. At the same time, Clayton had come to share the prevailing American fear of Russian pressure in the Eastern Mediterranean.[14] More important, even if he disagreed with EUR and Tasca as to the root causes of the Italian crisis, by late 1946 he accepted their contention that a local fifth column was exploiting the economic situation to the detriment of American interests.

Departmental agreement on the need to fortify De Gasperi paved the way for the invitation to visit the United States in early January.[15] His itinerary would include well-publicized appearances in New York and Cleveland as well as discussions with the State Department and president. For Clayton, the visit would provide an opportunity to discuss the ITO and related economic matters. Italy was not a UN member and had not been at London in October. For EUR, such issues were essentially a pretext in order to bolster De Gasperi's political standing in Italy and the United States. Both EUR and Clayton were determined to secure more aid for De Gasperi. Both realized that aid was hostage to the NAC and Congress. The invitation was therefore very much a gamble, and department officials no doubt pondered the odds of success while awaiting De Gasperi's arrival.

THE DE GASPERI MISSION

De Gasperi's ten-day visit to the United States (January 5–14, 1947) has engendered historical controversy and myth. The evidence suggests that the two sides made no agreement whereby De Gasperi would expel the left from his cabinet in return for American aid. Historians have continued to debate whether U.S. officials demanded such a quid pro quo in a more subtle fashion or whether De Gasperi used alleged American conditions in his subsequent campaign to isolate the PCI and PSIUP. Undoubtedly, De Gasperi made every effort to convince his hosts that his political future depended on a successful outcome of the trip. Some Italian circles wanted the Americans to attach explicitly political strings to their material aid, even if they proved reluctant to do so.[16] However, discussions of this kind tend to obscure the essential facts surrounding the De Gasperi mission.

State Department officials were well aware of De Gasperi's stake in the visit. The discussions before his arrival indicate that executive officials did not seek a commitment – explicit or otherwise – from De Gasperi to expel the left from his government. Instead they sought to forestall a possible Communist bid to bring down the government, and more important, to strengthen De Gasperi's hand in the upcoming (as yet unscheduled) national elections. Most accounts of the visit have failed to grasp this simple fact: The mission was a defensive move in the aftermath of the November 1946 local elections, not an offensive one aimed at the rapid elimination of the left.[17]

The minimum definition of success was the same for both sides: obtaining the Export–Import loan. Dowling had given the loan top priority in his November 21 proposal. On the eve of De Gasperi's arrival, Hickerson told Byrnes that the loan had "become a barometer of American confidence in Italy. . . . De Gasperi feels that the loan has now acquired an importance far beyond its financial significance, and is therefore the greatest single factor in what we can do for Italy."[18] If obtaining the loan was the most important purpose of the visit, historians have tended to neglect the important reasons. Obviously, De Gasperi wanted the loan in order to prove to the left and to the Italian public that he could deliver concrete benefits from his American friends. His desire was understandable at a time when it was widely believed that the United States had done nothing to help Italy during the peace treaty negotiations. De Gasperi was also concerned to placate the hostile *quarto partito* (fourth party) of business and financial interests, some of whom supported Uomo Qualunque and had called for the prime minister's head after the November elections. Italian business, needless to say, would be the beneficiary of an industrial reconstruction loan, and the Confindustria made no secret of its high expectations for the trip.[19]

As suggested, the department ran a serious, if calculated, risk in inviting the Italian prime minister to the United States. For this reason, on December 17, Dowling told the embassy to advise De Gasperi that "no (repeat no) promises can be made."[20] The department hoped that De Gasperi's presence in Washington would force the hand of bank and NAC officials and break the year-long stalemate on the loan. De Gasperi thus became an instrument of interdepartmental warfare. The State Department and De Gasperi also shared a broader common purpose: to convince the public and Congress that Italy needed substantial aid beyond the long-discussed suspense account and Export–Import dollars. The risk and promise of the mission must be understood within the immediate political context in Washington, another fact largely ignored by historians.

That context included the announcement of James Byrnes's resignation on January 7. Byrnes's intention to quit at the end of the New York session of the CFM had been known to Truman and a few top officials for some time. Most observers, including the De Gasperi delegation, were taken totally by surprise. The resignation had no direct effect on the negotiations (it took effect on January 20, well after De Gasperi's departure), but it served to emphasize that American policy had entered a crucial transition period. The *New York Times* noted the "urgent necessity of choosing a man with sufficient ability and prestige to carry the brunt of conducting our foreign policy in the two critical years of the Truman administration." The president's choice of General Marshall was almost universally applauded.[21]

The *Times* referred to the domestic as well as international difficulties facing the incoming secretary. Indeed, the Byrnes resignation and De Gasperi mission coincided with the opening salvoes of a GOP attack on Truman's domestic and foreign policies. On January 10, the president proposed a $37.5 billion budget for fiscal year 1947–48. The administration described the figure as "rock bottom" and noted that it was the lowest request in six years. The Republican response was immediate and predictable. Taft called for a $3 to $4 billion cut and income tax reductions of 20 percent. House Republicans demanded cuts of up to $8 billion in the Truman figure.[22] Truman's foreign economic policy provoked a similar reaction. On January 5, Taft called for "reasonable assistance" to foreign countries rather than "huge loans" and also for "reasonable tariffs" but not "free trade." Again, House Republicans took a more aggressive stance. On January 16, Representative Thomas Jenkins of Ohio called for a "scientific study" of U.S. commercial policy before additional tariff cuts. Jenkins and his colleagues responded to mounting protests from the cotton textile, liquor, chemical, and other manufacturing groups and aimed to scuttle the Geneva tariff conference.[23]

As usual, Vandenberg tried to mediate between the administration and Republican back-bench militants. He warned Clayton to "go easy," or face a basic review of existing commercial legislation. At issue was the Trade Agreements Act, renewed periodically since 1934, which authorized the executive to lower U.S. tariffs up to 50 percent without congressional approval. Vandenberg was hard-pressed to keep order in the ranks. On January 16, Representative Paul Shafer of Michigan demanded Clayton's removal for reaping personal profit from the British loan and other aid programs. According to Shafer, Clayton was "a well-known one worlder in do-gooder circles, and I must admit that he does believe in one world – one world for Will Clayton and family."[24] Clayton refuted the charges, but the incident reflected a widely held suspicion of the Hullian ideology espoused by the under secretary of state.

Such was the local political atmosphere as the De Gasperi visit began.

De Gasperi was accompanied by a high-powered entourage, including Trade Minister Pietro Campilli, Guido Carli of the UIC, Donato Menichella of the Bank of Italy, and Ambassador Tarchiani. Also present was James Clement Dunn, former director of EUR and newly appointed ambassador to Rome. On January 6, De Gasperi presented a long list of future aid requirements to Byrnes. The secretary (who would announce his resignation the following day) delivered a warning repeated to De Gasperi on subsequent occasions: With the Republicans in command, "it was not possible at the present time to tell how economic and other matters would be dealt with. . . ."[25]

Discussions with Clayton began on January 7. In response to urgent requests for wheat and coal, Clayton promised to do his best to secure greater supplies.[26] The main purpose of the meeting was to prepare a common strategy for the Export–Import loan. Tarchiani repeated that the loan had become a political test at home. Menichella observed – disingenuously – that the government had not yet called on the Bank of Italy to finance its expenditures, but that "drastic measure [would] soon become necessary. . . ." Ideally, the Italians desired a long-term credit, usable for balance of payments support as well as for industrial raw materials, but Menichella emphasized that he would discuss it on any basis, "whether for short, medium, or long term . . . obtaining the loan [was] an absolute necessity for the success of the De Gasperi mission." Menichella found himself in the uncomfortable position familiar to Tarchiani since early 1945 of having to prove both Italian creditworthiness and dire dependence on U.S. loans. Fortunately for the Italians, Clayton had always opposed the politically myopic "banker's mentality" within the NAC. He told the Italians that a short-term credit for industrial raw materials would be easier to obtain but agreed to support their request for a long-term reconstruction and balance-of-payments loan.[27]

President Martin and the bank were not oblivious to the political importance of an Italian loan. They were also aware that it would further the commercial policy objectives of the U.S. government. (Clayton's lieutenant, Assistant Secretary Willard Thorp, met with Campilli on January 8 to discuss Italian membership in the ITO.) With appropriations hostage to budget-cutting Republicans, however, Martin was more than ever compelled to conduct his operations in a "strictly business basis." Given Italy's economic and political problems, the risk of default could hardly be denied. The bank also knew that private American creditors would press claims on Italian debts incurred as far back as the mid-1920s by the Fascist regime and thus further tax Italy's limited ability to repay.[28]

It therefore came as no surprise that Clayton and the Italians met stiff resistance at the Export–Import Bank. Before his first meeting with De Gasperi, Clayton had learned that Martin did not even wish to discuss

Italy at the next session of the NAC. Following their initial contact with the bank, moreover, the Italians abandoned any hope of the long-term multipurpose loan discussed with Clayton on January 7. During a second meeting with Byrnes on January 8, De Gasperi hinted at a "new plan" involving an Italian government guarantee of loans for raw materials. Byrnes telephoned Clayton for clarification. Clayton was unaware of the proposal but assured Byrnes that he was doing everything possible to sell a loan to the bank and the NAC.[29]

The new plan had apparently been proposed by the bank itself as the only basis for discussion, and the Italians outlined the details to Clayton later in the day. A $100 million credit would be extended to IMI (Istituto Mobiliare Italiano), the parastatal banking institution. IMI would reloan the money to individual firms, control the foreign exchange from result-ing exports, and, along with the government itself, guarantee repayment to the United States. The arrangement would provide emergency raw materials only, forcing the Italians to look elsewhere for longer-term assistance. They expected the average length of the loans to be eight or nine years, but the bank would insist on four to five.[30]

De Gasperi departed for his appearance in Cleveland the same after-noon (January 8), leaving the fate of the loan in the hands of Clayton and his own assistants. It is impossible to document the discussions that ensued, but Martin and other members of the NAC approved the new plan on the eve of De Gasperi's departure for Rome (January 13). A department official later recalled that the agreement came only after vigorous efforts by Clayton, who was forced "to solicit a direct interven-tion by the White House on De Gasperi's behalf."[31] Along with the transfer of a check for $50 million in suspense account money (these funds, it will be recalled, had been committed in principle since July 1946) in front of the Italian newsreel cameras, the Export–Import loan agreement ensured the success of the De Gasperi mission.

However, it was obvious that $150 million provided at most a breathing space in which to consider Italy's longer-term requirements. The Export–Import loan had far more significance as a political gesture than as a practical instrument of economic aid in January 1947. As such, it was vital to De Gasperi, but the actual credits would not be available until the bank had completed long and complicated technical arrange-ments, including a firsthand survey of Italian industry. With a 1947 balance-of-payments deficit projected at anywhere between $300 and $600 million, Italy could scarcely be expected, in the words of a *New York Times* editorial, "to get back on its feet without future aid."[32]

The second, public relations phase of the mission was designed pre-cisely to persuade informed American opinion that Italy under De Gas-peri was severely dependent on yet worthy of future economic aid. In public appearances and private meetings, De Gasperi stressed that the future of Italy was bright, and Tarchiani later called this aspect of the visit an unqualified success. But De Gasperi continually encountered the question "Who will govern tomorrow?" Such skepticism was widespread, especially in Congress. It was also politically useful in Italy. In explaining to the Rome press his failure to obtain a bigger loan, De Gasperi observed – accurately enough – "underlying hesitation, there is always doubt: is our democratic system stable, or is there fear of falling again into chaos and dictatorship?"[33] The anticommunist susceptibilities of spendthrift congressmen would eventually prove exploitable by State Department lobbyists. De Gasperi, however, had encountered the new Republican legislature in an aggressive, budget-slashing mood. His propaganda efforts produced no commitment to the major reconstruction and balance-of-payments support required for 1947 and beyond.

THE JANUARY CRISIS AND BEYOND

De Gasperi arrived home scarcely better equipped to cope with his familiar quandary, but he now found affairs altered to his advantage by an important political development. On January 11, 1947, in the midst of the National Congress of the PSIUP, the leader of the party's right wing, Giuseppe Saragat, led a group of dissident delegates (including fifty members of the Constituent Assembly) to the Palazzo Barberini, where they declared themselves the Socialist Party of Italian Workers (PSLI). The formation of a social democratic party was the climax of a long and bitter disagreement between Saragat and Nenni over the PSIUP's alliance with the communists.[34] The split provoked Nenni's resignation from the cabinet (the Nenni majority assumed the name Italian Socialist Party, or PSI), followed by De Gasperi and the rest of the cabinet on January 20.

First-hand U.S. observers including Tasca hoped the way was now paved for a Catholic–Social Democratic alliance, and De Gasperi considered broadening the tripartite formula by including the so-called "*piccola intesa*" of Republicans (PRI), Labor Democrats (DL), Actionists (Pd'A), and social democrats (PSLI) in the government.[35] However, the small parties had little desire to share responsibility for the growing economic crisis, nor, perhaps, for the peace treaty scheduled to be signed in Paris on February 10. De Gasperi, in any event, was not yet ready to exclude the PSI and PCI, nor did American officials expect him or ask him to, according to a deal struck during his visit to the United States. He wanted both parties in the cabinet when the treaty was adopted and was probably also looking forward to the vote on the inclusion of the 1929 Lateran Pacts in the new constitution. The ratification of the pacts was vital to the DC, and De Gasperi feared the opposition of a PCI-led alliance. He gambled that the Communists would vote in favor if they were still in the government. Indeed, to the dismay of the other left-wing parties, the Communist deputies voted yes on March 24, and the Lateran Pacts were preserved.[36]

At the same time, De Gasperi used the occasion to weaken the left. The Socialists were badly shaken by Saragat's defection. Despite harsh attacks on the DC during the U.S. visit, Togliatti and the Communists were still committed to their policy of active collaboration. De Gasperi made them pay a price. The treasury and finance ministries were consolidated and given to Campilli. The PCI thus relinquished the major economics ministry (finance) it had held since December 1944. De Gasperi added new allies, the independents Luigi Gasparotto at defense and Count Carlo Sforza (replacing Nenni) at the Foreign Ministry, while substituting himself at the Interior Ministry with his trusted protege, Mario Scelba.

Several weeks later, Ambassador James Dunn cabled Washington that the crisis had produced "a stabilizing effect" by demonstrating that there was no other workable basis for government than the three-party formula. "It is therefore improbable that there will be any further basis for a government crisis during the final interim period leading up to elections for parliament under the new constitution. . . ."[37] Tasca, a more seasoned analyst, offered a view based on the latest economic developments:

> It is clear that the recent reconstruction loan was a disappointment . . . the short-term Treasury bill market has practically disappeared. . . . Currency circulation is again expanding under the impetus of deficit financing through the Central Bank. Finally, Government expenditures continue to increase as a result of political pressure on a weak government, the component parties of which appear to have their sights fixed on the elections probably to be held sometime next summer.[38]

Tasca's analysis was overly optimistic. Inflation gathered momentum during the first months of the year. Wracked by dissension, the tripartite government offered feeble answers to the country's economic problems. Despite the vaunted efficiency of its new interior minister, the government could not stem rising violence in the streets or defuse the hostility of right-wing and business forces. De Gasperi and the Christian Democrats turned to the United States with a series of plaintive, increasingly desperate appeals for aid. They found Washington engaged in an all-out effort to change the domestic political climate. In the meantime, the message from Tasca was clear and unequivocal: De Gasperi would have to take his own decisive steps to arrest the slide towards political and financial chaos.

8

The "whirlwind of disintegration"

American foreign policy toward Western Europe entered a decisive phase in early 1947. In March, the Council of Foreign Ministers would convene in Moscow to decide the fate of Germany. The Geneva tariff conference scheduled to begin in April would determine the future international trading order. Simultaneously, the United States strove to cover the gaping balance-of-payments deficits of Britain, France, and Italy. In the midst of these preoccupations, the British announced their imminent withdrawal from the Eastern Mediterranean.

Washington officials also faced a showdown at home, for without a breakthrough on Capitol Hill, the Truman administration saw little hope of salvaging its European position. Thus, the British announcement was both an occasion for new anxieties and an opportunity to seize. During the famous fifteen weeks culminating in Marshall's Harvard address, the administration mounted a systematic campaign to gain additional aid for Europe. During the same span of time, there emerged in high circles of the bureaucracy outlines for what later – as it turned out, much later – became the European Recovery Program (ERP).

Alcide De Gasperi watched these developments like a man adrift with his eye on a distant rescue vessel. It was apparent that major changes were underway in Washington, but the shape of these changes and their eventual consequences for Italy were vague. In late April 1947, De Gasperi was forced to confront the raging political storm. He acted in the hope that the Americans might ease the pain of the unpleasant measures he was obliged to take but eventually realized that the United States could not rescue him from his sea of troubles, at least not before he had moved decisively on his own.

De Gasperi opened the crucial government crisis of the postwar period in early May. The tense interlude leading to the formation of a DC-technician cabinet demonstrated the oblique and tenuous nature of American influence. The United States could offer little more than moral encouragement to De Gasperi in his hour of greatest need and could not affect the makeup of the new coalition in order to satisfy illusory hopes for the "democratic left." The expulsion of the Communists and Socialists from the cabinet marked the close of the "heroic" period of postwar reconstruction. The June 5 Harvard speech also represented the end of American dreams for rapid recovery and universal liberal order.

However, the political clarification and subsequent deflation led to a new set of dilemmas for U.S. policy makers. One need not endorse John Gimbel's unorthodox view of the origins of the ERP in order to accept one of his more modest conclusions: There was no Marshall Plan in the summer of 1947. U.S. officials were at a loss to reconcile the imperative of deflation with the rapid economic recovery they considered essential to longer-term plans. Also, despite the emergence of domestic support for massive foreign aid, the United States could not impose its will on the diverse collection of local interests to whom, willy nilly, it had entrusted the fate of its new Italian policy.[1]

TRANSITION IN WASHINGTON

As the architect of victory in World War II, George Marshall enjoyed an esteem unmatched by any other U.S. public figure, and his arrival did much to raise morale from the doldrums of the Byrnes period. Byrnes had spent much of his time on the road, pointedly ignoring the problems created by a large influx of personnel – not to mention the advice of the geographic and economic divisions.

Marshall immediately imposed his stamp, creating a central secretariat and Policy Planning Staff (PPS), the latter to look "far enough ahead to see the emerging form of things to come and outline what should be done to meet or anticipate them."[2] Marshall gave that task to George Kennan, the brightest star of the EUR professional corps. The form of things on the congressional front was already clear enough, and Marshall kept Acheson as under secretary of state.

Marshall, a department official later marvelled, had "tremendous power of decision and his batting average [was] phenomenally high."[3] It is also true that Marshall arrived at a moment when domestic and foreign pressures had already brought a considerable degree of consensus among the department's rival factions. EUR's preoccupations remained geopolitical; Clayton's, the creation of liberal economic order. These concerns, however, were more than ever inseparable. Western European recovery and interdependence were vital to counter Russia and the local Communist Parties. Even though he did not think communism was the basic cause of Europe's troubles, Clayton realized that radical forces posed a threat to his economic schemes. Differences of style and tactics existed with respect to domestic politics. Marshall and Clayton had little taste for the inflammatory rhetoric that marked Acheson's approach to Congress. Ironically, neither did Kennan, whose impulsively written long telegram had galvanized anti-Soviet opinion in early 1946. At the same time, however, there was no disagreement on the urgent need to create a broad consensus in support of massive foreign aid.

The department took up that task under the inauspicious circumstances of early 1947. Republican Congressmen had promised to slash Truman's $37.7 billion budget down to size, and the Joint Budget Committee recommended a ceiling of $31.5 billion for 1947–48. Vandenberg helped salvage what he could, and his efforts eventually produced a compromise of $34.7 billion.[4] Such was the atmosphere when Truman approached Congress for $350 million in post-UNRRA relief aid for Italy and other liberated areas. Congress's attitude toward Europe at the time, according to Acheson, was "one of hardly suppressed skepticism."[5] Truman spoke to Congress on February 21. On the same day, the Foreign Office informed the State Department that British aid to Greece and Turkey would end in six weeks.

Acheson, more than anyone else, made a virtue of necessity. He set Joseph Jones to work on a presidential speech asking aid for Greece and Turkey, a speech, Jones later observed, "*specifically intended to add to the policy foundations of large-scale United States reconstruction aid to Europe*" (his emphasis).[6] On February 25, Truman, Marshall, and Acheson faced the leaders of Congress. The under secretary of state delivered the first barrage in what became a full-scale assault on congressional and public opinion:

> My distinguished chief [Marshall], most unusually and unhappily, flubbed his opening statement. In desperation I whispered to him a request to speak. This was my crisis. For a week I had nurtured it. These Congressmen had no conception of what challenged them; it was my task to bring it home. Both my superiors, equally perturbed, gave me the floor. Never have I spoken under such a pressing sense that the issue was up to me alone. No time was left for measured appraisal. In the past eighteen months, I said, Soviet pressure on the Straits, on Iran, and on northern Greece had brought the Balkans to the point where a highly possible Soviet breakthrough might open three continents to Soviet penetration. Like apples in a barrel infected by one rotten one, the corruption of Greece would affect Iran and all to the east. It would also carry infection to Africa through Asia Minor and Egypt, and to Europe through Italy and France, already threatened by the strongest domestic Communist parties in Western Europe. The Soviet Union was playing one of the greatest gambles in history at minimal cost. It did not need to win all the possibilities. Even one or two offered immense gains. We and we alone were in a position to break

up the play. These were the stakes that British withdrawal from the eastern Mediterranean offered to an eager and ruthless opponent.[7]

Whether Acheson fully believed his own words is subject to doubt. How the infection would spread directly from Greece to Iran was, in any case, a question for geographers and other skeptics to ponder. It is possible that he took his cue from Vandenberg, who, according to tradition, had advised Acheson to "scare hell" out of the American people. In any event, he sought to set the stage for a more ambitious program for Western Europe. On March 5, Marshall departed for the Moscow meeting of the CFM. The same day, Acheson wrote the War and Navy Departments urging study of "situations elsewhere in the world which may require analogous financial, technical, and military aid on our part." In a memo also dated March 5, Clayton called for $5 billion in special aid. "The U.S.," he warned, "must take world leadership and quickly, to avert world disaster."[8]

The immediate result of these efforts was Truman's famous address of March 12, requesting $400 million in aid for Greece and Turkey. With Marshall in Moscow, the speech did not mention the USSR. But the statement – dubbed the Truman Doctrine – was couched in now familiar Cold War rhetoric: ". . . It must be the policy of the United States to support free peoples who are resisting attempted subjugation by armed minorities or by outside pressure." The open-ended proposal was immediately attacked by Taft on the right and Wallace on the left. Walter Lippmann noted that the administration had conspicuously ignored its own creation, the United Nations Organization. Acheson and Forrestal fended off such arguments and concentrated their forensic skills on Capitol Hill. Clayton did the same, though his testimony was characteristically free of jingoism. With Vandenberg's help, the campaign bore fruit some weeks later. The Senate passed the Greek–Turkish aid bill on April 22. The House followed suit on May 9.[9]

THE TASCA LINE

Acheson's passing reference to Italy on February 25 reflected a growing anxiety about that country's vulnerability.[10] Like most high officials, Acheson was neither well versed nor deeply interested in Italy's internal situation. He was, however, convinced that it was precarious and would continue to deteriorate without major American aid. If U.S. officials had any doubt as to the inadequacy of their efforts, Tarchiani undertook to convince them otherwise. When he learned that Truman's February 21 request included a mere $107 million for Italy, the ambassador protested to Clayton. De Gasperi made a similar appeal, but the department had no choice but to urge them to look for help from other friendly countries.[11]

The "whirlwind of disintegration"

Tarchiani and De Gasperi pled their case in the midst of the gravest crisis of the postwar era. The international polarization, reflected and reinforced by Truman's March 12 address, ended any pretence of resistance unity. By March 1947, moreover, Italy faced runaway inflation and financial chaos. The shape of the crisis had been visible for some time. Since 1944, the Bank of Italy had allowed the free expansion of private credit in hopes of promoting productive investment. Likewise, the treasury had kept its hands off the financial markets between early 1945 and late 1946. But the attempt to limit government borrowing from the Central Bank had been doomed from the start by political demands for higher wages, subsidized prices, and industrial subventions. Private economic operators, meanwhile, sought quick killings in the financial markets while funnelling their profits to Switzerland and Argentina. A major crisis had been averted in September 1946, but the political stalemate allowed no coherent financial policy. Between January and May 1947, the lira's free-market value fell from 528 to 909 per dollar.[12] The cost of living index rose almost 20 percent between December 1946 and March 1947 and another 30 percent by June. Wage earners took to the streets to protest dwindling food supplies and rising prices, and bloody clashes with Scelba's police became a daily affair.

By early 1947, Paolo Baffi has argued, the "preeminent cause" of inflation was the uncontrolled expansion of private credit that fueled speculation.[13] Luigi Einaudi took a different view at the time. On March 31, the governor of the Bank of Italy appealed for new sacrifices in order to avoid the impending "critical moment" of inflation. Einaudi condemned wage indexation as "an instrument of privilege for the few and immiseration of the many," but he singled out the subsidized price of bread as the main cause of rising monetary circulation. The Central Bank had been obliged to rediscount the so-called wheat bills presented by the treasury; they covered the loss to the government when it sold grain at less than cost. Einaudi's "cry of alarm" was echoed by the Confindustria, whose *Notiziario* condemned a "monstrous complex" of social expenditures and warned that Italy had "reached the extreme limits within which the economy . . . can be saved."[14]

The tripartite coalition, meanwhile, lacked either cohesion or authority. On April 4, it proposed a fourteen-point economic program (authored largely by the Socialist Minister of Industry Morandi) calling for spending cuts and gradual elimination of political prices, import and exchange controls, tax increases, and restrictions on private bank credit. However, the program pleased no one, least of all the banks, who had already warned of a "dangerous run" should restrictions be imposed. This program represented, in any case, a mere statement of intentions to be debated by the Constituent Assembly. On April 13, Confindustria President Angelo Costa announced his own radically different program, including a devaluation of from 20 percent to 30 percent, abolition of exchange controls and political prices, major cuts in social spending, and the firing of workers in the private and public sectors. The Bank of Italy's representative in New York, Giuseppe Cigliana, wrote Einaudi on April 16 that Wall Street was "perplexed and worried" by recent government statements, including Einaudi's own. Cigliana had done his best to counter the "hysteria," but the New York banks seemed convinced that "wider and more rapid steps" were necessary to deal with the economic crisis.[15]

Such pressures left De Gasperi no choice but to consider ways of breaking the political stalemate. Since September 1946, if not before, he had seen a showdown as inevitable. By late April, neither the Peace Treaty (signed February 10) nor the Lateran Pacts (adopted March 24) constituted a reason to delay it. However, a confrontation involved serious risks, and De Gasperi proceeded with his usual care. During April, Campilli and Foreign Minister Sforza sought to test U.S. readiness to grant more aid and to clarify the political conditions that were likely to be attached. On April 12, the Rome embassy reported that the Italian Foreign Ministry believed that loans of from $100 to $200 million to Greece and Turkey, "on the basis of relative populations, would indicate that a loan of around $800,000,000 would be needed to ensure similar stability for Italy." Two days later, the economic director of the Foreign Ministry told Tasca that the Export–Import loan was "of little use in view of restrictions imposed by the Bank. . . ." Therefore, ". . . some Italians perhaps felt an Italian request for a loan from the Russian government might convince the U.S."[16]

Throughout the month of April, the Rome embassy was largely cut off from Washington. Until April 26, when the department requested information on the economic situation, the embassy received no orders or advice. The reasons are not difficult to surmise. The department was engaged in four time-consuming initiatives: both the Moscow and Geneva Conferences, the Capitol Hill campaign to sell Greek–Turkish aid, and the long-range studies ordered by Acheson on March 5. The embassy thus behaved according to its own intuition and predilictions. With Tarchiani temporarily in Rome, moreover, the embassy became the sole American interlocutor for the Italian government in its hour of greatest need.

Henry Tasca moved to center stage. Since late 1944, Tasca had been the economic and financial mind of the embassy, as well as its eyes and ears in the Italian business and political world. Inevitably, that experience had shaped his political outlook.[17] The willful, socially insecure treasury representative was something of a loner within the American diplomatic community. He gravitated naturally toward the attractions of Roman society, while his wide powers and access to information made him a magnet for the local elite. (He would shortly be engaged to marry Natalia Federici, daughter of the Roman construction magnate Federico Federici, a union that lasted until his tragic death in 1979.) By April 1947, Tasca's prescription differed little from the Confindustria's, and the young man's constant exposure to conservative circles undoubtedly contributed to the hardening of his views. Throughout his Italian career, however, those views were never reconciled with another, more original strain in Tasca's temperament and philosophy. The progressive spirit of his original masters, Roosevelt and Morgenthau, inclined him to support Giuseppe Saragat and the democratic left, while his Italian-American background created a permanent ambivalence and distance vis-à-vis the Italian bourgeoisie.

There is no doubt that Tasca's was the most important voice in U.S. policy toward Italy during the spring of 1947. The presence of James Dunn served only to reinforce the Tasca line. The ambassador knew little about economics and left such matters to the old-hand Tasca. As a veteran of EUR, moreover, Dunn's analysis did not differ from Tasca's in any important respect.[18] Neither man was amused by the amateurish threat to seek a Russian loan, and Tasca had a message that served to reinforce the mounting pressure on De Gasperi. On April 21, he was urgently called to the office of Treasury–Finance Minister Campilli. The apparent purpose of the visit was to ask that all lira funds still held by the AC be transferred to the Italian treasury. The proposal, according to Tasca, reflected "the desperate internal financial position of Italy, which, if not halted soon, may lead to a complete financial breakdown." The minister then appealed for "the importation on a vast scale of consumer goods" into Italy. Tasca's reply was blunt: "There were, as far as the Embassy was concerned, no plans for any further requests for aid from Congress on the part of the administration." It was his personal opinion, moreover, that "the U.S. Government would not be convinced that the halting of internal inflation was directly dependent upon foreign aid, and that the present psychological crisis appeared to be more an internal problem." The Italian government would have to take steps to control both wages and "internal disturbances and unrest." Campilli referred to harsh personal attacks on De Gasperi from both right-wing separatists and the PCI–PSI "Blocco del Popolo" during regional election campaigning in Sicily. Party leaders including Gronchi, Attilio Piccioni, and Don Luigi Sturzo leaned strongly toward a withdrawal from the coalition. But if De Gasperi was looking for some extraordinary remedy from the United States, the April 21 conversation indicated that such hopes were all but illusory. Tasca's message was undoubtedly in his mind as he prepared to take decisive action.[19]

In a brief, dramatic radio announcement on April 28, De Gasperi appealed for an end to the "wave of panic and madness" sweeping the country and condemned the speculators and profiteers who held the economy hostage. His real purpose was a call for participation in the government by representatives of those same business forces whose confidence was desperately lacking. Echoing Tasca, De Gasperi described the immediate barrier to recovery as essentially psychological. The restoration of calm would require courageous measures, to be carried out by unnamed "technicians" enjoying the respect of the private economic operators.

The showdown was now at hand. Severe economic measures required at the very least a further weakening of the PCI and PSI. Even though the chances of their elimination from the coalition were slim, De Gasperi was determined to try.[20] As always, he was cautious and "empirical," hedging his bets and attending signals from abroad. He did not have long to wait. The airwaves contained other important messages on April 28.

The Moscow conference had ended on April 24 with no agreement on the question of Germany. Marshall told General Clay to accelerate the bizonal merger and arrived home on April 28. Unbeknownst to De Gasperi, the secretary spoke the same evening by radio:

> The recovery of Europe has been far slower than had been expected. Disintegrating forces are becoming evident. The patient is sinking while the doctors deliberate. So I believe that action cannot await compromise through exhaustion. New issues arise daily. Whatever action is possible to meet these pressing problems must be taken without delay.

Marshall ordered Kennan to begin planning a major aid program integrating German recovery with that of Europe as a whole. Kennan had already cabled urgent requests for information on the European economies. Such a cable, noting that the department was "now investigating needs for the immediate and longer run stabilization of the Italian economy," arrived at the Rome embassy on April 26.[21]

The crucial events of May 1947 have been given varying interpretations.[22] All sources agree that the interval between De Gasperi's April 28 speech and resignation on May 12 was one of high tension and uncertainty. If, how, and when a crisis would begin remained unclear. De Gasperi proceeded very much by ear and was therefore encouraged by Marshall's speech, as well as by other developments abroad. At the same time, De Gasperi's radio address served to reinforce Tasca's position. In response to an anxious request (May 1) for information, Dunn emphasized to Washington that no improvement was possible under the present circumstances. The Communist Party "would of course, fight hard against any effort to form a Government without its participation but I do not believe it is too late for a Government to be formed without their participation and there appears to be a growing realization that the Communist Party is not really trying to bring about the restoration of economic stability. . . ." In the meantime, the United States should provide only emergency coal and food, also a presidential statement linking future aid to the rejection by Italians of "totalitarian" forces.[23]

De Gasperi summoned Dunn to test American intentions on May 5. He would not deliberately provoke a crisis that "might result in a financial panic." If the crisis were "brought about in the assembly," that was another matter. Following this ambiguous pronouncement, De Gasperi raised the presumably unwelcome prospect of his own departure. Various figures, including the eighty-one-year-old Francesco Nitti, had been mentioned as replacements, and De Gasperi "was ready to retire at any moment that he felt an able and efficient successor could be chosen."

De Gasperi then came to the point by inquiring about new American aid. Dunn's account suggests that he remained impassive until this point in the conversation, but his reply left De Gasperi with little margin for maneuver:

> I said that our Government was deeply interested in the Italian situation and wished to be of such assistance as they could, but that it was necessary for us to see some effective measures taken by the Italians themselves to put their house in order before we could give consideration to aid for Italy other than direct relief.

De Gasperi feared that the aid would arrive too late to save the situation, but Dunn was not moved:

> I told him that we all had the greatest confidence in him personally and that we wanted to be of all the help we could and that we were sincerely hopeful that he would find the means of correcting the present situation and take advantage of the splendid attitude and will to work of the Italian people at this present time.[24]

The embassy reiterated this view to Washington on May 7. In a preliminary reply to Kennan's request for information, Dunn's (or perhaps Tasca's) prose waxed lurid and sensational:

> . . . Only Draconian measures, and the longer they are delayed the more severe they must be, appear adequate to arrest the drift, which may become a plunge, and to start Italy on the upward path. The requirements to meet and vanquish the forces of this whirlwind of disintegration are:
>
> (1) Political leadership both competent and courageous.
> (2) Political and economic policy reforms against the opposition of many special interests. . . .

126

(3) Effective implementation of policies through fundamental reforms of practices and procedures.[25]

De Gasperi was probably unaware that Dunn (like Tasca on April 21) had expressed an essentially personal view on May 5. Whether, had it been less preoccupied, Washington might have offered De Gasperi more concrete encouragement will never be known. Tarchiani (who had returned to the United States by early May) was hard at work to obtain a better deal, but as far as De Gasperi was concerned, the Dunn–Tasca position constituted the official U.S. line during the last days before the crisis.

Other developments, however, tended to mitigate the harshness of the message. First was the news from Paris. In the wake of labor unrest and a Communist vote against the government's colonial policy, Premier Ramadier invited the PCF ministers to leave his cabinet. On May 5, they graciously complied. Four days later, the World Bank wrote its first loan, totaling $250 million, to the order of the French Republic.[26] On May 8, Acheson told an audience in Cleveland, Mississippi, that the United States was "going to have to undertake further emergency financing of foreign purchases if foreign countries are to continue to buy in 1948 and 1949 the commodities which they need to sustain life and at the same time to rebuild their economies. . . ."[27] On May 12, the Constituent Assembly prepared to debate the government's economic program. The executive of the PCI announced that the Communist members of the cabinet had formally disassociated themselves from any new proposals the prime minister might offer. This news came as no surprise, but De Gasperi seized the opportunity to resign, thus opening the decisive governmental crisis of the early postwar era.

TASCA IN WASHINGTON

In order to understand the complex diplomacy leading to the new, *monocolore* government on May 31, attention must first be given to the State Department. The record indicates no contact between the Rome embassy and Italian officials between May 5 and 27. After his disappointing meeting with Dunn, De Gasperi took his case directly to Washington, and the crisis found two other important actors in the United States. The right-wing Socialist leader, Ivan Matteo Lombardo, made his second visit to Washington in late April, this time to settle financial claims arising from the war and occupation. On May 5, treasury and state recalled Henry Tasca for consultation. He left by plane on May 8, carrying a long response to Kennan's request. Following discussions with Tasca, Washington would issue its first precise instructions on May 20. In the meantime, the embassy cabled routine reports, drawn largely from the press. Their quality in Tasca's absence prompted EUR Director Matthews to write Dunn on May 26, "We all feel that the political reporting from your Embassy is woefully inadequate."[28]

Joseph Jones exaggerates perhaps only slightly in his description of the atmosphere awaiting Tasca: "All . . . were aware that a major turning point in American history was taking place. The convergence of massive historical trends upon that moment was so real as to be almost tangible. . . ."[29] Tasca's reaction presumably included surprise and anticipation. From his Rome vantage point, he had had only vague indications that something dramatic was afoot. His concerns were parochial in the bigger scheme of things, but he no doubt relished the chance to participate in the great decisions of the day.

Tasca carried with him a summary and distillation of his remarkable Italian experience.[30] The economic and financial position of Italy, he began, reflected "the lack of confidence on the part of strategic economic groups in the ability of the government to direct and control the country." Tasca knew those groups intimately, and his report contained much evidence of his own ambivalence towards them and implicit criticism of their lack of courage and cohesion. The divided middle classes were prey to a resourceful Moscow-directed Communist Party. Public unrest created "a psychosis of fear which, in turn [was] politically exploited." In short, the PCI had set in motion a self-serving vicious cycle: "The fear of Communist seizure of power, paradoxically, increases the number of adherents to the Party."

Tasca's analysis left no doubt that a Communist conspiracy, rather than genuine "economic difficulties and the relatively low standard of living," was chiefly responsible for the current, essentially political and psychological crisis. "Indices of consumption and real wages would appear to indicate that the position with respect to the masses in Italy has not deteriorated substantially during the last year, and that in fact, the probability is that the political agitation is retarding economic recovery rather than economic difficulties retarding the achievement of political stability and equilibrium." Nor, Tasca added, was there much doubt about how to deal with the situation: "If it is true that the economic position could be substantially improved through political measures, then aid to Italy perhaps should be based upon the *quid pro quo* of necessary changes in political orientation and policies."

Once the political situation had been corrected, the Italians must adopt a broad series of reforms designed to streamline and update the government's technical performance. Tasca attacked such measures as the capital levy and the tax on both the increase in monetary value of stocks and profits derived from activities of the previous regime. The latter tax was particularly odious in that it weakened the already enfeebled classes who "constituted the backbone of opposition to Communism." Tasca also urged a complete overhaul of the fiscal system, including the introduction of an income tax, the removal of regressive factors, and the modernization of government accounting and budgetary procedures.

On crucial questions of wages, employment, and inflation, Tasca shared the Confindustria view that the *scala mobile* be retained for short-term political reasons. The Government, however, would have to take direct control of wages, especially with the Communists in opposition, and the firing of industrial and public employees must be freely resumed. In the longer run, Italy's unemployment problem could be solved only through "large scale emigration and foreign investment." Tasca rejected new controls on private economic activity (with the exception of foreign exchange). Price controls, unlike wage controls, were impractical, and public utility and other prices had to be raised in order "to restore normal price and cost relationships." Even though he acknowledged that the lack of "effective credit control" on private banks had resulted in speculation and inflation. Tasca's recommendations fell short of reserve requirements or other restrictions.

Unfortunately, no record exists of Tasca's consultations in Washington, but his report was widely distributed.[31] Tasca's pointed emphasis on the political and psychological roots of the economic crisis arose in part from his fear that a craven and disorganized Italian bourgeoisie might extort new aid from Washington, or failing that, cave in to Communist demands. In either case, the Italians would avoid taking the harsh medicine and housecleaning measures that Tasca's temperament and political instinct convinced him were indispensable. Even though it was no doubt well-founded, such an analysis aroused skepticism in Washington. Detached from the fray, neither Kennan nor Clayton could easily accept Tasca's view that Communist subversion was the root cause of the Italian crisis or that the problem was merely political and psychological in nature. Tasca's assertion to that effect led an unknown reader to write a large question mark and the notation "logic?" in the margin of the report.[32]

Kennan and Clayton, by contrast, believed that Communist strength was the by-product of previous economic problems. Even though the Communists profited from those difficulties, their mere removal from government would not suffice to restore stability and growth. In his first report (May 20) on the problem of U.S. aid to Western Europe, Kennan observed:

> The Policy Planning Staff does not see communist activities as the root of the difficulties of western Europe. It believes that the present crisis results in large part from the disruptive effect of the war on the economic, politi-

cal, and social structure of Europe and from a profound exhaustion of physical plant and of spiritual vigor. . . ."[33]

Several days later, a somewhat distraught Clayton returned from the trade conference in Geneva. His proposals had met resistance both at home and from the British Empire bloc, and he appeared deeply affected by the "economic horror stories" (no doubt exaggerated for his benefit) circulating throughout Europe. On May 27, Clayton wrote Acheson:

> Europe is steadily deteriorating. The political position reflects the economic. . . .
> It will be necessary for the President and the Secretary of State to make a strong spiritual appeal to the American people to sacrifice a little themselves, to draw in their own belts just a little in order to save Europe from starvation and chaos (*not* from the Russians). . . .[34]

Those people who shared the Clayton–Kennan view were inclined to see Tasca's appraisal as superficial or exaggerated. Tasca in effect was arguing that there was no basic economic crisis at all. At the same time, his plea for further dilution of the Communist role struck a responsive chord. Whatever the source of Italy's difficulties, there was general agreement that the PCI constituted a political and psychological barrier to a potential European recovery program. Even though plans were in the early embryonic stage, it was clear that participating countries would have to adopt tough stabilization measures in return for American funds. The nature and scope of such measures were undefined, but they would surely create unemployment in the short run and would not easily be supported by Communist ministers. Finally, the Communists would show little enthusiasm for an aid program that excluded the Russians. By May 1947, their exclusion was necessary and inevitable.

Therefore, Kennan argued, the United States must have guarantees from the Europeans to "preclude Communist sabotage or misuse of economic aid."[35] The maximum possible reduction, if not complete elimination, of Communist power in Western governments was an obvious first step. Also desirable was the inclusion in Western European governments of the democratic working class. This idea was naturally attractive to American liberal Democrats, steeped in the 1930s New Deal experience. For reasons of *realpolitik* rather than ideological conviction, the idea also struck a responsive chord at EUR. Happily enough, the French Socialists had remained in alliance with the Catholic MRP after May 5, and Tasca and other Truman administration officials entertained hopes for a Catholic–Socialist entente in Italy. There was a final reason for purging the extreme left from the Italian government. The public and Congress were unlikely to support massive outlays of American money to countries in which Communists held power. This fact was all the more obvious after the recent campaign to render the menace of Russian Communism "clearer than the truth."

Such were the general considerations as the department prepared to respond to the Italian crisis. However, achieving internal consensus did not solve the department's domestic political or diplomatic problems. Never were the two sets of problems more inextricably bound up. Since new Congressional appropriations would not be available for months, Tasca's April 21 warning to Campilli reflected the actual state of affairs in Washington. At the crucial moment in its postwar Italian diplomacy, the State Department could offer De Gasperi only the most paltry of concrete guarantees.

THE MAY CRISIS

On De Gasperi's resignation on May 12, the president of the republic offered the mandate to form a government to the noted economic expert Francesco Nitti. One argument suggests that Nitti was supported by Vittorio Valletta, managing director of FIAT, and other business figures seeking an alternative to De Gasperi and the DC.[36] The evidence for this line is scanty. Valletta was no fool, and Nitti's chances were very slim. Aside from his advanced age, he lacked a mass base and wide appeal. The position of his potential allies, moreover, was intractable. De Gasperi demanded an enlargement of the tripartite formula in return for Christian Democratic support. Nitti's own Liberal Party refused to enter the government as long as the PCI and PSI remained. The *piccola intesa* of PRI, Actionists, DL, and PSLI (a bloc of ninety deputies, including Saragat and La Malfa) refused to be party to what they saw as a DC-inspired maneuver to strengthen the right and demanded substantial economic powers in return for their support. Such powers neither Nitti, nor, in his turn, De Gasperi, was willing to concede. Saragat's veto on May 20 spelled the end for Nitti. In an equally futile gesture, President De Nicola passed the mandate to another octogenarian Liberal, Vittorio Orlando, on May 21.

As De Gasperi waited in the wings, Tarchiani sought concrete guarantees in Washington. On May 16, the ambassador spoke to Marshall and Matthews from a script worthy of Acheson himself:

> If Moscow succeeds in establishing a Communist Italy it will have gained a highly strategic position. Italy as a base would serve to flank Greece and Turkey, to extend Communist influence north to Germany and Austria and west to France and Spain. It would also facilitate Communist penetration into North Africa, an area to which Moscow is attaching increasing importance.

Tarchiani did not count on the exclusion of the PCI and sought to ensure American aid if the Communists remained in the government. Adopting a reassuring tone, he observed that the crisis would soon be resolved by Nitti or De Gasperi. In either case, the DC would remain the biggest party and De Gasperi would exercise the real power. In return, Marshall promised a list of items offered months before: the Export–Import loan and post-UNRRA relief, return of Italian assets in the United States, as well as support for Italian UN membership. On the central question of additional aid, he was conspicuously silent.[37]

Four days later, on May 20, Tarchiani spoke to Matthews of a "very private secret message" from De Gasperi. Nitti's failure was a foregone conclusion. De Gasperi would try to form a government, but, according to Tarchiani, he "seemed somewhat dubious of success and apparently in need of encouragement." Specifically, he sought a U.S. guarantee of more financial aid before undertaking the mandate.[38] This news prompted the department to dangle the carrot of possible future assistance. After consulting with Marshall, Matthews told Tarchiani to inform De Gasperi: "You may count on the strong moral support of the United States and that we will make a serious effort to assist Italy in meeting her essential financial needs."[39] The gesture was vague and ambiguous, but the department could offer nothing more specific in May 1947.

The same evening, the department cabled instructions to the Rome embassy. For the first time, it attached specific conditions to Marshall's May 16 list:

> It is evident that any non-Communist government formed following De Gasperi's resignation must achieve early, visible improvement in economic conditions and demonstrate to the Italian people it enjoys Western support. . . . Foregoing naturally applies also and in almost equal measure to any new government in which Communist participation is reduced to minimum.

The difference in measure apparently referred to the support the United States was prepared to offer. However, the proposals included in the cable represented a mere dressing-up of the threadbare package outlined by Marshall to Tarchiani on May 16.[40] Even though De Gasperi did not officially receive this message until May 27, he was aware of its substance via Tarchiani when he took up the mandate on May 24. Neither the political conditions nor the aid items came as any surprise, and the latter fell far short of what De Gasperi sought. Still, the U.S. gesture left him little choice but to press on in the hope that bold action might yet secure the elusive future assistance.

In the meantime, discordant signals were emanating from Washington. On May 24, De Gasperi received urgent cables from Lombardo and Tarchiani reporting that U.S. officials were angered by a recent *l'Unità* attack on the United States. In a May 18 broadcast, retired diplomat Sumner Welles had accused the communists of receiving large subsidies from the Kremlin. Togliatti replied in a caustic editorial entitled "How Stupid They Are!" According to Lombardo, the editorial would have "vast repercussions" and had undermined his own position. Lombardo's talks concerned, *inter alia*, approximately $60 million in Italian frozen assets to which the department's May 20 cable had referred. There is no evidence that the department intended to withdraw this concession, but it clearly used the occasion to put additional pressure on De Gasperi. Once the crisis was resolved, Lombardo reported a marked change in the American attitude.[41]

The episode further convinced De Gasperi that the time had come for a decisive move against the PCI. That possibility provoked deep anxiety within the DC, and De Gasperi sought to determine what, if anything, the Americans were holding in reserve. De Gasperi summoned Dunn on May 27. The prime minister–designate now revealed that he was giving serious consideration to a government of Christian Democrats and technical experts alone. Dunn took the occasion to relate the substance of Marshall's May 20 cable. De Gasperi listened patiently, but his mind was on another matter. According to the ambassador's account, De Gasperi wished to:

> dispense with discussion of the attitude of the U.S. toward the Italian situation as he was fully conversant with and fully appreciative of what we had done. . . . What he needed for the survival of the new single party government, if he undertook it, was some new and substantial evidence of economic aid which could be applied to the support of the lira and the financial position of the government.

With that support in hand, he was ready to do battle with the left.[42] On the same day, Campilli made an identical plea to Tasca, who had now returned to Rome. A noncommunist government would need "something spectacular" to offer the Italian people. At least 200 million dollars over and above post-UNRRA aid would be necessary in order to meet the deficit in the balance of payments.[43] Dunn made no reply to De Gasperi but urged Washington to find the desperately needed aid. He recommended a package including the return of Italian gold and a second Export–Import loan to be taken from funds still allocated for China.

If either De Gasperi or Dunn suspected that the department was holding back some major concession, they soon learned otherwise. Dunn's items involved long delays, and the department promptly vetoed any reduction of the China "set-aside."[44] The truth of the matter was once again bluntly put to Campilli on May 27. Nothing had transpired in Washington to alter Tasca's position. Obviously, he did not foresee Marshall's June 5 speech at Harvard, but that proposal would do nothing to ameliorate immediate conditions, and Tasca's was the message that the new government would have to live with during the months ahead: Italy would have to take the "necessary internal measures" to correct its economic and financial position.[45]

The May 27 meetings left De Gasperi little choice but to take the decisive step down the course embarked upon on April 28. Following last-minute arrangements, De Gasperi announced the formation of a new government, composed solely of Christian Democrats and technicians, on May 31. The cabinet contained a new "high command," composed to win the confidence of industry and finance. The Ministry of the Treasury and Finance was redivided to accommodate Gustavo Del Vecchio (Independent), a prominent liberal economist, and Giuseppe Pella (DC), a Peidmontese businessman. Cesare Merzagora (PLI), a Milan industrialist and financier, became minister of trade.[46] The major innovation was the appointment of Luigi Einaudi to a specially created post, the Ministry of the Budget. He also assumed the rank of vice-premier. Einaudi had demanded both positions in return for his entry into the government for the first time. In addition to his control of the Bank of Italy through Menichella, Einaudi now acquired wide powers over government spending and economic policy. With the support of the DC, PLI, and Uomo Qualunque, the cabinet won a narrow vote of confidence (274 to 231) on June 21. A handful of Republicans and Social Democrats abstained. All others joined the opposition.

THE END OF AN ERA

Preparations for the State Department's momentous departure proceeded apace during the last week of May 1947. On May 28, high officials met to discuss Clayton's memo written on his return from Geneva. After a vivid description of the crisis, he called for an annual grant of $6 to $7 billion worth of U.S. goods for three years and a plan for economic federation. Countries like Canada could help with food and raw materials, but Clayton left no doubt about who would call the shots: "We must avoid getting into another UNRRA. The *United States must run this show*" (emphasis in original).[47] No one disputed Clayton's point. The UNRRA experience was best forgotten. As for Eastern Europe, it was agreed that "the plan should be drawn with such conditions that Eastern Europe could participate, provided the countries would abandon the near-exclusive Soviet orientation of their economies."[48] The remaining issue of United States versus European responsibility and initiative was resolved by Marshall's historic announcement eight days later:

> It is logical that the United States should do whatever it is able to do to assist in the return of normal economic health in the world, without which

there can be no political stability and no assured peace. Our policy is directed not against any country or doctrines but against hunger, poverty desperation and chaos. . . . It would be neither fitting nor efficacious for this Government to undertake to draw up unilaterally a program designed to place Europe on its feet economically. This is the business of the Europeans. The initiative, I think must come from Europe. . . .[49]

Dunn cabled on June 8 that the address was "most happy as to both substance and timing."[50] Despite its considerable psychological value, however, the speech was the beginning of a long and complicated initiative that bore fruit only in the summer of 1948. Marshall indicated that Europe must take the initiative, but the department had extensive ground rules in mind and would eventually try to dictate the plan's design. Acheson emphasized the domestic pitfalls even before the secretary spoke. He knew then, as he later observed, that Congress would not reach into its pockets for "as Platonic a purpose as combatting 'hunger, poverty, desperation, and chaos'. . . ."[51] On July 1, Acheson bequeathed the domestic political problem to his successor, Robert Lovett.

It is clear in retrospect that the June 5, 1947, speech in effect admitted the failure of America's original postwar foreign economic policy. This admission was more explicit in Clayton's memo of May 27, on which Marshall's words were closely based. Clayton abandoned his old dream of integrating the entire European continent into a single economic unit. America's prospective collaborators in the West, meanwhile, appeared to be on the verge of economic collapse. Clayton had his own explanation for this unhappy state of affairs. He freely admitted his failure to grasp the economic consequences of the war. However, his warning against future UNRRAs was an equally telling admission of the philosophical disharmony and bureaucratic divisions that had plagued the internationalist community. If from now on the United States must "run the show," its leadership must speak with a single voice. Finally, in his call for a "spiritual appeal" to the American people, Clayton acknowledged a fundamental flaw in the multilateral blueprint. He had tried to build his lofty edifice on the shifting, treacherous ground of domestic interests and opinion. Throughout the early postwar years, Clayton had lacked the financial leverage and political support necessary to raise his structure into place.

For Clayton, the Marshall Plan represented a second chance, an opportunity to build a scaled-down, Western European version of his original design. He would discover, however, that the United States (not to mention Western Europe) continued to speak with many voices. Clayton's effort to run the plan within the State Department faced imminent defeat at the hands of his old antagonists on Capitol Hill, the same "Congressional masters" who would help to kill the ITO. The ERP spawned a vast new bureaucracy, beyond the State Department's grasp.

There is some irony in the fact that the foreign policy of the United States after June 5, 1947, would lack both the ambitions and the influence of the immediate postwar period. What was conceived as a major new offensive in fact became a strategic withdrawal from the pretentions of the earlier heroic phase. This withdrawal would be forced by continued delays and internal divisions at home. Henceforth, it would be reinforced by the growing sense of independence and self-interest on the part of the Western Europeans themselves. This is perhaps most obvious in the case of the British, who, after the disastrous sterling crisis of July 1947, refused to submit themselves to the Hullian logic of the United States.

This was also true in Italy, where the United States would prove unable to foster a new and contradictory scenario for financial stabilization, economic recovery, and social-political reform on the loose and internally divided coalition who took power in May 1947. The United States could offer Italy only the mildest of palliatives during the patient's gravest hour. Einaudi's was therefore the only available medicine, though for some people his sternly administered cure would seem nearly as insidious as the original disease. The Truman administration would be forced to mount a second emergency response designed to limit the damage wrought by deflation and to salvage the elections of April 1948. Thereafter, once ensconced in power, the new regime would be in a position to select only the items of abundantly available American aid and advice that served to consolidate its newly won control.

9

The dilemmas of deflation

INTRODUCTION

The Italian financial stabilization of 1947–48 has provoked a heated controversy among economists and historians. The debate revolves around three related issues: the economic wisdom of deflation, its political-ideological motivation, and the role of external forces, in particular, of the United States. The first issue has generated the most discussion yet is probably the easiest to resolve. Keynesian and left-wing critics have tended to endorse De Cecco's judgment that ". . . from September 1947 to the outbreak of the Korean War, the authorities' conduct was totally inexcusable."[1] This school contends that the liberal economists pursued misguided policies in defiance of the latest economic science. They mistakenly presumed that the economy was operating at full capacity, and their monetary stringency condemned the country to a wasteful, needless depression. Devaluation alone, according to some, would have sufficed to spur exports and augment essential imports and reserves, thus easing inflationary pressures. The stubborn pursuit of tight money in a period of high unemployment and excess industrial capacity is impossible to justify on economic grounds alone.[2]

Einaudi's defenders, on the other hand, have argued more convincingly that Keynesian doctrine did not apply to an economy still dominated by a large agricultural sector and suffering from extensive dislocation, shortages, and other bottlenecks. Devaluation, accompanied by the stimulation of internal demand, would have induced a flood of imports at higher prices, bringing renewed inflation and severe pressure on limited foreign currency holdings.[3] In order to guarantee sustained recovery, the task was to break inflationary expectations once and for all, restore confidence in the currency, and build up a cushion of international reserves.

Other observers divide their analysis into two distinct periods, based on the availability of large-scale American aid. Bruno Foa, a devastating critic of Corbino, calls Einaudi's policies a "financial masterpiece."[4] The historian Ugo Ruffolo agrees that Einaudi's credit controls responded precisely and effectively to the circumstances of late 1947 and early 1948. His endorsement is based on an all-important yet oddly neglected fact: During the six months after June 1947, the Americans provided only a trickle of emergency relief. The Italian government faced a foreign exchange crisis of unparalleled dimensions. As will be seen, Ruffolo's conclusion seems indisputable: For purely economic reasons, the authorities had no choice but to constrict demand until greater foreign credits became available.[5] Foa and Ruffolo take a different view of the continuation of deflationary policies after June 1948. Like the ERP authorities themselves, Foa is harshly critical of the government's reluctance to stimulate production with Marshall Plan backing. For Ruffolo and others, the post-June 1948 policy raises a second basic question: What were the political and ideological considerations underlying the stabilization?

The historian Antonio Gambino offers a typical response. Although conducted by De Gasperi and Einaudi, the stabilization was orchestrated by an industrial-financial elite. Having profited from inflation for many months, the elite was eventually convinced by Einaudi's reasoning that the "critical moment" had arrived. By mid-1947, "even those who had exploited (and stimulated) the inflation had real reason to fear its continuation could have negative social effects far greater than the economic benefits which by then were decreasing. The moment of stabilization, therefore, had clearly arrived."[6] Such arguments hardly do justice to the complexity of motives behind the stabilization or of the political and social coalition who supported it. It is impossible to accept Gambino's assertion that the internally divided Italian *padronato* suddenly changed its mind about inflation and then proceeded, as a group, to dictate an abrupt reversal in policy. What became known as the Einaudi line resembled only in part the program advanced by Angelo Costa and the Confindustria in April 1947. The gist of that program was a budget balanced by cuts in social spending. For obvious reasons, the Costa plan did not include the strict controls on private banks, which eventually formed the heart of the Einaudi approach. Indeed, Italian business and finance would find themselves in a strange, if temporary, alliance with the left against Einaudi.

Over the longer run, of course, deflation strengthened the large, independent firms vis-à-vis their smaller, more vulnerable competitors. Deflation also helped break the rigid labor market and destroy the bargaining power enjoyed by the CGIL during the immediate postwar period. Such factors help explain the Confindustria's toleration of deflation after the ERP began. It is not clear, however, that Italian big business foresaw

Introduction

these benefits in 1947, and it was reconciled to Einaudi's policies only through a series of quid pro quos, including additional state subsidies and a free hand with labor inside the factory walls.

Einaudi's personal agenda was of little interest to the state-bred and private industrial monopolies. For him, the unprecedented powers demanded and received in May 1947 provided the opportunity to recast the domestic economy along liberal lines and link it to the world according to the precepts of comparative advantage. The concessions demanded and received, in turn, by business served only to thwart the transformation Einaudi hoped to carry out. As Foa observed in 1948, "Whether one likes the fact or not, it appears increasingly clear that an unexpected by-product of the policies of Professor Einaudi has been to increase the already large area of Government power, and ultimate control, in the industrial field."[7]

This basic conflict of purpose was embodied in the new economic high command itself. Einaudi and Menichella clashed with Industry Minister Giuseppe Togni and also with Trade Minister Merzagora, who represented private business interests. Einaudi and his eventual successor, Giuseppe Pella, would also come under strong attack from Gronchi, Fanfani, and the Christian Democratic left. The economists held tenaciously to the path of monetary stabilization, but their broader vision was compromised beyond recognition by the demands of big industry and DC social planners.

These contradictions emerged clearly during the summer of 1947. At the same time, the anti-Marxist forces had a common interest in currency stabilization during the period of mid-1947 to early 1948. In his classic study of the pre-1940 Italian political economy, Pietro Grifone observed that the decision of the Fascists to embark on a painful monetary stabilization in the mid-1920s arose, above all, from the necessity to avoid a collapse of the lira and consequent immiseration and radicalization of groups whose support was vital to the regime – middle- and lower-middle class savers, rural property owners, and urban *commercianti*.[8] Similar considerations loomed large for De Gasperi, the leader and mediator of the center–right coalition that assumed power in May 1947. The immediate concern was to win the national elections scheduled to follow the completion of the work of the Constituent Assembly in late 1947 and thereafter to monopolize the political game in the interests of the victorious electoral bloc. One need not belabor the obvious political as well as economic imperatives that dictated the stabilization.

Grifone also invoked the role of international factors, in particular, Mussolini's desire to restore the confidence of foreign investors in the lira and in the local political system. Such factors seem equally evident in 1947, but the nature of external pressures has rarely been identified.

The dilemmas of deflation

Pietro Armani, for one, speaks of "concrete links, especially of an international political nature, which pushed us fatally toward the choice of monetary measures."[9] As to the substance of those links, Armani does not elaborate. Gambino is one of few to address directly the question of American involvement, concluding, "Washington's intervention did not play any determinant role in the adoption of the Einaudi measures." De Gasperi welcomed, indeed solicited, pressure from the United States, but the business-financial hierarchy had made a prior and independent decision to deflate.[10]

It is clear from the discussion of April–May 1947 (see Chapter 8) that Gambino's argument cannot be sustained.[11] History offers few examples of political leadership willing to undertake severe measures to halt inflation unless forced to do so by international pressures. Italy in 1947 is no exception. Understandably, De Gasperi approached the stabilization with extreme trepidation and sought an extraordinary financial remedy from the United States until the final moment of the May crisis. Even then, he and Einaudi hesitated, appealing for "quick extra aid" to bolster their position.[12] The government made its preparations in hopes that the United States might still ease the pain of the contemplated deflation, and Einaudi undertook his program only when external pressures were no longer escapable. By September 1947, it was obvious that the United States could not rescue Italy from its balance-of-payments crisis, at this point badly aggravated by the British decision to suspend the convertibility of sterling. It was equally obvious by September 1947 that the United States demanded tough internal measures as a precondition for future assistance. Those conditions had been articulated – quite without Italian solicitation – by the embassy since April and were reiterated throughout the summer and fall.

It is another matter to argue, however, that, following the collapse of its original timetable for recovery and liberalization, the United States was better equipped intellectually or diplomatically to confront Italian realities after May 1947. In his revisionist critique of the Marshall Plan, Gabriel Kolko observes that a fundamental contradiction underlay the new American scenario. The requirements of its two basic objectives – sound currencies and balanced budgets on one hand, and sustained production and full employment on the other – were effectively incompatible.[13] Kolko is wrong to contend that the Economic Cooperation Administration (ECA) officials gave priority to the task of monetary stabilization, at least in Italy. Indeed, New Deal and Keynesian-inspired FEA and UNRRA officials migrated to the ECA in large numbers in 1948. At the same time, however, the dilemma identified by Kolko was the main obstacle to America's new plans for Italy after June 1947.

The State Department and embassy were naturally concerned that the stabilization operation be brief and coherently executed, and that its political effects be limited and contained. The objective of the stabilization, after all, was to set the stage for the European Recovery Program, that is, for the economic growth and social reconciliation required to guarantee political stability and American interests over the longer run. But U.S. officials could not control the technical conduct, duration, or political-economic consequences of deflation. They were forced to mount another emergency response to reconcile the contradictory goals of currency stabilization and increased production and also to try to shift the center of gravity within the coalition modestly to the left in order to weaken the mass-based Marxist parties.

However, more unwelcome surprises were in store after 1947. Efforts to rally a democratic left behind the Christian Democratic government stood little chance of success in a country in which non-Catholic, non-Marxist socialism had little respectability or appeal. American officials, moreover, resorted to the doubtful notion that Keynesian gimmickry could substitute for a painful, conclusive financial stabilization. Einaudi and his colleagues would resist what they saw as shortsighted efforts to abort the stabilization, both before and after the elections of April 1948. If capitalist recovery were to be guaranteed, the foundations could not be laid on the cheap.

Once committed to the DC-led alliance, the United States would fall prey to the dilemmas inherent in the complex relationship of a great power to a smaller local client. Events would be determined less by the architects of the Marshall Plan than by factors essentially beyond the American executive's control: Congress, objective economic circumstances, and, above all, by the Italian political forces themselves.

THE EINAUDI LINE

The need for stable European currencies and exchange rates provoked little debate among U.S. officials working on the Marshall Plan in the summer of 1947. Monetary stabilization would become a precondition for participation because it made patent economic and domestic political sense. Clayton personally conveyed this message to the sixteen member nations of the Committee for European Economic Cooperation (CEEC) who met in Paris between July and September 1947 to draw up the European proposal solicited by Marshall. According to Clayton, U.S. public opinion "attached great importance to satisfactory assurances that participating countries will take all reasonable action to place their budgetary affairs in a manageable position as soon as possible, as an essential preliminary step towards the stability and convertibility of their currencies." Such a clause was included in the CEEC's report (a document prepared with considerable American guidance) of September 1947.[14]

U.S. officials also hoped that monetary stabilization in such countries as Italy would be rapid, allowing the ERP to promote investment, employment, and social-administrative reform. Not the least of their reasons was political. With elections in early 1948, deflation was a ready-made issue for the Socialist–Communist alliance. In mid-June 1947, the embassy emphasized the need to "shift from the present phase of an emergency hand-to-mouth-economy to one providing maximum employment and production. . . . For democratic leadership in Italy to survive it must accomplish this in the foreseeable future."[15] Time, the message suggested, was of the essence.

But the events of May 1947 did nothing to alter the financial plight of both the State Department and the De Gasperi government. In August, the Italians would be obliged to bear the consequences of earlier illusions and miscalculations embodied in the Anglo-American financial agreement of 1946. Until late 1947, when Truman summoned Congress to consider a special "interim aid" appropriation, the department could offer little or nothing to stave off the collapse of Italy's reserve position. Throughout the summer, officials in Washington labored to stitch together a package of aid concessions, but they were forced to admit that a substantial gap in Italy's July–December foreign exchange requirements would remain.

Among the items available were $115 million in long-anticipated post-UNRRA relief, the Aid United States of America, or AUSA, program that began July 1. In mid-July, the United States sold the Italians $148 million in surplus military property at the price of $18 million. The United States–Italian financial agreement concluded by Ivan Matteo Lombardo and the department on August 14 provided for the return of $60 million in blocked and vested Italian assets in the United States, the waiver of all U.S. claims arising from the wartime military relief and FEA programs (approximately $523 million), and the transfer of the remaining net troop pay offsets (amounting to $312 million), which had begun in late 1944.[16]

Although extremely generous, the final financial settlement did little to relieve Italy's desperate situation at the time. On July 25, the department estimated Italy's July–December deficit at $83 million. This figure represented a severe slashing of a $236 million shortfall calculated by Lombardo. The Italian government made its case directly to Clayton, who arrived in Rome for two days of talks on July 22. Einaudi had prepared a long memo asking for a minimum of $4 billion in U.S. aid over five years. For the 12 months ending July 1948 alone, Italy would require from $850 to $900 million. "The diseases of Italy," Einaudi noted, "can be healed in several years of severe economic administration at home, but along with a substantial foreign assistance." In meetings with De Gasperi, Sforza, and Einaudi, Clayton displayed his well-known sympathy for Italy but could offer nothing of substance. Italy would have to restrict internal demand and give attention to "the restoration of a sound currency . . . as a means of promoting the exchange of goods and thereby increasing production generally."[17]

If Clayton's visit was a severe disappointment, the Italians were in for a much ruder shock. On July 15, 1947, in accordance with the Anglo-American agreement, sterling balances in the hands of third parties became freely convertible. During the six-day period of August 10–15 alone, Britain lost 176 million in dollar reserves. On August 18, Foreign Secretary Bevin told the United States that the $3.5 billion loan would be exhausted within two weeks. On August 20, Chancellor of the Exchequer Dalton announced the indefinite suspension of convertibility, effective the following day.[18]

As a former enemy, Italy had been excluded from the stampede to trade in sterling for dollars. The Italians, however, had made bilateral arrangements in April permitting the gradual conversion of 20 million pounds in frozen assets and export revenues. The crisis radically altered even the State Department's conservative estimate of Italy's foreign currency needs. The dollars allocated for October coal purchases in the United States were now unavailable, and Tarchiani importuned Under Secretary Lovett to pressure the British government.[19] But the British refused to budge. Following a mission to London in September for the annual meeting of the IMF, Einaudi, Menichella, and Carli reported that the British had "categorically declined to permit conversion of even one Pound." Einaudi warned Clayton and Treasury Secretary Snyder, "If within the next few weeks no extra-ordinary help in dollars will be granted to Italy, the collapse of the Italian economy will be inevitable."[20]

Such were the international realities that combined with unforeseen internal developments to belie the earlier hopes and calculations of both Einaudi and the United States. A most transparent illusion concerned the potential role of the Italian democratic left. One week after the formation of the DC-technician government, Secretary Marshall told the Rome embassy to express its disappointment to both De Gasperi and social democratic party leaders about the failure to agree on the inclusion of the PSLI. The message emphasized the need "which applies to all European governments today, for support of the democratic left and of the fullest possible representation of the working classes."[21]

There is no reason to doubt the sincerity of this plea. For pragmatic reasons, the hard-line anticommunists in EUR shared hopes for the emergence of a genuine social-democratic movement following the ex-

pulsion of the Marxist parties. But the message reflected little apprecia-
tion of Italian realities. The PSLI was and would remain a small, divided,
and ineffectual force. It had scant appeal to the industrial working class
and was widely seen as a creature of American interests. De Gasperi had
approached the leaders of the small parties during the May crisis, but La
Malfa later noted that "no real effort" had been made to win them over.
This is because the PSLI, PRI, and Pd'A leaders had demanded real
powers to implement a reformist program, and Gambino correctly observes that De Gasperi did not receive their refusal with "excessive displeasure."[22] The embassy assiduously courted the PSLI and PRI (Saragat
visited the United States in August), and De Gasperi was made aware of
U.S. wishes. The two parties were in no hurry to collaborate, however,
and, along with the PCI and PSI, introduced motions of no-confidence in
De Gasperi's government in September. The department reacted in exasperation on September 4: "Obviously, we shall not support extremists,
but it must be clear also that we cannot support those who, while not
themselves of extreme left or right, make common cause with extremists
to the detriment of the general welfare." Saragat and PRI leader Randolfo Pacciardi were finally prevailed on to join the cabinet as vice-
premiers in December 1947. Even though the move ended De Gasperi's
dependence on the neofascists, the PSLI–PRI presence did little to alleviate the consequences of deflation or the expulsion of the left.[23]

Still other unwelcome developments were in store during the summer
of 1947. The stabilization and reform scenario outlined by Henry Tasca
in May contemplated a brief if inevitably unpleasant period of *risana-
mento* and recovery. Tasca presumed the presence of "competent and
courageous" but also unified leadership while at the heart of his anti-
inflation plan lay two basic recommendations: strict wage control and a
balanced budget.[24] The embassy's early contact with the economic "high
command" offered room for optimism in these respects. However, the
new leadership soon proved far less than coherent, and its economic
policy unfolded quite at variance with Tasca's recommendations. By
March 1948, the initial optimism had given way to dismay and bitterness
on Tasca's part and to near panic at the State Department.

The government's economic program, announced on June 9, included
virtually all of the measures discussed by the DC–PCI–PSI cabinet in
April. After a conversation with Einaudi, Tasca informed Washington
that retaining the program was "a political tactic to lessen the open
opposition of the extreme left." Einaudi also outlined a plan for quantitative restrictions on private commercial banks but assured Tasca that
the controls would be similar to those of the U.S. Federal Reserve. The
budget minister was committed to the severe control of government expenditures as the "basic technical key to the control of inflation." Tasca

noted that the program had ignored wages, but strict controls would come once the government was more secure politically.[25]

Einaudi also intended to overhaul the multiple exchange rate structure and bilateral trade agreements, while the new Treasury Minister, Gustavo Del Vecchio, told Tasca that he would take steps to put industry on a self-financing basis as soon as possible. Ending the ban on dismissals was a top priority. In response to a question about IRI, Del Vecchio replied that its whole structure, "including personnel, must be reorganized and trimmed down to a few basic industries with the bulk of the remaining holdings disposed of." Tasca observed that the success of the new approach would depend on vigorous cabinet action, effective administration, and the "ability of the government to maintain public order and keep the Communists and fusionist Socialists under control." For the moment, he was satisfied: The Government appeared ready to carry out "drastic measures to halt inflation."[26]

Indeed, the government proceeded to make good on several of its pledges. On June 28, the price of bread was raised by 35 percent. The stock and foreign exchange markets reflected a shift in expectations. The export rate rose from 939 on May 31, to about 700 lire per dollar by the end of August.[27] It was soon clear, however, that the most important objective would not be readily accomplished. Einaudi had unprecedented authority over the budget (including the option to veto spending appropriations over one billion lire) and he tried to adhere to the principle that no new appropriations be permitted unless the corresponding revenue could be guaranteed to his personal satisfaction. However, Einaudi, like Corbino, hoped to use the influx and sale of U.S. goods to help restore budgetary equilibrium. Those goods would not be available for an indefinite period, and Einaudi was soon forced to live with other, more immediate realities. Despite his prestige, he had no mass support or responsibility to a political constituency. De Gasperi and his DC colleagues were far more sensitive to the consequences of major spending cuts. There were signs of rivalry and friction within the cabinet, and Einaudi met early resistance to his budget-cutting program.

In late June, Del Vecchio told Tasca that Einaudi was working too hard and showing "definite signs of strain. . . ."[28] On July 9, Tasca reported that Del Vecchio opposed the plan to transfer power over credit controls to Einaudi's ally Menichella at the Bank of Italy. Del Vecchio's views foreshadowed serious problems for Einaudi and Menichella, as did his accurate prediction that many businessmen would oppose credit restrictions, preferring continued inflation for speculative purposes.[29]

Trade Minister Cesare Merzagora was a sharper thorn in Einaudi's side. Merzagora had been included in the cabinet to ensure the good graces of Northern export industry. In early August, he removed all restrictions on the import of foreign goods financed by capital held abroad. (Such purchases were known as "franco valuta" imports and had been restricted since the war.) The purpose of the move was to induce the repatriation of illegally exported capital, or, according to Merzagora's famous quip, "to win the war with deserters." In further response to demands from industrial pressure groups, he changed the official lira–dollar rate from 225 to 350 and the proportion of hard currency earnings exporters could retain from 50 percent to 70–75 percent. In the case of shipbuilders, the proportion was raised to 90–95 percent.

Both the new rate and franco valuta measure were accepted, though not actively supported, by Einaudi. Granting preferential treatment to certain industries through multiple exchange rates was another matter, however. Merzagora acted without agreement or even previous consultation with his fellow ministers. Tasca was incensed. Merzagora had defied earlier State Department advice to limit cotton imports and cut down local inventories. Moreover, as Tasca cabled Washington, the Italians were now "developing techniques which will make the return to a more simply definitive exchange rate system considerably more difficult." Tasca was told to threaten countervailing duties. Del Vecchio and Einaudi welcomed such pressure on Merzagora, but the dispute dragged on for a number of months.[30]

The most dramatic and controversial departure from the program foreseen by both Einaudi and Tasca involved the famous credit restrictions themselves. Tasca had not suggested such measures to either the State Department or Italian government. When Einaudi explained his intentions in June, the embassy endorsed the idea as one element in a broader approach. Cutting the budget rather than limiting credit to private investors would be the centerpiece of the program, and Einaudi himself had resisted the idea of controls throughout the postwar period. In 1947, however, he was obliged to follow the line of least political resistance, and thus quantitative credit controls rather than the budget would become the "basic technical key" to the government's stabilization program.

Einaudi and Menichella prepared the controls in July and August, and an interministerial Committee on Credit and Savings held consultations with the banks. The financial markets were thus well informed as to what to expect at some future date, but Einaudi's hand was forced by the sudden suspension of convertibility in London on August 21. The next day, the committee announced a set of policies known to posterity as the Einaudi measures. Bruno Foa has summarized their main provisions:

> All banks were required to invest in government securities, to be pledged with the Bank of Italy, or alternatively to deposit in a special reserve with

the Bank of Italy or with the Treasury, 20 percent of their deposits in excess of an amount equal to ten times the net value of their assets. The amount thus invested or deposited, however, was limited to 15 percent of total deposits. The measure became effective as of September 30, 1947. Effective October 1, banks were required to invest or deposit as above 40 percent of all increases in deposits in excess of their September 30 volume, up to the limit of 25 percent of their total deposits.[31]

In a complementary move, the discount rate was raised from 4 percent to 5.5 percent on October 1. The private banks began to ration credit immediately, and the effects were felt well before the restrictions became official on September 30.

Einaudi and Menichella went to great lengths to argue that the measures did not involve an absolute deflation of credit. Indeed, they were careful to establish reserve requirements at a level corresponding to existing holdings of public securities and balances with the Bank of Italy. But the impact on expectations was immediate and dramatic. Inventories were quickly liquidated and the stock market boom fizzled out for lack of easy credit. Large firms, particularly in the troubled mechanical sector, found themselves unable to borrow for payrolls and other current expenses. Einaudi and Menichella soon confronted a wave of savage criticism from business and labor.

In October, the embassy reported "almost desperate appeals by industrialists to the Government for assistance. . . ." Many protested that controls were crudely quantitative rather than selective. Others did not appear overly concerned by inflation: "On the contrary, they tell the Government they are willing to meet almost any demands of labor as long as they are permitted full freedom in their business." The embassy endorsed the government's moves but noted the futility of credit controls "without at the same time halting the other source of credit – the printing of new currency."[32]

Hemmed in by local and international forces, however, Einaudi came to rely on the controls as the only available tool. The restrictions, in turn, produced new demands on the government printing press, which Einaudi was unable to resist. In early October, following intense pressure from heavy industry and the unions, the cabinet announced a 55 billion lire emergency fund – known as the Mechanical Industry Fund, or FIM – to bail out the foundering mechanical sector.[33] Einaudi's reacted to this and similar measures in a famous article, "Non contabit": "To rush to the salvation of this or that tottering business . . . may be in certain cases a political necessity, [but it remains] morally condemnable, socially iniquitous, and economically dangerous."[34] Such demands on the treasury led Einaudi and Menichella to pursue their credit control policy with redoubled vehemence. The deepening recession in turn provoked more calls for help from industrial pressure groups. By fall 1947, Einaudi was caught in a vicious cycle that shattered his old dream of a basic economic transformation along classical liberal lines.

THE EMERGING CRISIS

From the distant vantage point of Washington, the Einaudi measures appeared to be a necessary, even exemplary, step towards the European Recovery Program. Only in February 1948 did the department turn serious attention to deflation in Italy.[35] However, more general political developments were a source of growing anxiety. In early September, each of the major opposition parties introduced motions of no-confidence centering on the government's economic policies. With the assembly debate to begin on September 23, the embassy appealed on the 17th for a second Export–Import loan and an advance against Italy's frozen sterling balances. Dunn painted a bleak picture of the local situation:

> While the Marshall Plan is still a light of hope on the dismal road Italy walks, it is a dim and distant one for the weary traveller. . . . In a short time, perhaps a very short time, it will be a question no longer whether this government or even a broadened one can survive; it will be a question when Communists find it suits their purpose to seize initiative, which is passing to them, to assume the Government by legal means.[36]

By September 1947, frustrated hopes and geopolitical anxieties had spawned an obsessive fear of the Italian Communist Party and Nenni's fellow travelers. On September 24, the policy planning staff produced the first of several contingency plans entitled "Possible Action by the U.S. to assist Italian Government in the Event of Communist Seizure of North Italy and the Establishment of an Italian Communist 'Government' in that Area." The peace treaty had been ratified by the Constituent Assembly on July 31 and took effect on September 16. Accordingly, foreign troops were to leave Italian soil in ninety days. In the case of a PCI uprising, the plan called for suspension of the Allied pull-out and measures to isolate Northern Italy. Meanwhile, frantic efforts were being made to transfer military hardware to the Italian Army and Carabinieri. On the eve of the December withdrawal, Truman made a thinly veiled threat of U.S. intervention in the case of armed action by the PCI.[37]

The Communist mood was indeed hostile and aggressive, and there was daily agitation in the streets and piazzas during the summer and fall. On September 7, Togliatti delivered a well-publicized address to a rally of former resistance fighters in Modena. According to a *New York Times* dispatch, Togliatti stated the party had 30,000 well-armed partisans and

148

might have to fight to obtain positive results. The PPS attributed such provocation to a basic shift in Soviet strategy. Shortly after Togliatti's speech, Moscow revived the Communist International and severely rebuked the Italian Communists for their pre-May 1947 errors. Kennan discounted the possibility of general war but warned that in view of the temporary halt in the advance of Western European Communism, the Kremlin might now order the French and Italian parties to launch civil war once U.S. troops had left Italy.[38]

Whatever the nature of Soviet pressures on the PCI – they are difficult to document – there is little reason to believe that either Togliatti or the Russians were considering such a dramatic – and suicidal – departure from their strategy of collaboration within the new political system. Work on the new constitution was almost complete in late 1947, and such Communist jurists as Umberto Terracini had made a major contribution. The September 7 speech was undoubtedly designed to intimidate De Gasperi and also to deflect criticism from such party hard-liners as Pietro Secchia. Both the PCI and PSI had been stunned and humiliated by their expulsion from the government and aimed to restore the pre-May state of affairs. Public agitation would continue to that end, and the economic crisis of late 1947 provided ready-made political capital. However, the Communists were clearly on the defensive. The base of the party would soon feel the heat of the Confindustria campaign to fire industrial workers in the mechanical sector as well as of Scelba's offensive in the streets.

De Gasperi understood the left's position well enough and did not really fear an open insurrection. He and Tarchiani continued to exploit America's by now acute susceptibility, but their goal was less military aid than a new "emergency response" to relieve deflation and the desperate payments crisis. On September 22, Dunn reported the prime minister's deep concern about the political debate, noting "immediate measures of support . . . prior to the vote of confidence, may be the decisive factor." Dunn recommended immediate restoration of $28 million in Fascist gold held since 1945. On October 1, the department cabled the text of a press release announcing the gold's return.[39] In the event, De Gasperi's government easily weathered PSI, PSLI, and PRI motions of no-confidence on October 4. Following the defeat of Nenni's motion, Togliatti prudently withdrew his own. Dunn reported that the "extremist Marxian parties emerged not only proportionately weaker, in parliamentary terms, but also somewhat discredited in absolute terms vis-à-vis the public."[40]

The October 4 vote was followed by a period of calm. Wholesale prices began a marked decline in October, and the embassy praised the "great persistence and sincere efforts" of the economic leadership. Del Vecchio told Tasca that the credit controls were now working but that several more months would be needed before the full effects were felt. Merzagora, meanwhile, attributed the slowing of inflation to his own policies – the increase in imports paid for with capital held abroad and a trade agreement with Argentina. In late November, the government also announced a new exchange system designed to consolidate the existing multiplicity of rates. The UIC would no longer purchase 50 percent of export earnings at the official rate of 350 (established in August), but at a price approximately equivalent to the average quotation of each hard currency in the free market during the previous month. The system thus created a single rate, fluctuating on a monthly basis. Special facilities for textiles and shipbuilding were abolished. Tasca, one of the main architects, called the system "a long step forward in the clarification and rationalization of the Italian exchange rate structure. . . ."[41]

These signs of stabilization could only reinforce De Gasperi's view that underlying trends favored the government camp. Thanks in part to the prime minister and Tarchiani, however, fall developments did little to allay American fears. On October 20, Tarchiani warned that Italy's reserves were "exhausted to all practical effects" and asked for $334 million for the period from October 1947 to April 1948. On November 1, Dunn warned that without new aid, "the persons who have been contributing their share will be discredited among their own countrymen and Italy will revert to slum conditions which are what doctor ordered for Communists."[42] It was increasingly obvious, however, that deflation itself was aggravating existing slum conditions in major urban areas. According to the minister of labor's conservative estimate, unemployment stood at 1.4 million persons in October 1947, with thousands more joining the rolls in the coming months. The Confindustria took advantage of the PCI's parliamentary setback to press for the dismissal of redundant workers concentrated in Genoa and Milan. According to the embassy, the Confindustria's hardline reflected its "increasing confidence" in the trend away from the extreme left. The CGIL had agreed in principle to the resumption of dismissals in August but protested the heavy-handed methods of the industrialists. Rodolfo Morandi called the firings "pure and simple decimation" and demanded actuation of the works councils (*consigli di gestione*) in return. De Gasperi ignored this demand and quietly jettisoned the Christian Democratic Party's wartime commitment to employee participation in the workplace.[43]

The shape of the pre-electoral crisis was now visible. The requirements of monetary stabilization on one hand and production, employment, and political calm on the other were not reconcilable within the electoral timetable. Economic hardship would produce an even wider political polarization in the coming months, as well as calls from within and without the government for an about-face on economic policy. By fall

1947, earlier American hopes had given way to fear of civil war and general collapse. In September, the Truman administration set up an Advisory Steering Committee (ASC) to prepare an emergency response to the plight of Western Europe. An ASC memo, dated September 29, warned that the "virus of totalitarianism" was about to attack the European continent. At a news conference the same week, Truman announced he would write the chairmen of key congressional committees requesting that they address the urgent need for aid to Western Europe. On October 23, the president called Congress into special session, beginning November 10, to consider an emergency request for $597 million in so-called interim aid to Western Europe.[44]

THE SECOND EMERGENCY RESPONSE

The purpose of the Italian interim aid program of early 1948 was to provide badly needed raw materials and food to the Italian population while permitting the government to pursue its anti-inflationary campaign. In contrast to the UNRRA ground rules, those of interim aid allowed the Italian treasury to use the local currency proceeds – or counterpart fund – from the sale of imported goods to meet current expenses and balance the budget. UNRRA's attempt to use the fund as a stimulus now appeared not feasible and unsound. In late 1947, the lire generated by interim aid were better used to sustain the financial stabilization. Thereafter, according to an emerging scenario, the far greater funds generated by the Marshall Plan would provide a Keynesian infusion restoring production, employment, and prosperity.

An August 30, 1947, embassy report on the possible uses of ERP counterpart funds observed that "any far-reaching control exercised with respect to such proceeds, on the assumption that such proceeds are identifiable, would be difficult politically . . . and from an administrative point of view, unwieldy." At the same time, lira proceeds must be used in a manner consistent with American goals and were a potential "political fighting fund to reinforce the effects of direct U.S. aid in areas providing fertile terrain for totalitarian tendencies." From the standpoint of August 1947, however, embassy officials felt that the main use of the fund should be "achieving internal budgetary equilibrium."[45]

This ordering of priorities also made good sense to the State Department. Along with provisions to cut off aid to communist governments, sound currencies and balanced budgets were the prime concerns of the skeptical Congressmen who reviewed Truman's emergency request. After heavy lobbying by Marshall and Lovett, Congress passed an aid bill of $522 million (PL 389, the Foreign Assistance Act of 1947, or USFAP), including $211 million for Italy, on December 15. On December 19, the president presented Congress a proposal for the European recovery program calling for a staggering $17 billion in aid to sixteen European nations over four-and-a-half years. The program would be administered directly by the State Department; all Marshall Plan officials were to be Foreign Service officers.

On December 20, the department cabled the Rome embassy a draft agreement spelling out the operation of interim aid and the use of its local currency counterpart. The proposal reflected the earlier consensus on the priority of monetary stabilization and the hope that the aid would permit the Italians to stop inflation before the ERP began. According to the agreement, lira proceeds were to be used for "net retirement of the national debt" and other programs, "including measures to promote the stabilization of the Italian currency" agreed on by the two sides.[46] Once again, however, events would unfold at variance with the official scenario. The embassy was first to recognize the flaws in Washington's design. By mid-December 1947, Italy was in the grips of a recession that could only be reinforced by a rigid application of the new ground rules. With elections approaching in early 1948, U.S. and Italian officials came face-to-face with the political consequences of deflation.

As early as mid-October, the embassy had distinguished between the minimum interim aid needed to prevent "economic retrogression" and maintain political stability, on one hand, and the amount of aid Italy could actually use, on the other. Washington had suggested $284 million to cover the six-month period ending March 31, but the embassy argued that, given the depressed state of the economy, Italy could absorb "as little perhaps as $150,000,000."[47] The economy's absorptive capacity had scarcely increased by December, and in view of the growing polarization, Washington's counterpart fund provisions struck the embassy as seriously misguided. On December 31, Dunn sent an urgent cable to Washington outlining his objections. Proceeds from the new program would amount to from 75 to 125 billion lire and "could work great harm or great good depending on the policies adopted."

In view of the political situation, Washington's rules were ill-conceived in their almost exclusive emphasis on monetary stabilization, and the embassy urged "the greatest amount of flexibility" in any formal agreement. In that way, the fund could become "a powerful weapon of versatile uses to handle new and difficult situations" that the communists might create. The embassy listed a series of possible uses, including aid to small landowners and artisans, the natural base of the Christian Democratic Party. In conclusion, the embassy urged a political decision by Washington, "to retain the maximum amount of discretion and maneuverability . . . in order to promote in the most effective way the economical and social stability of Italy, and, to attain at a minimum cost to the American taxpayer our national security goals."[48]

The Embassy received no immediate reply. The department was now caught up in the delicate business of the ERP itself, and administration officials were not inclined to risk the wrath of Congress by fiddling with the interim aid law. Following a ceremony in Rome on January 3, 1948, the State Department's December 20 draft became the formal interim aid agreement between the U.S. and Italian governments.

But the interim aid controversy had only just begun on January 3. Revision of the official scenario became an urgent matter as elections approached in April 1948. Students of the period have naturally focused their attention on the frenzied U.S. efforts to arm the Italian police, bankroll the DC–PSLI–PRI alliance, and lend a sufficiently Manichean tone to the anticommunist campaign.[49] Throughout early 1948, the embassy pursued a complementary objective: to reverse the Italian government's financial policies. Although unavoidable and commendable in the fall of 1947, the Einaudi measures had become a serious political liability. The disposition of the lira fund foreseen in the new emergency response served only to reinforce the downward cycle, and a coalition of embassy and Italian officials emerged to arrest the slide toward economic and political disaster.

By January 1948, the rifts within the cabinet had widened considerably. At the center of the controversy was Donato Menichella, whose rigid administration of the credit controls had won him few friends in the world of business or politics. Menichella also tended to deflect criticism from the more eminent and venerable figure of Einaudi himself. Merzagora complained bitterly to Tasca that Menichella refused to ease the money markets and was thus responsible for the crisis. Giovanni Gronchi, chief spokesman for the DC left, told Tasca that the depression was "attributable entirely to Einaudi, Del Vecchio and Menichella," with principal responsibility on the shoulders of the latter. Gronchi also had harsh words for De Gasperi, citing the prime minister's admission of total ignorance of economic and financial matters. The embassy cabled its own gloomy analysis, predicting more business failures and unemployment that would only help the communists.[50]

The embassy meanwhile prepared to take the offensive against the Einaudi–Menichella line. On January 27, Dunn called on De Gasperi to discuss the economic situation. In an urgent, top-secret cable the following day, the ambassador warned of the "serious danger of industrial depression." Dunn had urged De Gasperi to take action to increase production and review the government's credit policies. The cable attributed the decline in industrial activity to 58 percent of 1938 levels to the

153

"exaggerated measures taken by the government." De Gasperi had assured Dunn that he was fully aware of the problem and would give it his "immediate personal attention."[51]

Dunn's intervention brought an angry reply from the Bank of Italy. On February 2, Menichella insisted to Tasca that the credit measures were working. The political and psychological atmosphere had been transformed, and industry in general did lack working capital. The heavy mechanical sector was a special case since it had grown artificially under Fascism and had to be cut down to size. Tasca dismissed this rosy assessment in his cable to Washington, but Menichella was not to be intimidated.[52] With the complete support of Einaudi, he refused to alter the credit policies. De Gasperi meanwhile labored to preserve his characteristic neutrality and integrity as mediator. Despite his apparent agreement with Dunn on January 27, he took a hands-off position that in effect allowed the restrictions to continue.

Tasca found his hands full with the consequences of the stabilization he had so vehemently encouraged since early 1947. Gradually, he joined the chorus of demands for freer credit and extraordinary expenditures. But the pressure for a pre-electoral stimulation of demand and wider governmental intervention served in turn to strengthen the resolve of Einaudi and Menichella. Amidst warnings to Washington about an imminent "vast emotional upheaval" and growing strength of the left, the embassy attempted to use interim aid as a tool of reflation and recovery.[53]

On February 4, the embassy informed the department that 70 percent of locally produced coking coal was being stockpiled and fifty thousand tons had even been earmarked for export to Switzerland. The "real solution," the embassy repeated, "can only be found by the government taking action to maximize production."[54] The same day, state and treasury cabled a reply to the embassy's December 31 critique of interim aid. Washington was aware that Italian efforts had resulted in "some deflation" by late 1947. Still, the local counterpart funds were best used to facilitate financial and economic stabilization in anticipation of the Marshall Plan. The "impetus to financial and economic stability through appropriate use of these funds will aid greatly in achieving our general objective." They would consider funding projects already included in the Italian budget. By "appropriate uses," however, the departments intended "sterilization to assist in measures of financial reform and currency stabilization . . . [and] non-inflationary retirement of the national debt."[55]

The bureaucrats in Washington were obviously loath to deviate from their original scenario, which foresaw the restoration of financial stability before the ERP. By February, moreover, the administration was caught in the confrontation of the decade to salvage the Marshall Plan legislation. Despite pleas from Clayton and Marshall that there could not be "two Secretaries of State," Congress had insisted that the Plan be placed in the hands of a new, independent agency. Vandenberg, moreover, had immediately rejected the request for $17 billion over four years. The battle raged to secure $5 to $6 billion for an initial fifteen-month period.

The department's dilemma emerged in sharp focus from a message to the embassy of February 6. The February 4 orders on the use of counterpart funds had apparently been prepared before receiving Dunn's urgent and alarming message of January 28. The department noted that officials had commented frequently and favorably on the Einaudi measures during their Capitol Hill appearances.[56] If the Einaudi measures had been portrayed to skeptical congressmen as a paragon of European competence and responsibility, the department's reluctance to change its attitude was natural and understandable. Thus, the logic of the ERP scenario and the fear of congressional retaliation against tinkering with the interim aid program militated strongly against any U.S. decision to encourage reflation in Italy. By March 1948, moreover, time was growing short. With elections now scheduled for April 18, expansionist measures were unlikely to have any great effect before the voting. These factors, combined with the atmosphere of near hysteria created by the February coup in Czechoslovakia, explain the decision in Washington to launch an unprecedented propaganda and clandestine financial campaign.

On March 8, the recently formed National Security Council (NSC) recommended covert funding of the government bloc, as well as coordinated public statements by prominent U.S. officials, journalists, and private citizens. In the case of communist victory, there should be military and economic assistance to the pro-Western forces.[57] Several weeks later, Secretary Marshall delivered a major address at Berkeley, California. If the Italians chose to elect a government hostile to the ERP, the United States "would have to conclude that Italy had removed itself from the benefits of the European Recovery Program." The Justice Department meanwhile announced that anyone who voted for the PCI would be denied entry into the United States according to a 1924 law prohibiting immigration by those advocating the overthrow of the U.S. government by force.[58]

The embassy heartily endorsed these and similar measures. At the same time, it moved to change the government's economic policies by exploiting a clause in Washington's February 4 instructions that authorized the funding of projects already in the current budget. Following the cabinet's approval of the January agreement on February 13, U.S. officials met with Einaudi and his fellow ministers to discuss the lira fund. Under great embassy pressure, the cabinet agreed to take steps to reverse the 20 percent to 25 percent decline in industrial production since September 1947. With Einaudi's reluctant approval, 25 billion in interim aid counterpart funds were committed to an existing public works program.[59] Henry Tasca was unimpressed. On March 5, he cabled a sarcastically worded review of a recent article praising Einaudi's policies. Since Washington's hesitation to press for a shift in Italian policies was linked to domestic political concerns, in a March 17 letter, he took his case to Rep. Christian Herter (Republican of Massachusetts), an important figure in the on-going contest to prepare the ERP. Tasca's letter was deeply pessimistic and discounted DC predictions of victory. Einaudi's policies could "only be described as disastrous." The Budget Minister had failed to improve the budget situation while causing a notable slowdown in industrial production.[60]

In the meantime, Tasca and his colleagues continued to press the Italians for a major stimulatory program. On March 26, the embassy and cabinet agreed on a series of projects: 20 billion lire for agricultural development in Sardinia and the South, 28 billion for state railway reconstruction and repair, and 4 billion to refit two Italian passenger vessels. According to the embassy, the government had agreed that currency stabilization should no longer constitute the sole purpose of interim aid.[61] Einaudi and Menichella fought hard for their original priorities but were forced to give ground to the reflationary coalition of Merzagora, Gronchi, and Tasca. With elections in three weeks, De Gasperi could not pass up the chance to announce major spending programs.

The State Department cabled its approval of the new projects on April 3.[62] The small remaining balance of the fund should be applied to the original objective (retirement of the national debt), but the decision represented a contravention of the original legislation. Italian electoral considerations by now held sway in Washington as well. Fears of congressional retaliation had also eased by early April. On March 31, following a final administration barrage stressing the threat of imminent Soviet aggression, Congress approved $4.3 billion, covering the first year of the Marshall Plan.

Following a similar last-minute barrage, including special radio broadcasts by Bing Crosby and Dinah Shore, the DC-led coalition swept to an overwhelming victory on April 18.[63] Indeed, the magnitude of the victory surpassed the most optimistic expectations. For the first and last time in their history, the Christian Democrats achieved an absolute majority in the Chamber of Deputies, with 48.5 percent of the popular vote. Their smaller allies, the PSLI, PRI, and PLI, together accounted for 13.4 percent. The PCI–PSI Blocco del Popolo fell from nearly 40 percent in June 1946 to 31 percent. Observers offered a variety of explanations, including the great maturity of the Italian electorate. It is clear that the climate of profound anxiety generated by American, Christian Democratic, and Vatican propaganda played an important role. The decisive factor, however, was probably the European recovery program itself – both the U.S. pledge to exclude Italy in the event of a Communist victory and the great promise embodied in the plan of higher standards of living.

CONCLUSION

U.S. officials breathed a collective sigh of relief on the morrow of April 18. The ground had been cleared for implementing the Marshall Plan and adopting long-delayed internal social and economic reforms designed to heal the wounds exacerbated by the bitter election campaign. In an April 27 conversation with Tarchiani, John Hickerson emphasized the need for measures to counteract the dissent of that 30 percent of the Italian population who had voted for the left despite its opposition to the Marshall Plan. Tarchiani agreed that the time had come to move from negative anticommunism to a "positive policy of reconstruction" including social and economic reforms promised during the campaign.[64] These reforms had included greater employment, new housing construction, and a major land redistribution.

Hickerson may have been reassured, but Henry Tasca remained unimpressed. Tasca was astute enough to realize that America's problems after May 1947 had something to do with the nature of the social forces he himself referred to as the "backbone" of anticommunism. His intimate knowledge of the Italian bourgeoisie accounted for some of his pessimism in March 1948. In his pre-electoral letter to Christian Herter, Tasca observed that industrialists, large landholders, and much of the right were "disorganized or disoriented and incapable of realizing their social responsibilities." They tended to deal with the left by either preparing to escape abroad or doing an undercover deal for their own protection. The Italian bourgeoisie, he lamented, was not a self-possessed and confident ruling class but a collection of individualists "organically incapable of combining as a group to meet a common threat."[65] In addition, Tasca probably anticipated, the Italian bourgeoisie did not necessarily intend to manage the country according to American wishes once their position was secure after April 1948.

Tasca's pre-electoral frustrations also arose from the flaws and self-deceptions inherent in the revised U.S. scenario for European economic recovery that emerged after June 1947. Indeed, the evolution of Tasca's own position is testimony to the internal contradictions of the interim aid–Marshall Plan design. Tasca had pushed "tough internal measures" on the Italians since early 1947. By early 1948, he had resorted to Keynesian interventionism in order to offset the political and economic consequences of his original advice. Tasca blamed the recession and political crisis on Einaudi's technically ill-conceived and overzealous deflation. Indeed, Einaudi was not a political leader and may have been more concerned about the integrity of his liberal program than Christian Democracy's electoral fortunes. In fairness to Einaudi, however, once the left had been expelled from the government, it was Tasca's DC and business allies whose corporatist demands constituted the main obstacle to budgetary equilibrium. Einaudi, moreover, grasped what any perceptive economist or historian, whether liberal, Catholic, or Marxist, might have realized in mid-1947: There were no political quick-fixes or technical panaceas at hand to ease the pain of the long-delayed financial stabilization. Tasca and his colleagues seemed unable or unwilling to accept this fact.[66]

10

Conclusion: the Marshall Plan and after

Throughout the occupation and early postwar period, American attempts to promote and guide Italian economic recovery had been hindered by bureaucratic and ideological disunity within the foreign policy community. Those conflicts tended to produce contradictory policies toward Italy, policies, moreover, that lacked the financial leverage to make U.S. influence felt in a sustained and effective way. Those essentially American problems had not disappeared by the spring of 1948. Congress had forced the State Department to relinquish control of its brainchild, the ERP, to a new, specially created agency, the Economic Cooperation Administration. The ERP's proper relationship to the department's latest initiative – the creation of an Atlantic security system – would soon perplex and trouble such officials as George Kennan.[1] These continuing difficulties notwithstanding, the American executive had achieved an unprecedented degree of internal consensus by mid-1948, based on the twin tenets of anticommunism and massive foreign aid. The New Deal and Hullian idealism of earlier days had given way to a more sober reassessment of U.S. capabilities and European needs. At the same time, thanks to the Truman administration's relentless public campaign, the U.S. Congress and people had authorized an undreamed of financial commitment to European economic recovery. The years 1948–49 marked the high noon of bipartisan foreign policy.

From the standpoint of U.S. strategic interests newly defined to include the Mediterranean basin, America's Italian policy had achieved a hardly negligible success. American largesse and military presence had prevented the sort of political breakdown and social-economic chaos that had beset the defeated powers after November 1918. In May 1947, the U.S. had overseen the expulsion of its adversary's local client from the highest levels of government, thus breaking a debilitating political stalemate that had prevailed since 1944. Finally, the United States had estab-

159

lished a partnership with a coalition of conservative and middle-class forces whose victory helped guarantee American military and political predominance in the Mediterranean. Thenceforth, according to the American view, the integrity of that guarantee depended in part on the adoption by the victorious coalition of the new U.S. recipe for economic recovery and social stability. To that task, U.S. officials turned in earnest as the Marshall Plan began.

However, the experience of May 1947–April 1948 scarcely suggested that greater unity and domestic support would make U.S. officials either wiser or more effective in their approach to Italy's economic and political problems. Nor did relations between the United States and the DC-led coalition during that period offer much indication that, once firmly in power, the new regime would take a greater interest in American advice. Indeed, at the moment of triumph in April 1948, the United States largely forfeited its already feeble control over the internal economy and politics to the Italian forces themselves. Those forces were already conscious of both their autonomy and indispensability vis-à-vis their U.S. protector and ally.

To be sure, many Italians were concerned to demonstrate the appearance of scrupulous adherence to U.S. wishes as the Marshall Plan began. As usual, they were motivated not by any great faith or confidence in American economic and political schemes but by a lucid sense of Italian national interest in the face of their former enemies and traditional European rivals. Such sentiment was captured in a brilliant analysis of Italy's position by the Ambassador to Paris, Pietro Quaroni. On May 19, 1948, Quaroni wrote Foreign Minister Sforza that, in order to avoid becoming another Egypt, Italy would have to pay lip service to American "*bestialità*" in the case of intra-European cooperation and other strings attached to ERP money. Sooner or later, the "*bestialità*" would "become obvious," even to the Americans. Quaroni urged his government to go along with the United States on the controversial Marshall Plan bilateral agreement, "not for reasons of general principle, but exclusively for our interest. The Americans, and only the Americans can defend us."[2]

Moreover, not unlike the coalition that consolidated power after 1922, the victorious bloc of April 1948 was loosely constituted and heterogeneous, representing widely disparate and openly contradictory interests and ideologies. The new class of political leaders drew what strength and cohesion they had largely from their common opposition to the Marxist left and from the determination to control state resources and outside aid to the benefit of their respective constituencies.

It was a coalition with no common vision of the future, hardly capable of imposing its own coherent program of economic recovery or social reform, let alone one imported from the United States. The internal contradictions visible during the Einaudi deflation became institutionalized in the DC–PSLI–PRI–PLI cabinet formed after the elections.[3] Classical liberals, Social Democratic reformers, Catholic corporatists, Republican technocrats, and parochial-minded industrialists all prepared for the intense contest to direct the Marshall Plan. That battle produced no clear-cut victory, largely because De Gasperi preferred to balance and conciliate a broad range of interests. At the same time, DC political mediation and administration of ERP funds strengthened the party's hold on the state apparatus and honed the skills of a now familiar political generation.[4] The list of ministers and under secretaries in the May 1948 cabinet included Fanfani, Colombo, Andreotti, and Moro. The competing interests would also vie for the imprimatur of the United States. In this respect, the experience of the immediate postwar years gave De Gasperi and his disciples a decisive advantage. They would refine their techniques to a fine precision during the period of uninterrupted power after 1948.

The shell-shocked, sullen forces of the left, meanwhile, looked on from the political sidelines. New blows were in store later in the year – the attempted assassination of Togliatti and the American-financed break-up of the CGIL. The Communists would nurse their grievances in bitter opposition, but given the stark contrast between ERP propaganda and everyday reality in the factories, their electoral strength would rise steadily, if slowly, from the nadir of April 1948.[5] The period of the Marshall Plan and after constitutes the epilogue of the story recounted here. However, the shape of things to come was visible in May 1948. Indeed, the inflated American hopes and expectations surrounding the DC victory and the Marshall Plan were put to the test in the immediate aftermath of April 1948.

On May 12, the embassy advised Washington to expect a "basic review of the credit policies of the Italian government." To the relief of many of his former collaborators, Luigi Einaudi had been elevated to the presidency of the republic following the elections. The embassy's DC contacts, including Giuseppe Togni and Party Secretary Attilio Piccioni, agreed that his measures had been far too drastic and had created serious problems during the election campaign. Both the DC and the embassy were confident, moreover, that Donato Menichella could be eased out of his key position at the Bank of Italy.[6] This prospect dovetailed nicely with the plans of ERP officials in Washington. On May 28, the ERP area committee for France and Italy issued a preliminary report on the use of the Marshall Plan counterpart fund by the Italian government. The report estimated that lira proceeds would amount to 365 billion lire during the first year of the plan, equal to 49 percent of the total anticipated revenues of the Italian government for 1947–48. The report left little doubt as to how the lira proceeds should be used. The recent deflation had succeeded in restoring the stability of the lira but "only at the expense of the decline in economic activity and production, and an increase in the already high level of unemployment." Either to withhold the fund from circulation by sterilization or to substitute it for available noninflationary financing would have a deflationary effect at an unfortunate time and would "deter rather than foster reemployment and economic recovery. In the immediate future, the Lira fund should be returned to circulation. The important issue [was] how best to return it." The report recommended capital formation as the highest priority.[7] Such Keynesian sentiment was echoed by contemporary economic experts. Bruno Foa observed in 1948, "It would obviously be ludicrous if a monetary bottleneck should stand in the way of the full use of the resources which may become available under the Marshall Plan."[8]

It should come as no surprise that the liberal economists profoundly disagreed. They had never had any use for Keynesian economics. Some saw it as simply Bloomsbury hedonism in the guise of economic science. For almost all, Keynesianism threatened sound finance, the free market, and conservative social values. In practice, the liberal critique of Keynes differed little from that of such Catholic interventionists as Pasquale Saraceno. Saraceno considered Keynesian macroeconomic policies irrelevant, even dangerous, to an open, fragile, and dualistic economy like Italy's. The problem was not one of excess capacity or temporary disequilibrium susceptible to expansionary monetary and fiscal policies – Italy's archaic and regressive tax system was completely unsuited to "demand management" in any case – but of external vulnerabilities and deep structural problems.[9]

The classical school had strong evidence to support its orthodox approach: Both the government budget and foreign accounts were in serious deficit in 1948. Thus, the spirit of Corbino and Einaudi haunted the ECA and would-be Italian reflationists throughout the Marshall Plan period. To veterans of the UNRRA–treasury contest of 1946, the story was familiar. Even though his constitutional powers were limited, Einaudi did not hesitate to bring his prestige and power to bear. In August 1948, the president of the republic intervened to save Menichella. When he learned that the central directory of the DC had settled on the more pliable Costantino Bresciani Turroni to replace Menichella, Einaudi summoned De Gasperi to the Quirinale Palace and informed him that the present governor would remain. De Gasperi declined to challenge Einaudi, and Menichella was confirmed as permanent governor of the Bank. DC politicians complained to the embassy of the "unheard of

manner" in which Einaudi had pushed through the election of Menichella.[10]

Einaudi's successor at the Budget Ministry was an equally determined
opponent of the Keynesian recovery program. Giuseppe Pella gained
favor with the ECA and embassy during the summer of 1948 by resisting
Merzagora's pressure for a precipitous devaluation of the lira. It was
gradually apparent, however, that Pella intended to carry out his men-
tor's project regardless of the ECA. Despite pressure from within and
without the cabinet, Pella and Menichella attempted to divert ERP funds
to alleviate the budget deficit. Meanwhile, as aggregate demand, industrial production, and employment stagnated at early 1948 levels, Italy's
foreign exchange reserves mounted from $149 million in 1948 to more
than $1 billion in December 1949.[11]

In accordance with ECA requirements, the Italian government presented (September 1948) a long-term plan governing the use of the counterpart fund for the years 1948–1952. Like subsequent documents of the
kind, it represented a complex set of compromises among the diverse
interests represented in the cabinet and bureaucratic apparatus: liberals,
DC, PRI, and socialist interventionists, public and private industry. In its
widely publicized rebuke of the Italian government issued in February
1949, the ECA called the Italian document "a very tentative expression
of views rather than a firm program of goals and the means to achieve
them." In the discussion of the current situation "in Government circles
there has perhaps been generally speaking, an exaggerated fear of a new
inflation, while a good part of the business community hopes for precisely such an inflation in the expectation that it will postpone difficult
cost price adjustments and permit large speculative profits to be made
without serious risks." The situation demanded "a more aggressive public investment policy" resulting from a "careful analysis of the directions
in which Italy's capital plant should be expanded."[12] The ECA line of
1949 was a direct descendent of UNRRA and of Tasca's anticommunist
Keynesianism of 1947–48. Both hoped to use American aid to foster a
political economic strategy based on what was later called the "politics
of productivity" – the promotion of administrative and fiscal reform,
Keynesian stimulation of demand and investment, and the loyal opposition of social democratic unions.[13] De Gasperi committed his government to a rather different formula – orthodox financial management
combined with the break-up and isolation of the organized working
class.

Pella eventually (after late 1949) could not resist the intense, conflicting demands for ERP counterpart funds from powerful industrial
groups – notably Finsider steel, FIAT, and Edison Electric – as well as

agricultural interests and the DC left, who pressed for a major housing construction project. In the meantime, the Confindustria was reconciled to deflation through additional political concessions – suppression of the remaining factory councils, full freedom to fire workers, and tough police action (the so-called "linea Scelba") against labor unrest. The ruling bloc, however, was unwilling and probably incapable of providing the sort of planning, careful analysis, and coherent investment strategy urged by the ECA. Both Mario Ferrari Aggradi, De Gasperi's personal economic advisor after 1948, and the treasury and Bank of Italy remained skeptical of the practicability and relevance of American advice. Pella fought hard to complete the task of monetary stabilization and publicly rejected the technical analysis of the Marshall Plan authorities: "We will continue . . . with all our force along the road to a balanced budget."[14]

The long-awaited reforms, meanwhile, were not forthcoming. A Central Intelligence Agency study, dated April 9, 1949, observed that the "De Gasperi Government has failed so far to show any signs of having or soon developing any program of long range economic reform in Italy." The failure to carry out promised land tenure reforms in the South was particularly galling to high American officials, and following the outbreak of violence between tenants and landlords in Calabria in 1949, Ambassador Dunn and Secretary of State Dean Acheson called Italian officials on the carpet on the issue.[15] But De Gasperi and the DC left were hostage to the right. When the government pushed through a diluted land redistribution program in the early 1950s, it incurred the wrath of Liberals, conservative landlords, Vatican hierarchs, and suspicious industrialists. Their defection would cost the DC its parliamentary majority in 1953, despite De Gasperi's attempt (the so-called *legge truffa*) to rig the electoral machinery in favor of the ruling bloc. The left scored impressive gains in the 1953 elections. Although the documentation remains beyond reach, it seems safe to assume that the State Department was not overly pleased with the *legge truffa* ploy. American pressure and material incentives during the first postwar legislature had produced neither hoped-for reforms nor a decline of the left. According to the pattern established in 1948, the CIA responded with a multimillion dollar covert funding and propaganda operation after the 1953 elections designed to avert "another Czechoslovakia" in the heart of NATO territory.[16]

The faltering victors of 1948 were saved by the spectacular recovery of the Italian economy. For this, it seems clear that Tasca and the ECA Keynesians owed a debt of gratitude to the monetary authorities whom they had tried to undermine. This is not to belittle the important contribution of Marshall aid to Italian recovery. The provision of U.S. food, capital goods, and raw materials relieved severe internal bottlenecks and foreign exchange constraints. However, Einaudi's successors knew better than their would-be American mentors how to manage the local economy. Monetary stabilization and replenished international reserves were undoubtedly a necessary, though not sufficient, condition for sustained economic growth. Like any deflation, that of 1947–48 hit the poorer regions and politically impotent social strata hardest, but the point is simply that rigid labor markets and inflationary expectations were broken in the process.

Italy's new economic vitality also owed much to such dynamic and persistent technocrat-enterpreneurs as Oscar Sinigaglia and Enrico Mattei. Sinigaglia was a product of the peculiarly Italian state industrial experience of the 1930s. He defied local and outside pressures to scale down or sell off the Fascist-bred complete-cycle steel industry. His updating and expansion of IRI's Finsider holding flew in the face of Hullian or Einaudian logic, but it laid the basis for success in the automobile and mechanical sectors. Under De Gasperi's protection, Mattei played a similar role in the new hydrocarbons sector. His economic empire became a bastion of Christian Democratic power.

The remarkable export-led growth of the 1950s was sustained by the gradual dismantling of tariff barriers within the nascent common market, combined with the continuing weakness and remarkable mobility of the Italian working class. These happy circumstances allowed for a virtuous circle of high productivity, exports, profits, and investment. Both the contradictions within the ruling coalition and the sharp division between right and left were temporarily soothed in an atmosphere of expanding wealth and *dolce vita*. The Christian Democratic Party partially compensated for its lack of a parliamentary majority after 1953 by taking firm hold of the state and its subsidiary institutions. In the tradition of both the pre-1914 liberal and Fascist regimes, the Christian Democrats used their control of the public purse to foster a vast network of clients and supporters. Despite his new recognition in academic circles, Keynes still had little to teach the Italian political class. If Keynesian doctrine is relevant to the Italian experience of the fifties and sixties, it served mainly to provide an ex-post rationalization for an ad hoc, politically inspired, and uniquely Italian spending strategy.

That these felicitous arrangements contained the seeds of their own undoing was visible well before the general crisis of the Western mixed economies and welfare states. The steadily expanding social and industrial projects sponsored by the Christian Democratic power system rent deep fissures in the bedrock of monetary stability. The guardians of the public purse, Carli and Baffi (they had received their baptism of fire under Menichella and Einaudi) were hard-pressed to resist the demands of their profligate political masters.[17] The long-isolated losers of April

1948, moreover, pressed home their own demands for higher wages and social services as the labor market tightened after 1960. If, as some contend, the progressive rhetoric of the PCI served in part to mask the extravagant claims of its employed and privileged constituency, the party learned its lesson well from those who monopolized the state at communist expense during much of the postwar period.

The Americans, meanwhile, suffered their DC partners with frequent frustration and bewilderment. Successive American interventions, both public and covert, failed to fulfill the promise of April 1948. Long after the 1940s, the United States continued to indulge its expectations for the right-wing socialists and a Catholic-social democratic alliance. But the "transformation" of the PSI, encouraged by the Kennedy White House, produced the result feared by its conservative opponents: reinforcement of the Communists. The agony of the *apertura a sinistra* tempted the United States to flirt with right-wing conspirators in the late 1960s.[18] At a time when social democratic movements have withered in their more natural Northern European soil, some continue to place hopes in the latest, Craxian incarnation of the democratic left. But the Socialists' relationship with their Christian Democratic "ally" is as always marked by mutual bad faith and bitter rivalry for the political center.

The policy of recent U.S. administrations appears on the surface to reflect at least one basic lesson of the postwar period: American interference has never served to affect basic political trends in Italy, nor to foster American-inspired social and economic schemes. Hopes in the late 1970s and early 1980s lay instead with increased U.S.-Italian contact and exchange in the areas of education, business, government administration, and defense. According to one of its Italian enthusiasts, the new approach was based on the assumption that "American influence is strongest, almost irresistible, when it is the unconscious irradiation of its national ideas, of its example, of its immense economic might." Thus Luigi Barzini was confident that "increased familiarity with American historical ideals would solve many Italian problems and add votes to the pro-Western parties. Unfortunately, he noted, this will happen "only in the long run, within a generation."[19]

But beneath that "new" approach lay two old and time-worn premises. The Anglo-Saxons, as Admiral Ellery Stone observed in June 1945, "have much to teach and the Italians much to learn."[20] In the meantime, as a key strategic entity, Italy's fate remained too important for Italians alone to decide. The first premise was called into serious doubt during the period 1945–9. Events thereafter have not enhanced its credibility. What the cold warriors of 1947–8 conceived as an alliance for progress with the Italian people was only the latest marriage of convenience for the predominant political class. The second premise has perhaps been accepted too complacently by the Italians themselves. A commanding plurality of Italian voters have consistently endorsed the bargain struck by their political leaders that cedes a degree of national sovereignty and dignity for American leadership and physical protection. Yet the value and reliability of the American connection becomes problematical as U.S. behavior grows more erratic and self-centered and U.S. and European interests diverge. The response of the reigning political class to the consequent erosion of their internal position will no doubt provide a rich field of study for future observers of the Italian scene.

Notes

1. INTRODUCTION AND OVERVIEW

1 Marcello De Cecco, "Economic Policy in the Reconstruction Period, 1945–51," in S. J. Woolf, ed., *The Rebirth of Italy* (New York: Humanities Press, 1972), 158.

2 Camillo Daneo, *La politica economica della ricostruzione, 1945–1949* (Turin: Einaudi, 1975), 11.

3 On Fascist financial policy, 1935–43, see Paolo Baffi, "Monetary Developments in Italy from the War Economy to Limited Convertibility (1935–1958)," *Banca Nazionale del Lavoro Quarterly Review* 12 (December 1958):401–5; Bruno Foa, *Monetary Reconstruction in Italy* (New York: King's Crown Press, 1948), 13; *Rapporto della commissione economica all 'assemblea costituente*, Part III *Problemi monetarie e commercio estero*, vol. I, *Relazione* (Rome, 1946), 9–10.

4 Baffi, "Monetary Developments," 407–8; Foa, 14–15.

5 Baffi, "Monetary Developments," 417; Pasquale Saraceno, *Intervista sulla ricostruzione* (Bari: Laterza, 1977), 77–9.

6 See Daneo, *La Politica Economica . . .* , Chapter 2. The four largest private companies were virtual monopolies by 1938. Montecatini controlled rayon production and 25 percent of chemical fertilizers. Snia Viscosa controlled 60 to 65 percent of other artificial fibers. FIAT controlled 83 percent of automobile production. Pirelli controlled 100 percent of tires, 60 to 70 percent of cables. Edison controlled 45.5 percent of electrical power capacity. See P. Profumieri, "Capital and Labor in Italy, 1929–1940, An Economic Interpretation," *Journal of European Economic History* 1 (Winter 1972): 684.

7 Roland Sarti, *Fascism and the Industrial Leadership in Italy* (Berkeley: University of California Press, 1971), 119.

8 Daneo, 306–8; Shepard Clough, *An Economic History of Modern Italy* (New York: Columbia University Press, 1964), 249–50. For the details of damage suffered by IRI, see Margherita Pelaja, "L'industria di stato nel dibattito del secondo dopoguerra: il caso dell'IRI," *Italia Contemporanea*, 124 (July–September, 1976): 50–1.

9 Piero Barucci, introduction, to Pasquale Saraceno, *Ricostruzione e pianificazione* (Bari: Laterza, 1969), 9.

10 In 1939, U.S. imports from Italy and its dependencies represented a mere 1.9 percent of total U.S. purchases abroad. U.S. sales to Italy constituted an equally trivial proportion of total exports, 1.9 percent – compared to 5.6 percent

in 1919. U.S. Tariff Commission, *Italian Commercial Policy and Foreign Trade* (Washington, D.C.: Government Printing Office, 1941), 113. As of 1943, the value of U.S. investments in controlled enterprises in Italy amounted to $90 million (compared to $171.1 in France, $513.6 in Germany), concentrated ($35.4 million) in the Italian subsidiaries of two U.S. oil companies, Socony Vacuum and Standard of New Jersey. Total U.S. investment amounted to $272 million (compared to $379 million in France, $1 billion in Germany). Other investment was divided as follows: securities, $51.4 million; gold, currency, and deposits, $34.3 million; real property, $71.1 million; estates and trusts, $3.6 million; miscellaneous, $22.2 million. Department of the Treasury, *Census of U.S. Assets Abroad* (Washington, D.C.: Government Printing Office, 1947), 68–70.

11 See Gino Borgatta et al., *Ricostruzione dell'economia nel dopoguerra* (Pisa: CEDAM, 1942). See also Demaria's Introduzione, *Rapporto della commissione economica*, Part II, *Industria*, vol. I, *Relazione*, Tome I, 3–19.

12 Demaria, Introduzione.

13 The Piedmontese Luigi Einaudi was the dominant member of the classical school. Through personal or professional contacts, he exerted a moral and intellectual influence on most of the other economists destined to serve in the government. See Paolo Baffi, "Memoria sull'azione di Einaudi," in his *Studi sulla moneta* (Milan: Guiffre, 1965), 176–7. Einaudi shared the prevailing enthusiasm for free trade and distaste for the mixed banks and government intervention. He was not categorically opposed to state intervention, as in the case of natural monopolies such as transport and utilities. See his *Lezioni di politica sociale* (Turin: Einaudi, 1967), 63–71. It should be noted that there is a basic distinction in Italian thought between *liberismo,* the doctrine of free trade associated with the classical economists, and the *liberalismo* of Croce. According to Croce, Einaudi made a basic error in identifying economic liberalism with the broader, metapolitical notion of *liberalismo.* For Croce, *liberalismo* was the spirit that guided history toward the universal realization of human freedom and dignity. Its concrete embodiment could take many forms, not necessarily democratic or liberal in the economic sense. Economic *liberismo* was crudely utilitarian, aiming merely to satisfy the individual libido. Croce favored state intervention and supported Giolitti, whereas Einaudi was bitterly opposed to both. Croce and Einaudi conducted a running feud throughout the Fascist era. The debate has been collected in the volume *Liberismo e liberalismo,* edited by Paolo Solari (Milan: R. Ricciardi, 1957).

14 See Enzo Piscitelli, "Del cambio o meglio del mancato cambio della moneta nel secondo dopoguerra," *Quaderni dell'istituto romano per la storia d'italia dal fascismo alla resistenza,* 1 (1969): 9.

15 The State Department followed economic developments in wartime Italy and received regular intelligence reports from the Bern consulate. The views of Professor Mario Einaudi of Fordham University, and son of Luigi Einaudi, were also known and appreciated at the department. See memo of conversation between Einaudi and J. W. Jones, October 24, 1943, RG 59, 865.00/2–238, NA.

16 David Calleo and Benjamin Rowland, *America and the World Political Economy* (Bloomington: Indiana University Press, 1971), 37.

17 Frederick J. Dobney, editor of Clayton's papers, notes that the Texas businessman was an "economic ideologue of the first order. . . . Seldom has any individual been so dominated by ideological considerations, both in theory and in

practice." Clayton's role in postwar Italian economic affairs serves to confirm that basic judgement. See F. J. Dobney, ed., *Selected Papers of Will Clayton* (Baltimore: Johns Hopkins University Press, 1971), 1–6, 283–4.

18 "The Treatment of Italy," CAC document 248, August 31, 1944, RG 59, Harley Notter Files, Box 112, NA. Cited by David Ellwood, *L'Alleato nemico, la politica dell'occupazione anglo-americana in italia, 1943–1946* (Milan: Feltrinelli, 1977), 95, 330–9.

19 Sarceno, *Intervista*, 103.

20 From speech to the Constituent Assembly, September 18, 1946, cited in Enzo Piscitelli, 51. See also Gaulberto Gualerni, *Ricostruzione e industria* (Vita e Pensiero, Milan, 1980), Introduction.

21 The CLN was a coalition of six anti–Fascist parties – the Communists (Partito Comunista Italiano, or PCI), Socialists (Partito Socialista Italiano di Unità Prolitaria, or PSIUP), Christian Democrats (Democrazia Cristiana, or DC), Actionists (Partito d'Azione, or P d'A), Liberals (Partito Liberale Italiano, or PLI), and Labor Democrats (Democrazia del Lavoro, or DL).

22 On the DC's wartime program, see Gianni Baget-Bozzo, *Il partito cristiano al potere*, vol. I (Florence: Vallecchi, 1974), 57–9. On De Gasperi's progressive wartime vision, see Pietro Scoppola, *La proposta politica di De Gasperi* (Bologna: Il Mulino, 1977).

23 From an article written by Harlan Cleveland on leaving UNRRA in 1947. Draft copy in the United Nations Archives, New York, (UNA), RG 17, Records of UNRRA, Italy Mission, 1944–1947, Files of the Chief of Mission, Box 70,002.

24 Taylor's papers have been collected in *Stati Uniti e Vaticano, 1939–1952*, edited by Ennio Di Nolfo (Milan: Angelli, 1978).

25 Long's message is attached to a memo from Long to Mr. Geist, October 7, 1943, RG 59, 711.65/460 Confidential File (CF), NA.

26 See Martin Weil, *A Pretty Good Club, the Founding Fathers of the US Foreign Service* (New York: Norton, 1978), Chapters 1, 2.

27 George Kennan, *Memoirs, 1925–1950* (Boston: Little, Brown, 1957), 257. For Kennan letter to Bohlen, see Charles Bohlen, *Witness to History* (New York: Norton, 1973), 175–6. For evidence of the diversity of opinion within the Foreign Service, see Hugh De Santis, *The Diplomacy of Silence* (Chicago: University of Chicago), 1979.

28 Daniel Yergin, *The Shattered Peace, The Origins of the Cold War and the National Security State* (Boston: Houghton, Mifflin, 1977), 34. See Weil, *A Pretty Good Club*, 78, 82–3.

29 "Still a Little Bit Left of Center?" *Fortune*, 31 (March 1945): 118.

30 Weil, *A Pretty Good Club*, 83.

31 Dean Acheson, *Present at the Creation* (New York: Norton, 1969), 68, 88.

32 Congress increased the bank's lending authority by $2.8 billion in July 1945. For an account of the bank's early postwar activities, see *FRUS*, 1946, vol. 1, 1410–16. Truman set up the NAC in mid-1945. It met for the first time on August 21, 1945, under the chairmanship of Treasury Secretary Vinson. See *FRUS*, 1946, vol. 1, 1399.

33 "The U.S. Foreign Service," *Fortune*, 34 (July 1946): 85. On Stettinius, see Weil, *A Pretty Good Club*, 142, 179–80. For Acheson's scathing comments on his former boss, see *Present at the Creation*, pp. 88–91. Speaking of the U.S. corps of ambassadors at the time, *Fortune* observed, "As a whole the group is

marked by an amiable sort of mediocrity. There are some brilliant exceptions and some that fall just short of scandal" (p. 86).

34 See Ernest May, *"Lessons" of the Past: The Use and Abuse of History in American Foreign Policy* (New York: Oxford University Press, 1975), 22–30.

35 The Potsdam Protocol of August 2, 1945, created the Council of Foreign Ministers of the United States, United Kingdom, USSR, France, and China, to meet "as often as may be necessary, probably about every three or four months." The council's immediate task was to draft peace treaties for Italy, Hungary, Rumania, Bulgaria, and Finland. Once prepared, the drafts would be submitted to a peace conference for consideration and adoption by the twenty-one members of the United Nations. See J. Wheeler-Bennet and A. Nicholl, *The Semblance of Peace, the Political Settlement after the Second World War* (London: St. Martins Press, 1972), 419–30.

36 See the recollections of Charles Bohlen, who was attached to the secretary in 1946. When Bohlen complained that Byrnes rarely sent reports to Truman during diplomatic missions abroad, he was "put in his place." Bohlen, *Witness to History,* 247, 250.

37 See, for example, Piero Barucci, "La politica economica internazionale e le scelte di politica economica dell'italia (1945–1947)," in Aga Rossi-Sitzia et al., *Italia e stati uniti durante l'amministrazione Truman* (Padova: Franco Angeli, 1972).

38 See Togliatti's speech to the PCI convegno economico, held in Rome, August 21–23, 1945. Excerpts contained in Augusto Graziani, ed., *L'economia italiana, 1945–1970* (Bologna: Il Mulino, 1972), 111–13. See also Mauro Scoccimarro's speech on the same occasion, contained in Scoccimarro, *Il secondo dopoguerra* (Rome: Editori Riuniti, 1956), 8. Both emphasized to the party faithful that even if the PCI held power alone, it would have to rely on "l'iniziativa privata" to accomplish economic reconstruction. On the early postwar strategy of the PCI, see Donald L. M. Blackmer, "Continuity and Change in Postwar Italian Communism," in Blackmer and Sidney Tarrow, eds., *Communism in Italy and France* (Princeton: Princeton University Press, 1975), 21–45.

39 Barucci, "La politica," 84, 92.

40 Latter day critics have argued that the PCI shared Demaria's misunderstanding of the Fascist experience and tended to fall under the intellectual hegemony of the liberal economists. See Ester Fano Damascelli's penetrating critique of the "liberal-leftist" interpretation of the Fascist economy, "La 'restaurazione anti-fascista liberista,' ristagno e sviluppo durante il fascismo," in *Il movimento di liberazione in italia,* 103 (July–September 1971): 60–70. It is perhaps more accurate to conclude that the party was badly served by its Gramsican heritage – an excessive concern with control of the civil society and its institutions – and by undervaluation of the importance of economic forces. Clearly, the party's analysis of the international situation was deeply flawed. Its strategy was based in part on the assumption that the period of wartime collaboration between the United States and the USSR would continue, permitting the party to maneuver without the fear of excessive U.S. interference. After 1947, the party tended to accept the mistaken thesis that an imminent worldwide crisis of capitalism would shift the balance of power in favor of the Soviet Union and create an opening for its Western Communist allies. In so doing, some have argued, the PCI condemned itself to years of intense but sterile and uncreative opposition.

2. WARTIME DIPLOMACY

1 See Norman Kogan, *Italy and the Allies* (Cambridge: Harvard University Press, 1956), 61.

2 "Economic Guides," in Combined Chiefs of Staff (CCS) directive on Sicily, Coles and Weinberg, eds., *Civil Affairs: Soldiers Become Governors*, 179–80, 340. See also, Sarceno, *Intervista*, 10.

3 Coles and Weinberg, *Civil Affairs: Soldiers Become Governors*, 346.

4 Ibid., 346.

5 Paolo Baffi, "Monetary Developments," 408. Of the 35 percent of total national increase in the monetary supply accounted for by the South, almost 32 percent was constituted by AMlire.

6 *FEA Report on Italian Survey Mission*, submitted by Adlai Stevenson, February 5, 1944.

7 See also "Inflationary Developments in Liberated Italy," by Henry F. Grady, Acting Vice President, ACC Economic Section, March 21, 1944, Record Group 169, Records of the Foreign Economic Administration, Relief and Rehabilitation – General File, National Archives, Washington, D.C. (hereafter cited as RG 169, NA).

8 Coles and Weinberg, *Civil Affairs: Soldiers Become Governors*, 345, 366.

9 Ibid., 522. On the AC Economic Section vice-presidency, see Ellwood, *L'Alleato nemico*, 324–6; C. R. S. Harris, *Allied Military Administration of Italy, 1943–45* (London: HMSO, 1957), 240.

10 On the genesis of the Hyde Park Declaration, see James Edward Miller, "The Politics of Relief: Italian Americans, the Roosevelt Administration, and the Reconstruction of Italy, 1943–44," *Prologue*, 1 (Spring 1981): 54–75. For the text of the declaration, see Harris, *Allied Military Administration*, 251–2.

11 Following the capture of Rome in June 1944, the CLN had forced Badoglio's retirement. A new six-party coalition was formed under Ivanoe Bonomi, a veteran of pre-Fascist politics and leader of the social democratic Democracy of Labor Party (DL), made up largely of his personal followers.

12 See Harris, *Allied Military Administration*, 245–46. See also Ellwood, *Alleato nemico*, 101–02. Ellwood cites an August 1944 War Cabinet Memo: "In no case at the present time can we agree on any rehabilitation program for Italy."

13 According to the September 29, 1943, Instrument of Italian Surrender, Article 33: "A. The Italian Government will comply with such directives as the United Nations may prescribe regarding restitution, deliveries, services or payments by way of reparation and payment of the costs of occupation during the period of the present instrument." Coles and Weinberg, *Civil Affairs: Soldiers Become Governors*, 35.

14 Ibid., 356–7.

15 For the text of agenda, see memo from Matthews to Stettinius, November 24, 1944, RG 59 865.50/11–2444, NA. See also Memo by Lawler, AC officer accompanying the mission, to AC Chief Commissioner Stone, November 15, 1944, RG 331, Records of the Allied Control Commission, Italy, 10000/151/642, NA, Washington, D.C. (hereafter RG 331, NA).

16 For a brief summary of the U.S. view of the mission, see Grew to Kirk, January 13, 1945, *FRUS*, 1945, vol. 4, 1222–5. For British reaction to the proposed mission, see Memo of conversation between G. Middleton, UK Embassy, and J. W. Jones, Department of State, September 27, 1944, RG 59, 865.51/9–

2744, NA. The author learned of White's comments to Mattioli from a conversation with Egidio Ortona, March 1982, Bologna. For the U.S. embassy's observations, see Ambassador James Dunn to Secretary, July 22, 1947, RG 84, Records of the Rome Embassy, 851.5–Italy, NA, Washington, D.C.

17 See memo, Collado to Clayton, January 2, 1945, RG 59, NA. See also Lawler to Stone, November 15, 1944, RG 331, 10000/151/642, NA.

18 For an account of first meeting with treasury officials, see memo of November 16, 1944, RG 331, 10000/151/642, NA. See also memos of November 21 and 22 meetings with treasury and state officials, RG 331, 10000/151/642, NA.

19 Morgenthau to Stettinius, November 22, 1944. Stettinius to Morgenthau, December 11, 1944, RG 59, 865.50/11–2244, NA. See also Department of State memo, January 1, 1945, RG 59, 865.50/2–2345, NA.

20 Italian Note Verbale, Nov. 21, 1944, RG 59, 865.50/11–2944, NA.

21 Kirk to Secretary, January 26, 1945, paraphrasing the Italian government message *FRUS*. vol. 4, 1945, 1228–32.

22 On Cox's ties to Deltec and the Italian embassy, see Archivio Centrale dello Stato (hereafter ACS), Records of Deltec, Box 20, "Note on Consultants," May 14, 1947.

23 Crowley to Stettinius, January 11, 1945, *FRUS*, vol. 4, 1945, 1221–2.

24 *FRUS*, vol. 1, 1945, 1250–1.

25 See Minutes of Meeting between Mission and U.S. officials, December 4, 1944, RG 59 611. 6531/12–444, NA. Minutes of final meeting, March 6, 1945, RG 59 611.6531/3–645, NA. Memorandum handed Mission, March 6, 1945, RG 59 865.50/3–645, NA.

26 *FRUS*, vol. 4, 1945, 1252–3.

27 See Department Memorandum handed Mission, March 6, 1945, RG 59, 865.50/3–645, NA.

28 Eugene Rostow, "The Great Transition," *Fortune*, 31 (January 1945): 142–4.

29 For the details of this arrangement, see AC economic section memorandum by Harlan Cleveland, "Financing of Essential Italian Imports," June 19, 1945, RG 59, 865.50/6–1945, NA. See also Coles and Weinberg, 524–5, 627–9; Ellwood, 163–4.

30 For text of the CCS directive of January 31, 1945, see Coles and Weinberg, *Civil Affairs: Soldiers Become Governors*, 515–18.

31 See memo from office to Matthews, March 22, 1945, citing comments by Mr. Wade, UK Treasury representative in Washington. RG 59, 865.51/3–2245, NA.

32 Kirk to Secretary, February 13, 1945, *FRUS*, vol. 4, 1945, 1237.

33 "Problem Sheet–Italy" (for week ending February 17, 1945), RG 59. Records of the Department of Western European Affairs Relating to Italy, Box 3, NA.

34 For minutes of meeting, February 22, 1945, see Henry Morgenthau, *Diary*, vol. 821, 167–9, FDR Library, Hyde Park, New York. For British reaction, see memo from Office to Matthews, March 22, 1945, RG 59, Matthews–Hickerson Files, HF Matthews correspondence, Box 9, NA. For British reaction to Tasca's appointment, see memo of conversation between Hickerson (Department of State) and Roger Makins (UK Treasury), March 3, 1945, RG 59, Records of the Department of W. European Affairs, NA. Makins told Hickerson that Tasca's

"attitude of hostility was so apparent that he was a little surprised at his new designation."

35 See Morgenthau to Bonomi, March 7, 1945, ACS, Presidenza del Consiglio-Gabinetto, 31111/152. See also report by Coe (U.S. Treasury) to Pollack, November 28, 1945, RG 84 851/Italy, NA. The author is indebted to Mr. Elia Tasca, son of the late Henry Tasca, for speaking to me on several occasions about the career of his father.

36 On his return to Rome, Tasca told his British counterpart that if necessary, the Italians would have to be "forced" to accept their financial responsibilities. See Tasca to Harry White, March 17, 1945, RG 84, 851–Italy–General, NA. For the U.S. embassy's new position, see Kirk to Secretary, February 28, 1945, *FRUS,* vol. 4, 1945, 1248–9. Kirk asked for the department's views on the subject. The U.S. Treasury Department clarified its position in a March 14, 1945, press release: "It is perfectly clear that the US has not obligated itself in any way to 'redeem' any invasion currency issued in a foreign land, and we have no 'secret understandings' that we will do so." Release appears in Memo from G–5 to CCS, March 22, 1945, RG 84, 851, AMlire, NA. For details of net troop pay account, see Secretary to Kirk, March 20, 1945, RG 84, 851–Italy–Troop pay, NA. Placed in the account was $50 million, to bring the total to $100 million. This covered the period ending December 31, 1945.

37 For Soleri's reaction, see AFHQ to CCS, March 22, 1945, RG 84, 851, AMlire, NA.

38 See "United States Policy toward Italy," January 4, 1945, copy located in RG 169, Italy, R&R, General, Box 99, NA.

39 The basic documents concerning the preliminary peace proposals are contained in *FRUS,* vol. 4, 1945, 991–1055. For summaries of the Russian and British positions taken during the Potsdam conference in July, see *FRUS,* Conference of Berlin, vol. 2, 1086–7.

3. LIBERATION AND TRANSITION

1 The government included top leaders of the six CLN parties. In addition to Parri these leaders included Vice-Premiers Nenni (PSIUP) and Brosio (PLI); De Gasperi (DC), foreign minister; Togliatti (PCI), minister of justice; and Ruini (DL), minister of reconstruction.

2 Dulles to Kirk, June 20, 1945, RG 59, 865.00/6–2045, NA.

3 *FRUS,* Conference of Berlin, Vol. 1, 1945, 686–8. For Stone's views, see "Future Policy towards Italy," *FRUS,* Conference of Berlin, vol. 1, 1945, 688–94.

4 Salvemini letter to R. Bauer, ACS, Archivio Ugo La Malfa, Green Box 11; on Tarchiani's wartime career, see Antonio Varsori, *Gli Alleati e l'emigrazione democratica antifascista, 1940–1943* (Florence: Sansoni Editori, 1982).

5 See Memo of conversation between Tarchiani and Clayton, March 27, 1945, *FRUS,* vol. 4, 1945, 1252–3. The ambassador discussed FEA plans for a $600,000,000 credit to Italy, though, according to Clayton, "He did not indicate very clearly what the purpose of his visit was. . . ."

6 Tarchiani letter to Phillips, May 28, 1945, *FRUS,* vol. 4, 1945, 1256–7. Memo of conversation between Phillips and Tarchiani, May 30, 1945, *FRUS,* vol. 4, 1945, 1260–1.

7 Harlan Cleveland, "Some Conclusions and Recommendations on United States Policy and Organization in Italy," May 28, 1945. RG 163, Box 98, NA.

8 Stone, "Future Policy towards Italy," *FRUS*, Conference of Berlin, vol. 1, 1945, 688–94.

9 Clayton to Kirk, July 10, 1945, RG 59, 865.50/7–1045, CS/LE, NA.

10 Comment attributed to Emilio Collado in memo from J. Schairer to J. J. Reinstein, June 25, 1945, RG 59, 865.50/6–2545, CS/E, NA.

11 Acheson, *Present at the Creation*, 106.

12 "The US Foreign Service," *Fortune*, 34 (July 1946): 81–7. See also, Weil, *A Pretty Good Club*, 203–08.

13 Acheson, *Present at the Creation*, 28, 122; Yergin, *The Shattered Peace*, 93–4.

14 Acheson, *Present at the Creation*, 157–63; Weil, *A Pretty Good Club*, 140–50.

15 Weil, *A Pretty Good Club*, 234.

16 Kirk to Secretary, May 24, 1945, *FRUS*, vol. 4, 1945, 1005–08. Cleveland to Stone, May 28, 1945, RG 169, Italy–General, Box 99, NA; *FRUS* Conference of Berlin, vol. 1, 1945, 688–94.

17 For the story of FIAT's wartime and immediate postwar relationship with the Allies, see Valerio Castronovo, *Giovanni Agnelli* (Turin: UTET, 1972), 621–700.

18 B. Salvati, "The Rebirth of Italian Trade Unionism, 1943–54," in S. J. Woolf, *The Rebirth of Italy*, 187, 196. The CGIL was organized in June, 1944.

19 See "Labor Conditions in Northern Italy," report by Embassy Labor Attache, John Clark Adams, June 14, 1945, RG 84, 850.4–Italy, NA. See also minutes of meeting between AC ESC and Italian Cabinet, August 9, 1945, RG 331, 10000/136/637, NA; Coles and Weinberg, *Civil Affairs: Soldiers Become Governors*, 578.

20 See F. Parri, "La politica economica del CLNAI," in *Movimento di liberazione in italia*, 48 (July–September 1957), 42–51.

21 See UNRRA, *Survey* (Rome: 1947), 94. For a description of the cotton textile industry and its immediate postwar prospects, see *RAC, Industria Relazione*, vol. 1, 168–9. The textile and clothing industry suffered a mere 0.5 percent loss of its total 1938 value (compared to 25 percent for the metallurgical, and 12 percent for the mechanical industries). See Marcello De Cecco, "Economic Policy in the Reconstruction Period, 1945–51," in S. J. Woolf, *The Rebirth of Italy*, 158. On the industry's coal dependence, see Foa, *Monetary Reconstruction*, 43.

22 Italian banks were in an abnormally liquid position in late 1945, but they hesitated to commit themselves to industry until the political situation was clarified. Businessmen reported to the U.S. Consul in Milan that their recovery and expansion plans were blocked by the lack of credit. See Report by Coit McClean, Milan, to C. Livengood, Rome embassy, December 7, 1945, RG 84, 860–Italy, CF, NA.

23 Kirk to Secretary, September 12, 1945, RG 84, 868.1101–Italy–Cotton, CF, NA.

24 Clayton to Phillips, May 26, 1945, RG 59, 865.61321/5–2645, NA.

25 See Clayton to Russell, May 31, 1945, RG 59, 865.61321/5–3145, NA. For department's authorization of the Italo–Polish talks, see Secretary to Kirk, July 24, 1945, RG 59, 865.6362/7–2445, CS/D, NA. For Stone's reservations, see Kirk to Secretary, August 10, 1945, RG 59, 865.6362/8–1045 CF, NA. For

department complaints on delay, see Secretary to Kirk, RG 59, 865.6362/8–2145, NA. See Kirk to Secretary, September 27, 1945, RG 59, 865.6362/9–2745, NA; Kirk to Secretary, October 24, 1945, RG 59, 865/6362/10–2445, NA. On temporary breakdown of talks see Key to Secretary, May 27, 1946, RG 59, 865.6362/5–2746, NA. For details of the October, 1946 accord, see *UNRRA Survey*, 489.

26 For a detailed account of the early postwar coal problem and Allied efforts to deal with it, see John Harper, "The United States and the Italian Economy, 1945–48," Ph.D. dissertation, The Johns Hopkins University, 1981, 172–5.

27 The military aid "disease and unrest" formula did not provide for cotton imports. The FEA $100 million ("YB") program, which operated from August 31 to December 31, 1945, provided primarily coal and wheat. The Italians also had small amounts of foreign exchange available through the troop pay offset (YT) program, administered in Washington. In 1945, the mission spent $14 million for U.S. supplies, including about $6.5 million for raw cotton. See UNRRA, *Survey*, 447.

28 For the CCS financial directive of July 3, 1945, ending the AC's prior approval of Italian external transactions, see *FRUS,* vol. 4, 1945, 1266–71.

29 Kirk to Secretary, July 25, 1945, RG 59, 611.6531/7–2545, CS/LE, NA. See also Kirk to Secretary, October 22, 1945, RG 59, 611.6531/10–2245, CF, NA.

30 Stone to Parri, July 31, 1945, RG 331, 10000/136/452, NA. For Parri's reply of August 1, 1945 and Stone's subsequent letter to Parri (August 31, 1945), see Livengood to Secretary, September 25, 1945, containing correspondence and embassy summary, RG 59, 865.50/9–2545, CS/LE, NA.

31 For AC–Italian government discussion of ICE's problems, see letter from AC Acting Vice-President Kinley to Minister of Industry and Commerce Giovanni Gronchi, August 16, 1945; minutes of meeting between AC and Italian economics ministers September 1, 1945. Letters contained in dispatch from Kirk to Secretary, September 1, 1945, RG 59, 865.50/9–145, CS/MA, NA.

32 Kirk to Secretary, October 3, 1945, RG 59, 865.6132/10–345, NA.

33 *FRUS*, vol. 4, 1945, pp. 1290–1. For Kirk's reply see, Ibid., 1295.

34 The Export–Import Bank's lending authority had been increased by $2.8 billion in July, 1945. On the cotton loan and general bank policy, see Export–Import Bank, *Semiannual Report,* (July–December 1945).

35 Memo, *FRUS*, vol. 4, 1945, 1295–7.

36 On Giannini's press conference in Naples, November 15, 1945, see Key, Charge d'Affaires, to Secretary, November 16, 1945, RG 59, 865.51/11–1645, NA. On his visit, see also Julian Dana, *AP Giannini: Giant of the West* (New York: Prentice-Hall, 1947), pp. 326–30; Kogan, *Italy and the Allies,* 124. See also Kirk to Secretary, December 13, 1945, RG 84, 851–US–Industrial Credits, CF, NA.

37 On November 10, 1945, John White of Fulbright, Crooker, Freeman, and White, lawyers for Anderson, Clayton, and Company, delivered a memo on his client's problems to Walter Dowling of the State Department. The memo cited five sales to Italian textile firms for which partial payment had been received in dollars. The U.S. Treasury would not issue the necessary export licenses until the Italian government had given its approval. The department urged Kirk to push the Italians on the issue. Kirk reported that the Italian government would grant the necessary import licenses at the specific request of Anderson, Clayton, and

Company to import cotton and hold it on deposit. See Secretary to Kirk, November 15, 1945, RG 84, 851–Italy, CF, NA.

38 For a discussion of such measures taken elsewhere in Europe, see Frank Southard, *The Finances of European Liberation* (New York: King's Crown Press, 1946), 194–9.

39 Paolo Baffi, "Il problema monetario sullo scorcio del 1944," in *Studi sulla moneta*, 133–6. The piece was written during 1944. See also Harold Glasser to Secretary Morgenthau, December 18, 1945, Morgenthau *Diary*, FDR Library, Hyde Park, N.Y., vol. 821, 243. The Italian government's first major attempt to absorb excess monetary circulation was the bond issue (the so-called Soleri Loan, after the minister of the treasury, Marcello Soleri) of April–May 1945. The issue consisted of five-year bonds at 5 percent and raised almost 105 billion lire. Given the immensity of the relief burden, the loan provided little more than a drop in the bucket, and its success was due in part to rumors of a currency conversion, which caused people to convert cash into securities. Moreover, as Baffi reported to the Allies in June, the total, consolidated public debt stood at nearly 1,000 billion lire. Of this amount, a mere 233 billion lire was medium term, or funded; the rest, short-term, "floating" obligations. See OSS Report, June 13, 1945, RG 84, 851–Italy, CF, NA.

40 Piscitelli, "Il cambio," 18–19.

41 See discussion in *RAC*, Part II, *Problemi monetari e commercio estero*, vol. 1, 29. See also Piscitelli, "Il cambio," 9; Daneo, *La politica economica*, 24.

42 For text of Einaudi memo, see Piscitelli, "Il cambio," pp. 78–88.

43 See Demaria, "Il letto de Procruste," *Nuova Stampa*, February 7, 1946, reprinted in his *Problemi economici e sociali del dopoguerra* (Milan: Malfasi, 1951).

44 Writing in June 1946, Scoccimarro referred, *inter alia*, to "technical impediments" imposed by the AC, in explaining the *cambio's* delay. See Scoccimarro, "Il cambio della moneta e gli alleati," *Milano Sera* (June 26, 1946), contained in Scoccimarro, *Il secondo dopoguerra*. Christian Democrats who hesitated to show open opposition used similar arguments at the time. Other observers, both pro and con, would endorse the position of the PCI economist Luciano Barca: ". . . this was fundamentally a period of relative autonomy, independence and even national dignity. The basic choices of the period were, for better or worse, Italian choices. Choices for which all of us who were there bear a part of the responsibility." Referring specifically to the *cambio* issue, Barca recalls only two instances of Allied interference – a request for one month's advance notice of the date of the operation, and technical questions about the disputed Trieste area. See "Il condizionamento internazionale," in *Italia 1945–1975*, 351. See also Piscitelli, "Il cambio," 24–6.

45 *FRUS*, vol. 4, 1945, 1266–71.

46 Banca d'Italia, *Adunanza Generale*, Anno 1945, 71.

47 Venezia-Giulia province had been liberated by the Yugoslavs in April 1945. British troops entered Trieste in May. A temporary line of demarcation (the Morgan line) was worked out between General Sir William Morgan, chief of staff to Alexander, and the Yugoslav military, dividing the area into the so-called A and B Zones. The small Allied (A) zone included the city of Trieste. The Yugoslavs controlled the remaining bulk of the territory, with the exception of the city of Pola. Both Italy and Yugoslavia claimed the entire region. See Wheeler–Bennet, *The Semblance of Peace*, pp. 446–7. See minutes of meeting of AC FSC with Soleri and Einaudi, June 27, 1945, RG 331, 10000/136/442, NA.

48 Stone letter to Parri, July 18, 1945, *FRUS*, vol. 4, 1945, 1271–4. Parri's response to the letter did not raise the question of AMlire. Parri letter to Stone, September 4, 1945, RG 59, 865.51/9–425, NA.

49 AC FSC to U.S. and UK embassies, July 23, 1945, RG 84, 851–Italy–Financial Directive, CF, NA.

50 For contents of reply, see Livengood to Secretary, RG 59, 865.51/11–845 NA. See also *FRUS*, vol. 4, 1945, 1292–3.

51 Speaking of a fiscal decree already in effect, an embassy message observed in October 1945: "In the opinion of Embassy and Tasca, the administration of law had been a complete failure as a fiscal measure and it is clear that a basic reason for its failure had been the attempt to transform it into a weapon to destroy private enterprise and the economic basis of opposition to Communism in Italy." See Kirk to Secretary, October 17, 1945, RG 59, 865.00/10–1745, NA. For Clayton's position, see Department to Kirk, September 2, 1945, RG 59, 865.50/9–245, NA.

52 AC FSC Memo to Joint Director, FSC, September 5, 1945, RG 331, 10000/151/636, NA.

53 Report on August 27, 1945 meeting between Colonel Menapace, FSC, with Cigliani and d'Aroma of the Bank of Italy, FSC, to G–5 Financial Director, AFHQ, RG 331, 10000/136/636, NA. SACMED appeared unaware of the source of the delay. On August 31, Alexander urged that the currency agreement talks begin immediately in view of the "strong possibility that the Italian Government may undertake currency conversion in October," but he directed his appeal to the AC. SACMED to AC, Rome, RG 331, 10000/136/442, NA.

54 Kirk to Secretary, September 1, 1945, RG 59, 865.515/9–145, CF, NA. Such correspondence on economic and financial matters was invariably marked "from Tasca for Treasury Department" as well.

55 Kirk to Secretary, September 14, 1945, RG 59, 865.515/9–1445, CF, NA; Kirk to Secretary, September 15, 1945, RG 59, 865.515/9–1545, CF, NA.

56 AGWAR from CCS to AFHQ, October 23, 1945, RG 84, 851.5, CF, NA; Stone letter to Parri, November 1, 1945, RG 331, 10000/136/442, NA.

57 For Italian treasury memo, see ACS, Presidenza del Consiglio, Gabinetto, 116.44.8./19/11. Piscitelli, "Il cambio," 24.

58 Timmons to Stone, November 23, 1945, RG 331, 10000/136/442, NA. The question of the Yugoslav lire had not been resolved by the Allies themselves and was referred to G–5 AFHQ. See Timmons Report.

59 Kirk to Secretary, January 3, 1946, RG 49, 865.515/1–346, CF, NA.

60 Piscitelli, "Il cambio," 12. See Andreotti, *Intervista su De Gasperi*, 70.

61 Coe to Pollack, November 28, 1945, RG 84, 851–Italy, CF, NA.

62 Kirk to Secretary of State, August 25, 1945, *FRUS*, vol. 4, 1945, 983–4. Grew instructed Kirk to "see Parri again and inform him that this Government is unimpressed with his arguments cited for postponing elections . . . ," September 6, 1945, RG 59, 865.00/9–2645, NA. Grew added, "I would greatly appreciate it if you find occasion to express to Parri my personal best wishes to him in his difficult task."

63 Leone Cattini, "Dalla caduta del Fascismo al primo governo De Gasperi," *Storia Contemporanea*, (December 1974): Pietro Scoppola attempts quite unsuccessfully to play down the conspiratorial aspects of the meeting. See *La proposta politica di De Gasperi* (Bologna: Il Mulino, 1977), 183.

64 On British displeasure, see Ellwood, *L'alleato nemico*, 186. For Kirk conversations with Brosio and De Gasperi, see Kirk to Secretary of State, November

10, 1945, RG 59, 865.00/11–1045, NA. Kirk to Secretary of State, November 11, 1945, RG 59, 865.00/11–3045, NA. Byrnes to Kirk, November 23, 1945, RG 59, 865.00/11–2345, NA.

4. THE ADVENT OF DE GASPERI

1 Pietro Nenni, *Diaries,* entry for May 9, 1945; see also Giulio Andreotti, *Intervista su De Gasperi,* 54.

2 Speech contained in E. Corbino, *Discorsi elettorali e interventi parlamentari dal 1944 al 1958* (Naples: Istituto editoriale del Mezzogiorno, 1965), 44.

3 Speech to Third Congress of the PLI, May 1946, Corbino, *Discorsi elettorali,* 145.

4 Kirk to Secretary, January 3, 1946, RG 59, 865.515/1–546, CF, NA.

5 Kirk to Secretary, January 5, 1946, RG 59, 865.515/1–546, CF, NA. See also Timmons to Stone, January 24, 1946, RG 331, 10000/136/417, NA; De Gasperi letter to Stone January 24, 1946, RG 331, 10000/136/442, NA.

6 Kirk to Secretary, January 3, 1946, RG 59, 865.515/1–346, CF, NA, citing Corbino's presumed intention.

7 Embassy to Secretary, January 21, 1946, RG 59, 865.5151/1–2146, See also Ambassador to Secretary, February 8, 1946, RG 59, 865.5151/2–846, CF, NA.

8 Kirk to Secretary, January 7, 1946, RG 59, 865.51/1–746, NA, reporting on Stone's political meeting with De Gasperi. For Italian decision to postpone the conversion, see minutes of the Interministerial Committee on Reconstruction, January 5, 1946, ACS, Segreteria Particolare Presidenza del Consiglio; hereafter called (SPPC) 20/154.

9 Kirk to Secretary, December 21, 1945, RG 59, 611.6531./12–2145, NA. On resolution of procedural dispute, see Kirk to Secretary, January 4, 1946, RG 59, 611.6531/1–446, NA.

10 Kirk to Secretary, September 13, 1945, RG 59, 865.51551/9–1345, CF, NA.

11 For Parri's letter and AC comments, see AC Economic Section to G–5, AFHQ, November 1, 1945, RG 331, 10000/136/435, NA.

12 See Tasca letter to Corbino, transmitting Vinson's message and proposing extension of the new rate of U.S. government transactions. January 31, 1946, RG 84, 851–Italy–Military Exchange Rate, CF, NA. See also Kamarck, 134–8.

13 Secretary to Embassy, March 7, 1946, *FRUS,* vol. 1, 1946, 899.

14 Kirk to Secretary, January 11, 1946, RG 59, 865.655/1–1146, NA. On Italian protests, see Kirk to Secretary, January 22, 1946, RG 59, 865.655/1–2246, NA; Secretary to Kirk, February 8, 1946, RG 59, 865.655/2–846, NA.

15 See discussion between Riccardo Juker and Demaria's delegation from the Constituent Assembly's Economic Commission in March 1946. Demaria expressed his own fears of U.S. "economic imperialism" on a world scale. Neither he nor Juker were well-informed on cotton textile policy, but both were highly suspicious of U.S. motives. *RAC, Industria,* vol. II, *Appendice,* 113–123.

16 Key to Secretary, March 20, 1946, RG 84, 868.1101, Cotton Standards Conference, CF, NA.

17 See James Miller, "The Politics of Relief: Italian Americans, the Roosevelt Administration, and the Reconstruction of Italy, 1943–44," *Prologue,* 1 (Spring 1981): 54–75.

18 See memo from Department of War Strategic Services Unit (SSU) to Jack Neal, State Department, July 10, 1946, RG 59, 865.00/7–1046. Dunn to Secretary, March 28, 1947, RG 84, 851–Italy/US, CF, NA. See also Faenza and Fini, *Gli americani in italia*, 208, 223.

19 On Lombardo, see Acheson to Rome Embassy, April 25, 1946, RG 84, 868.1101/Cotton Standards Conference, CF, NA. See also Secretary to Key, April 1, 1946, *FRUS*, vol. 5, 1946, 901–02.

20 See Piccardi interview with the Constituent Assembly's Economic Commission, *RAC Industria*, Appendice II, 22–5. On impact of the "blocco dei licenziamenti," see Ernesto Rossi, *Lo stato industriale* (Bari: Laterza, 1953), 49.

21 IRI did not nationalize firms in the orthodox sense. It issued its own stock, of which large amounts were held by private investors. The vast bulk of industry remained in private hands in the thirties, increasingly dominated by an oligarchy of joint stock companies. See Palaja, "Industria di stato," 66–76; Daneo, *La politica economica*, 313–17.

22 For basic department policy, see Clayton to Kirk, July 10, 1945, RG 59, 865.50/7–1045, CS/LE, NA. Kirk to Secretary, October 13, 1945, RG 59, 865.504/10–1045, NA. In November, a U.S. Treasury official reported that given the cautious policy of the private banks, IRI penetration of private industry would inevitably increase. See Coe to Pollack, November 28, 1945, RG 84, 851–Italy, NA. On the unwillingness of banks to advance money to heavy industry, see report by Coit McClean, Milan Consul, to Rome Embassy, December 7, 1945, RG 84, 860–Italy, CF, NA.

23 Genoa Consul, Schnars, to Kirk, October 18, 1945, RG 84, 850.3. San Giorgio Co., CF, NA.

24 Kirk to Secretary, September 21, 1945, RG 59, 865.50/9–2145, NA.

25 Secretary to Kirk, September 21, 1945, RG 59, 865.50/9–2145, NA.

26 Key to Secretary, November 14, RG 59, 865.50/11–1445, NA. Memo from R. P. Terril, IR, to E. O. Anderson, IR, November 20, 1945, RG 59, 811.503165/11–2045, NA.

27 Memo from R. P. Terril, IR, to E. O. Anderson, IR, November 20, 1945, RG 59, 811.503165/11–2045, NA.

28 On Ansaldo, see Coe to Pollack, November 28, 1945, RG 84, 851–Italy, NA. See Kirk to Secretary, transmitting Permuda memo, November 28, 1945, RG 59, 865.50/11–2845, NA.

29 For a summary of Sinigaglia's views, see *RAC, Industria, Relazione* I, 29–32. See also Sinigaglia interview, *RAC, Industria*, Appendice II, 5–17. See also Rome Embassy Report on Finsider, including interview with Sinigaglia, prepared by H. Gardner Ainsworth, November 29, 1945, RG 84, 860–Italy, CF, NA.

30 See Genoa Consulate to Rome Embassy, January 16, 1946, RG 84, 850.3–San Giorgio Co., CF, NA; Rome Embassy Economic News Airgram, March 7, 1946, RG 59, 865.50/3–746, NA. In fact, Decree Law no. 86, March 5, 1946, authorized use of funds only in the case of firms in which IRI owned at least a majority share. See *Notizario della Confindustria* (April 5, 1946): p. 21.

31 See message from Tasca to State and Treasury Departments, enclosing a voluminous report on IRI holdings, March 14, 1946, RG 84, 860–Italy–IRI, CF, NA. On Embassy view of Paratore, see Key to Secretary, March 11, 1946, RG 59, 865.60/3–1146, NA.

32 See memo of conversation between Luigi Morandi and Department of State officials held in Washington, February 28, 1947. RG 59, 865.659/2–2847, NA. Morandi was on a forty-day visit to the United States. See Kirk to Secretary,

January 3, 1946, RG 84, Rome Embassy Files, 854–ICI. See also Ellwood, *L'alleato nemico*, 367, 370–1.

33 Letter from Peccei to Guido Soria, FIAT's New York representative, July 9, 1945, copy transmitted Kirk to Secretary, on July 17, 1945, RG 59, 611.6515/7–1745, NA. See also Valletta's testimony to the Economic Commission of the Constituent Assembly, *RAC, Industria, Relazione, Appendice*, 345–50. On GM takeover rumors, see Castronovo, *Giovanni Agnelli*, 632. See also Piero Bairati, *Valletta* (Turin: UTET, 1983), 149.

34 See Acheson, Acting, to Rome Embassy, September 7, 1945, RG 59, 865.70/9–745, NA.

35 The London embassy later reported that AE Vice-President and European Director Admiral W. S. Anderson, USNR, had discussed the purchase of Siemens–Halske's Italian properties during a visit to England. U.S. War Department Intelligence (SSU) reported, moreover, that Siemens–Halske had protected AE interests in Antwerp during the war. See Gallman, London, to Secretary, April 16, 1946, RG 59, 865.75/4–1646, CF, NA. For IT&T interest in OLAP, see report from K. E. Stockton, IT&T to C. Livengood, Rome Embassy, February 12, 1946, RG 84, 875–IT&T, CF, NA.

36 Letter from V. J. Shipman, Chicago, to S. R. Ryan, Washington, August 21, 1945, enclosed in letter from Ryan to Francis Colt de Wolf, Chief of Telecommunications Division, Department of State, August 22, 1945, RG 59, 865.75/8–2245, CS/LE, NA.

37 De Wolf, TD, to Wilcox, ITP, August 24, 1945, RG, FW 865.75/8–2445, NA. For Einaudi's views, see his *Lezioni di politica sociale* (Turin: Einaudi, 1967), first published in 1944, 71. On negotiations, see also Kirk to Secretary, September 21, 1945, RG 59, 865.70/10–2145, CF, NA. Kirk to Secretary, November 6, 1945, RG 59, 865.70/11–645, CF, NA. For AE protest, see letter from S. R. Ryan, AE–Washington, to de Wolf, October 17, 1945, enclosing letter from AE Vice-President Shipman, Chicago, to Ryan, of October 15, 1945. RG 59, 865.75/10–1745, CS/LE, NA. See also Department to Rome October 29, 1945, RG 59, 865.70/10–1745, CS/LE, NA. For TD reservations, see Secretary to Kirk, November 15, 1945, RG 59, 865.70/11–1545, NA.

38 Letter from Mario Scelba to Howard Bucknell, IT&T representative in Rome, December 15, 1945, transmitted from Rome to Department, December 21, 1945, RG 59, 865.70/12–2145, CF, NA.

39 Stone maintained close ties with the company during his AC service; his staff included Edward Behn, son of IT&T's founder, president, and board chairman, Col. Sosthnes Behn. On his retirement in 1947, Stone became president of the Commercial Cable Company, an IT&T subsidiary with interests in Italy. Umberto Merlin, DC minister of posts and telecommunications in a future De Gasperi government, told AE officials in 1947, "Mr. De Gasperi had been led to understand by Rear Admiral Stone, USNR, that the United States was particularly interested in the Italian Government consummating an agreement with the IT&T proposed by them which would give them a preferred and monopolistic position as respects the Italian telephone industry as a whole." Letter from Anderson, AE, to Ambassador James Dunn, October 6, 1947, citing comments made by Merlin to Anderson, in presence of AE Italian Managing Director Mr. Galassi. Letter transmitted from Embassy to Department, October 8, 1947, RG 59, 865.75/10–847, CS/A, CF, NA. For a brief account of Stone's IT&T career, see Anthony Sampson, *The Sovereign State, The Secret History of IT&T* (London: Hodder and Staughton, 1973).

40 See Scelba to Bucknell, December 15, 1945, RG 59, 865.70/12–2145, CF, NA. See also Secretary to Rome Embassy, January 23, 1946, RG 59, 865.70/12–1845, CS/VJ, NA. In a "Dear Howard" letter, February 1, 1946, Italian Desk Officer Walter Dowling transmitted a paraphrase of January 23 message to IT&T's Bucknell, RG 59, 865.70/2–146, CS.LE, NA.

41 Memo of conversation between General Wilson and S. W. Morgan, November 5, 1945, RG 59, 865.796/11–545, NA.

42 Opening up the international market in civil aviation was an intergral part of the Hull–Clayton program for a postwar liberal order. For documentation of the International Civil Aviation Conference held in Chicago in 1944, see *FRUS*, vol. 1, 1946, 1450. On department effort to gain nonreciprocal landing rights in Italy, see *FRUS*, vol. 4, 1945, 1323–9. For AV support of armistice revision, see Memo from AV to Mr. Hooker, TRC, May 10, 1945, RG 59, 865.796/5–1045, NA. Roosevelt's remarks are contained in Annex A of this memo, an excerpt from a confidential memo of conversation, prepared by A. A. Berle, dated November 11, 1943. Participants included Roosevelt, Hopkins, Berle, plus CAB and War Department officials.

43 Memo of conversation between General Wilson and S. W. Morgan, November 5, 1945, RG 59, NA. For De Gasperi's view, see Kirk to Secretary, December 26, 1945, RG 59, 865.796/12–2645, CF, NA. The details of the contract and a basic chronology of events are contained in a memo from Garrison Norton, TRC, to Clayton, April 10, 1946, RG 59, 865.796/4–1046 CS/V, NA.

44 Embassy to Secretary, January 10, 1946, RG 59, 865.50/1–1046, NA. See, for example, the following messages from the embassy to Washington: 865.51/3–1546, for Corbino's view that the *cambio* and tax program would be a "fatal error at this time"; RG 59, 865.51/5–3146, NA, for *Il Globo* article on Corbino's unequivocal opposition to the conversion; RG 59, 865.51/5–3146, NA, for excerpts from *L'idea Liberale* and full coverage of Corbino's May 19 address; RG 59, 865.51/6–546, NA, for *Il Sole's* coverage of a recent Corbino speech.

45 On this point see, Andreotti, *Intervista*, 74.

46 "US Financial Assistance to Italy," February 8, 1946, by the Office of Foreign Liquidation, Division of Investment and Economic Development, Italian Branch, RG 84, 851/Italy/US, CF, NA.

47 UNRRA was created in 1943, largely through American efforts. During the summer of 1944, an UNRRA observer mission recommended that $50 million be authorized for aid to Italy. The United States and Britain overcame opposition to this proposal by former enemy countries, and the first UNRRA mission was sent to Rome in November 1944. After extended negotiations involving Keeny, the Allied military bureaucracy, and the Italian government (represented by Lodovico Montini, brother of future Pope Giovanni Montini and a close associate of De Gasperi), a basic agreement was concluded in March 1945. The agreement created a Joint Committee – with Montini and Keeny as co-chairmen to administer the aid and conclude necessary supplementary accords. According to the terms, the Italian government pledged to provide matching funds to all UNRRA expenditures for goods and services supplied by UNRRA to Italy. The $50 million 1945 program was devoted almost exclusively to medical supplies, refugee care, and food for mothers and children. The Allies authorized the 1946 expanded program for Italy at Potsdam in July 1945. The United States proposed a specific $450 million program in August to finance a variety of relief and reconstruction projects. See George Woodbridge, *UNRRA, the History of the United Nations Relief and Rehabilitation Administration* (New York: Columbia

University Press, 1950), 257–67, UNRRA's official history. See also Coles and Weinberg, *Civil Affairs: Soldiers Become Governors*, 143.

48 See Cleveland to Stone, December 7, 1945, RG 84, 850–Italy, CF, NA.

5. CLAYTON AT BAY

1 John Lewis Gaddis, *The United States and the Origins of the Cold War, 1941–1947* (New York: Columbia University Press, 1971), 284, 312.

2 Ibid., 289–303.

3 Kennan, *Memoirs: 1925–1950*, 292–3.

4 Gaddis himself notes the importance of this political trend; see *The United States and the Origins of the Cold War*, 344.

5 Weil, *A Pretty Good Club*, 56–7, 254–5.

6 Cleveland to Stone, December 7, 1945, RG 84, 850–Italy, CF, NA.

7 See letter from Cesare Sacerdoti to Tarchiani, January 31, 1946, RG 59, FW 865.51/2–1446, NA. Cleveland to Stone, February 4, 1946, RG 331, 10000/136/422, NA. On department action see, *FRUS*, vol. 5, 1946, 892, 899.

8 *FRUS*, vol. 2, CFM, 1946, 221; also, vol. 5, 1946, 894–7.

9 Ibid., 900, 901. For documentation of 1946 effort to secure a preliminary peace settlement see *FRUS*, vol. 4, 1946, 830–40.

10 *FRUS*, vol. 5, 1946, 894–7.

11 Ibid., 902–6.

12 *FRUS*, vol. 2, CFM, 1946, 221; *FRUS*, vol. 5, 1946, 221.

13 *FRUS*, vol. 2, CFM, 1946, pp. 341–5, 360–1, 422–3.

14 *FRUS*, vol. 1, 1946, 1434 (footnote 50).

15 Ibid., pp. 1433, 1434.

16 On congressional appearance, see *FRUS*, vol. 5, 1946, 911–12. See also Memo of Conversation, May 16, 1946, RG 59, 865.51/5–1646, NA. See also *FRUS*, vol. 5, 1946, 914–15, for a version of the memo that deletes the phrase ". . . to influence the elections."

17 Kolko, *The Limits of Power* (New York: Harper & Row, 1972), 156.

18 For Clayton's defense of the UNRRA program in the USSR, see letter to Senator Kenneth McKellar of Tennessee, July 3, 1946, cited in Dobney, *Selected Papers of Will Clayton*, 164–7. On Exim Bank "set aside" for the USSR, see *FRUS*, vol. 1, 1946, 1435.

19 Acheson, *Present at the Creation*, 183–5. Rayburn quoted in Lloyd Gardner, *The Architects of Illusion* (Chicago: Quadrangle Books, 1970), 133.

20 *FRUS*, vol. 1, 1946, 1435–6.

21 Bank of Italy, Archivio Paolo Baffi, "Crediti all 'Italia," file, letter of Mario Einaudi to Cesare Sacerdoti, October 20, 1946.

22 Acheson, *Present at the Creation*, 183.

23 Norton (TRC) to Clayton, April 10, 1946, RG 59, 865.796/4–1046, NA.

24 See Key to Secretary, March 18, 1946, RG 59, 865.796/3–1846, CF, NA; Key to Secretary, March 31, 1946, RG 59, 865.796/3–3146, CF, NA; Norton to Clayton, April 10, 1946, RG 59, 865.796/4–1046, CS/V, NA. On March 18, Norton had discussed the contract with the Foreign Office in London. British officials said they were not worried, in part, because they could always veto the deal through CCS. The CCS, in fact, had already decided (March 16) to approve the Italian request for a local air service.

25 For documentation of the Bermuda conference, see *FRUS*, vol. 1, 1946,

1450–81. A preliminary agreement was reached in mid-February 1946. See also Norton to Clayton, April 16, 1946, RG 59, 865.796/4–1646, RG 59, 865.796/5–2546, CF, NA.

26 Italian press reports charged that the foreign airline deals had been the personal handiwork of Cevelotto and another prominent DL figure, Luigi Gasparotto. *Italia Nuovo* observed (June 11, 1946): "The reasons which induced first Gasparotto and afterward his friend Cevolotto to precipitate events must be varied and not only political in nature. . . ." Cevolotto had reportedly made plans to purchase foreign aircraft for the new company and came under strong attack from the Italian aircraft industry and unions. In early 1947, the *Giornale d'Italia* reported that Cevolotto had been promised the presidency of LAI in return for his services. Press reports transmitted in Key to Secretary, February 28, 1947, RG 59, 865.796/2–2847, CF, NA.

27 See Norton to Clayton, April 10, 1945, RG 59, 865.796/4–1046 CS/V, NA. For Acheson–Halifax conversation, see *FRUS*, vol. 1, 1946, 1451. For AV message, see RG 59, 865.796/1–346, CF, NA; Department to Rome, March 25, 1946, RG 59, 865.795/3–2546, CF, NA.

28 Norton to Clayton, April 10, 1946, RG 59, 865.796/4–1046 CS/V, NA; Terrill (IR) to Clayton, April 11, 1946, RG 59, 865.796/4–1146, CS/V, NA; Stinebower (ITP) to Clayton, April 11, 1946, RG 59, 865. 796/4–1146, CS/V, NA; Collado to Clayton, April 12, 1946, RG 59, 865.796/4–1246, NA; Durbrow to Norton, April 8, 1946, RG 59, 865.796/4–846, CS/V, NA.

29 Note Verbale to British Embassy, Washington, May 9, 1946 (including text; department's May 9 letter to TWA President Jack Frye), transmitted from Department to Rome Embassy, RG 59, 865.795/5–946, CS/VJ, NA. For substance of TWA reply to department's letter, see Acheson to Rome Embassy, May 14, 1946, RG 59, 865.795/5–1446, CS/VJ, NA. On subsequent Anglo-American negotiations on the Italian aviation issue, see Harper, "The United States and the Italian Economy," 279–81.

30 Key to Secretary, April 11, 1946, 865.70/4–1146, CF, NA. For earlier report from IT&T on British offer, see Memo of Conversation between Howard Bucknell of IT&T and department officials, January 16, 1946, RG 59, 865.70/1–1646, NA. See also Department to Rome, June 5, 1946, RG 59, 865.70/6–546, CF, NA.

31 "ITALY: Telecommunications Policy and Information Statement," July 17, 1946, RG 59, 865.70/7–2246, NA.

32 Memo by H. Van B. Cleveland to George Tesoro, May 14, 1947, RG 59, 865.51/5–1447, NA. See memo of conversation of department officials on IBRD loan for IT&T project, April 3, 1947, RG 59, 865.75/4–347, CF, NA.

33 See Note Verbale, transmitted by embassy to Secretary, September 18, 1946, RG 59, NA. For a detailed account of U.S. telecommunications diplomacy in Italy after 1947, see Harper, "The United States and the Italian Economy," pp. 282–6.

6. CORBINO, UNRRA, AND THE CRISIS OF THE LIBERAL LINE

1 See Baffi, "Monetary Developments," 425; De Cecco, "Economic Policy," 166–7.

2 Daneo, *La politica economica della ricostruzione*, 158; Baffi, "Monetary Developments," 426. On the expansion of bank credit, see also Friedrich A. Lutz

and Vera C. Lutz, *Monetary and Foreign Exchange Policy in Italy* (Princeton: Princeton University Press, 1950), 9–11.

3 De Cecco, "Economic Policy," 170.

4 Piscitelli, "Il cambio," 45–6; Lutz and Lutz, *Monetary and Foreign Exchange Policy in Italy*, 4–8.

5 Results of the election of June 2, 1946 for the Constituent Assembly:

Party	Percent	Seats
DC	35.2%	207
PSIUP	20.7	115
PCI	18.9	104
Unione Democratica Nazionale (PLI and DL)	6.8	41
Uomo Qualunque (neo-Fascist)	5.3	30
PRI	4.4	23
P d'A	1.5	7
Other Lists	5.5	28

The referendum gave victory to the republic by a narrow margin, 54.3 percent to 45.7 percent. The Constituent Assembly met for the first time on June 25 under the presidency of Giuseppe Saragat, leader of the conservative wing of the PSIUP. Liberal Enrico De Nicola was appointed provisional President of the republic on June 28.

6 Leigh Hunt to Secretary, October 24, 1946, RG 84, 848–UNRRA–Hunt Report, NA.

7 For embassy report see, Livengood to Secretary, October 24, 1946, RG 84, 848–UNRRA–Hunt Report, NA. See memo from Economic Affairs Officer of Foreign Office to Foreign Minister (De Gasperi), January 5, 1946, ACS (SPCC) 11–66. For Campilli visit to embassy, see Key to Secretary, September 17, 1946, RG 84, 848–UNRRA, Hunt Report. For rebuke of Keeny, see letter from Sir Humphrey Gale, personal representative of ERO director general, London, July 18, 1946. UNA RG 17, Chief of Mission (hereafter CM) File, CM, Box 70,002. On friction between mission and ERO, see also George Woodbridge, *UNRRA, the History of the United Nations Relief and Rehabilitation Administration* (New York: Columbia University Press, 1950), 268.

8 See Supplementary Agreement with Italy, January 17, 1946, contained in Woodbridge, Vol. 3, 296–316. See also Embassy to Secretary, August 20, 1945, RG 84, 865.102–Italy, NA. The embassy reported that Minister Gronchi had asked the AC for a directive on overall price policy. The AC declined, in accordance with CCS wishes to restore such responsibility to the Italian government.

9 See minutes of meeting, February 1, 1946, RG 331, 10000/136/649, NA.

10 Minutes of meeting, February 2, 1946, RG 331, 10000/136/166, NA.

11 Minutes of UNRRA cabinet meeting, April 17, 1946, UNA, RG 17, CM, Box 70,009; Cleveland memo to Keeny, May 14, 1946, UNA, RG 17, CM, Box 70,002.

12 Cleveland letter to David Weintraub, UNRRA deputy director general, May 6, 1946, UNA, RG 17, CM, Box 70,002; Minutes of UNRRA cabinet

meeting, May 17, 1946, UNA, RG 17, CM, Box 70, 012; Stone letter reported by Key to Secretary, March 21, 1946, RG 84, 869.5–Italy, CF, NA.

13 Minutes of meeting between Keeny and Italian government high commissioner for food, Pietro Mentasti, May 21, 1946, UNA, RG 17, CM, Box, 70,012. The description of the talks is Keeny's. See minutes of meeting between mission and UNRRA officials, June 4, 1946, RG 331, 10000/136/363, NA.

14 Woodbridge, *UNRRA*, pp. 270–1. On the creation of the Joint Price Committee, see also UNRRA *Economic Notes*, June 21, 1946, vol. 1, no. 23, 1. For details of Lira Fund Control Committee, see UNRRA *Economic Notes*, July 12, 1946, vol. 1, no. 26, 1–2.

15 Daneo, *La Politica economica della ricostruzione*, 153–4. Carli, "La disciplina degli scambi con l'estero e dei cambi nell'esperienza recente," *Critica Economica*, 1946, n. 3. For Jung's view, see RAC, *Industria*, vol. 2, *Appendice*, 505. La Malfa spoke of his earlier position in a speech to the Constituent Assembly, September 20, 1946. See La Malfa, *La politica economica italiana, 1946–1962* (Milan: Edizioni di Communita, 1962), 37–51. For Scoccimarro view, see minutes of CIR meeting of February 22, 1946, on that issue. ACS, Carte di Ugo La Malfa, Fasc. 6 Brown, "Atti politici 1946."

16 Foa, *Monetary Reconstruction in Italy*, 49.

17 Ibid., 49; see also, Karel Holbik, *Italy in International Cooperation* (Padua: CEDAM, 1959), 33.

18 See interventions by Einaudi and Corbino during February 22, 1946 meeting, cited above, note 15. De Cecco, "Economic Policy," 170.

19 American financiers like A. P. Giannini seized the opportunity. By the end of 1947, the Bank of America had advanced $37 million to Italian banks and industry for the purchase of raw materials. Marquis James, *Biography of a Bank: The Story of the Bank of America* (New York: Harper, 1954), 478.

20 Harlan Cleveland, speech to Italian Chamber of Commerce for the Americas and the Italo-American Association, Rome, January 16, 1946, RG 331, 10000/136/383, NA. Cleveland memo, August 27, 1946, UNA, RG 17, Files of Sub-Bureau of Industrial Rehabilitation (hereafter SIR), Box 70,116; Memo from Peter Treves to Harold Spiegel, H. Van Buren Cleveland, Walter Dowling, and Kermit Gordon, June 18, 1946, RG 59, 865.51/6–2046, CS/E, NA.

21 On Corbino's request for a raise, see letter from Corbino to De Gasperi, April 26, 1946, ACS, Segretaria Particolare Presidenza del Consiglio, (hereafter SPPC) fasc. 6, busta 32. See also Woodbridge, *UNRRA*, 293.

22 Raw cotton arrivals at Genoa:

Year	From USA	Total
1938	66,843 tons	108,922
1945	19,385	25,887
1946	163,076	219,099

Raffaele Sansone, "Italy's Textile Exports Expand Rapidly," *Cotton Trade Journal*, International Edition, 54 (1945–1946): 182.

23 Woodbridge, *UNRRA*, p. 298.

24 On the legal issues raised by the government's August decree naming two

mission officials to the committee, see September 13, 1946, memo by mission Legal Advisor, P. Contini. UNA, RG 17, SIR, Box 70,121. In mid-November, a mission official observed with reference to the wool program, "I am somewhat perturbed that manufacturers in this country are competing with foreign competition by making consumers at home pay exorbitant prices quite beyond the reach of vast numbers of people in Italy in order that export prices can be kept low." See draft report on wool program, November 1946, UNA, RG 17, SIR, Box 70,121.

25 Report by G. Morelli, mission textile division, December 18, 1946, UNA, RG 17, SIR, Box 70,121.

26 For details, see Harper, "The United States and the Italian Economy," 336–7.

27 Campilli cited in Key to Secretary, September 17, 1946, RG 84, 848–UNRRA–Hunt Report, NA.

28 The 1946 supply program totalled $418,322,000, divided as follows: food, 234,507,000; medical and sanitation supplies, 9,477,900; clothing, textiles, footwear, 50,269,600; agricultural rehabilitation, 13,320,500; industrial rehabilitation, 110,085,500. At its completion, UNRRA–Tessile had distributed $400 million (at free market prices) worth of textile products to the population at a cost of $220 million. Other major lira fund projects included UNRRA–CASAS (housing rehabilitation), the Sardinian malaria eradication program, aid to non-Italian displaced persons, and other health, welfare, and agricultural projects. See Woodbridge, *UNRRA*, 289, 294; also UNRRA *Economic Notes*, July 12, 1946, vol. 1, no. 26, 2. Keeny's remarks made in conversation with the author, Washington, D.C., February 22, 1984.

29 See *FRUS*, 1946, CFM, vol. 2, 55–69, 615; Byrnes, *Speaking Frankly* (London: William Heineman, 1948), 133; Kogan, *Italy and the Allies*, 137.

30 *FRUS*, 1946, vol. 2, CFM, 728–9.

31 For details of program, see Piscitelli, "Il cambio," 44. Rome Embassy Economic News Airgram, July 12, 1946, RG 59, 865.50/7–1246, LRC, NA.

32 Tasca remained in close touch with Corbino during the negotiations. For reports on his conversations with the minister, see Key to Secretary, July 5, 1946, RG 59, 865.51/7–546 NA; Key to Secretary, July 9, 1946, RG 59, 865.51/7–946, CF, NA. The embassy calculated that the indemnity would amount to a 5 percent salary increase, spread over a six-month period. See Rome Embassy Economic News Airgram, July 12, 1946, RG 59, NA. See also Daneo, 167–8; Mammarella, 142. De Gasperi became minister of the interior and foreign affairs, as well as president of the council. Nenni became minister without portfolio but took over the Foreign Ministry in October. Scoccimarro remained at finance; Togliatti left the Justice Ministry to concentrate on party affairs and was replaced by the Communist Fausto Gullo.

33 "Current Italian Economic Policies," by H. Gardner Ainsworth and Charles Livengood, transmitted to Secretary, July 25, 1946, RG 84, 850–Italy, CF, NA.

34 For De Gasperi's summer 1946 attitude toward the PCI, see Andreotti, *Intervista*, 65–8. On United States aid in strengthening the Italian police and military, see *FRUS*, 1946, vol. 5, 893, 932.

35 Interesting, albeit circumstantial, evidence of their differing approaches to the Communist question is provided by the so-called *giallo* – or mystery – of the stolen currency plates. For details, see Harper, "The United States and the Italian Economy," 341–4. De Gasperi made an eloquent, if utterly futile, denunciation

of the Italian treaty in Paris on August 10. Byrnes alone stood to greet him as he left the chamber. In a private meeting the same day, Byrnes told De Gasperi that the suspense account had been made available, but they agreed that its actual release should be delayed until the outstanding reparations claims were settled. For text of De Gasperi's speech, see *FRUS*, 1946, vol. 3, 172–4.

36 Key to Secretary, August 5, 1946, RG 59, 865.00/8–546, NA. On emergency steps, see Lutz and Lutz, *Monetary and Foreign Exchange Policy*, 30; Piscitelli, "Il cambio," pp. 45–7.

37 *Rinascita*, September 1946, no. 9. See also Luciano Barca et al., *I comunisti e l'economia italiana, 1944–1974*, (Bari: De Donato, 1974), 82–90; Scoccimarro interview to *l'Unità*, July 5, 1946 (reprinted in Scoccimarro, *Il secondo dopoguerra*, 119–24).

38 *FRUS*, 1946, vol. 5, 930–2.

39 Key to Secretary, September 9, 1946, RG 59, 865.00/9–946, CF, NA.

40 *FRUS*, 1946, vol. 5, 934–6. See also Agostino Giovagnoli, *Le premesse della ricostruzione* (Milan: Nuovo Istituto Editoriale Italiano, 1982), Chapter 7.

41 *FRUS*, 1946, vol. 3, 201–3.

42 *FRUS*, 1946, vol. 5, 936. On crisis, see also Ruggero Moscati, "Nota sulla 'svolta' del giugno 1947," *Storia Contemporanea*, 4 (December 1974): 573–4.

43 Minutes of conversation between the visiting Ward and UNRRA staff, October 28, 1946, UNA, RG 17, CM Box 70,115. Keeny's reaction from conversation with the author, March 1984.

7. THE EMERGENCY RESPONSE

1 The GOP achieved a majority of six seats in the Senate, fifty-eight in the House:

Senate	1944 elections	1946 elections
Democrats	56	45
Republicans	39	51
House		
Democrats	241	188
Republicans	192	246

2 See *New York Times*, November 7, 9, 1946.

3 James Reston, "Economic Foreign Policy is a Post-Election Problem," *New York Times*, November 7, 1946.

4 For Clayton remarks, see *New York Times*, November 10, 1946. See Report, dated December 27, 1946, *FRUS*, 1946, vol. 1, 1360–6. For a summary of proposed ITO charter, see *FRUS*, 1946, vol. 1, 1357–8.

5 On election results, see G. Mammarella, *L'Italia dopo il fascismo* (Bologna: Il Mulino, 1970), 143–4. On Montini–De Gasperi meeting, see Andreotti, *Intervista*, 71–4.

6 *FRUS*, 1946, vol. 5, 946.

7 Foa, *Monetary Reconstruction*, 96–7; Ugo Ruffolo, "La linea Einaudi," *Storia Contemporanea*, December, 1974, 643.

8 Embassy memo, "Italy's Transitional Problem and Italy's Foreign Exchange Position," October 28, 1946, RG 59, 865.50/10–2846, NA. See also, "Italian Financial Developments," December 16, 1946, by Edelen Fogarty, RG 84, 851–Italy, CF, NA.

9 In addition to $100 million to the USSR, Italy was required to pay the following amounts: $5 million to Albania; $25 million to Ethiopia; $105 million to Greece; and $125 million to Yugoslavia (Total = $360 million). An NAC study concluded that "the proposed peace treaty will probably not have major harmful effects on the Italian economy" and recommended a loan to Italian industry on November 15. See *FRUS*, 1946, vol. 5, 141–6.

10 Dowling to Matthews, November 21, 1946, RG 59, 865.00/11–2146, CF, NA.

11 Hickerson to Clayton, November 26, 1946, RG 59, FW 865.51/11–2646, NA.

12 Dallas Dort (AT) to Stillwell (IR), December 2, 1946, RG 59, 865.6131/12–246, NA. Willard Thorp was assistant secretary at the time. Nenni became foreign minister on October 18, 1946, and rumors circulated that he planned to replace Tarchiani with Ivan Matteo Lombardo. In an October 30 conversation with H. F. Matthews, Tarchiani observed that "Nenni was not a wise man and frequently made very wild and indiscreet statements." *FRUS*, 1946, CFM, 955.

13 *FRUS*, 1946, vol. 5, 948; see also 948 (footnote 99) for Clayton's comment.

14 See Clayton memo of March 5, 1947, contained in Dobney, *The Selected Papers of Will Clayton*, 198–200. See also his memo of May 1947, *FRUS*, 1947, vol. 3, 230–2. In a September 12, 1946, letter to Byrnes, Clayton noted Russian pressures in the Eastern Mediterranean and recommended that department policy be changed to permit the sale of surplus military equipment to Turkey and other countries in the area. Clayton expressed "grave doubt," however, about sending a military mission to Turkey. See *FRUS*, 1946, vol. 7, 209–13.

15 For invitation (sent via the embassy in Rome on December 9, 1946) and acceptance, see *FRUS*, 1947, vol. 3, 835–6.

16 On January 7, 1947, the Rome embassy reported that an Italian Foreign Ministry official had expressed "hope that any public announcement would make it clear that the loan was being granted to assist in development of free economic enterprise with implication that it would be subject to revocation if control of government passed to Communists or left-wing Socialists." See Embassy to Secretary, January 7, 1947, RG 59, 711.65/1–747, NA.

17 On December 20, 1946, the department told the embassy to tell De Gasperi that it understood "his concern for success of visit." See Department to Embassy, December 20, 1946, RG 59, 711.65/12–2046, CF, NA. The embassy feared that the visit might "boomerang . . . if De Gasperi got nothing." See Embassy to Secretary, January 2, 1947, RG 59, 711.65/1–247, CF, NA. For examples of misleading accounts, see Collotti, "La collocazione internazionale," and Antonio Gambino, *Storia del dopoguerra* (Bari: Laterza, 1975), 261–8.

18 *FRUS*, 1947, vol. 3, 837.

19 The Confindustria's biweekly *Notiziario* observed (January 5) that "The eyes of all Italy are focused on the trip, particularly those of business who hope for great positive results."

20 Department to Embassy, December 17, 1946, RG 59, 711.65/12–1746, CF, NA.

21 See *New York Times,* January 8, 1947. The Marshall transition is discussed in the next chapter.

22 Ibid., January 10, 1947; January 11, 1947.

23 Ibid., January 5, 1947; January 17, 1947; January 19, 1947.

24 Ibid., January 17, 1947.

25 De Gasperi's list included more coal and wheat, additional liberty (merchant) ships, the $50 million Suspense Account, return of Italian gold reserves, and a major post-UNRRA aid program. *FRUS,* 1947, vol. 3, 838–40.

26 Ibid., 845–7; also 841, for problems faced by the department in mobilizing wheat shipments. According to Tarchiani, the Italians appealed directly to Agriculture Secretary Clinton Anderson. See Tarchiani, *America–Italia: le dieci giornate di De Gasperi negli stati uniti* (Milan: Rizzoli, 1947).

27 *FRUS,* 1947, vol. 3, 848–9.

28 For Thorp–Campilli meeting, see *FRUS,* 1947, vol. 3, 852–4. The final peace treaty (article 78) made clear that all dollar debts incurred by Italy before the war were in no way affected by subsequent events. This provision was of particular interest to the holders of prewar Italian dollar bonds in default since 1940. On January 9, 1947, the department received a letter from A. M. Anderson, vice-President of J. P. Morgan & Company, noting De Gasperi's presence in the United States and expressing hope that the department "would not fail to take such steps in the interest of American bondholders as seems feasible at this time." Morgan held the bulk of the unpaid debt on loans dating from its close ties to Mussolini in the mid-1920s. See letter from Anderson to Secretary, January 8, 1947, RG 59, 865.51/1–847, CS/R, NA. See also letter from Morgan Bank to Secretary, August 8, 1944, RG 59, 865.51/8–844, NA. Morgan had lent $100 million to the Italian government in 1926 for support of the lira. This loan was followed by a credit of 12 million for steamship construction and a third issue of $30 million to the City of Rome for public works. In 1944, arrears amounted, respectively, to $66,174,000, $3,835,000, and $16,181,000. See also Secretary to Embassy, April 3, 1946, RG 59, 865.51/4–346, NA. The two sides discussed the question of claims briefly during the De Gasperi mission and set the stage for talks between Ivan Matteo Lombardo and the department in May and June, and the financial agreement concluded in August 1947. See *FRUS,* 1947, vol. 3, 857.

29 *FRUS,* 1947, vol. 3, pp. 843, 851–2.

30 Ibid., pp. 855–6.

31 Ibid., pp. 859, 860, 914.

32 For details of the credits that became available after October, 1947, see Harper, "The United States and the Italian Economy," 385–6. For editorial comment on De Gasperi's visit, see *New York Times,* January 16, 1947.

33 See Tarchiani, *Dieci anni,* 128. For summary of January 21 press conference, see Embassy to Secretary, January 21, 1947, RG 59, 711.65/2–147, NA; Embassy to Secretary, February 1, 1947, RG 59, 711.65/2–147, NA.

34 A covert campaign conducted by the Italian-American labor leader Luigi Antonini had encouraged Saragat, and he had met Byrnes in Paris in October to request U.S. "moral and spiritual support" for the "truly democratic elements including the Italian Socialist party." See Faenza and Fini, *Gli americani in italia,* 174–9; *FRUS,* 1946, vol. 3, 664–5. At the same time, there is no evidence of official U.S. complicity in the January events. The British Labour Government openly opposed Saragat's move.

35 Letter from Tasca to Andrew Overby, Special Assistant to Secretary of the Treasury John Snyder in Washington, January 16, 1947, Harry S. Truman Library, John Snyder Papers, Italy, 1946–49.
36 See Mammarella, *L'Italia dopo il fascismo*, 144–9; Moscati, "Nota sulla 'svolta' del giugno 1947," 580.
37 Dunn to Secretary, March 4, 1947, *FRUS*, 1947, vol. 3, 870–1.
38 Tasca letter of January 16, 1947, to Andrew Overby, Harry S. Truman Library, John Snyder Papers, Italy, 1946–49.

8. THE "WHIRLWIND OF DISINTEGRATION"

1 John Gimbel, *The Origins of the Marshall Plan* (Stanford, Calif.: Stanford University Press, 1976), 8–16. Alan Milward's interesting analysis of the "crisis of 1947" suggests that the view, held then and since, of Europe's imminent economic collapse was vastly exaggerated. Milward's picture, as the following chapter suggests, is perhaps overdrawn in the case of Italy. In addition to balance of payments difficulties, Italy faced an inflationary and political crisis that together threatened severe consequences. Italy, as Milward points out, was the only European country to take strong deflationary measures in 1947. See Milward, *The Reconstruction of Western Europe, 1945–51* (Berkeley: University of California Press, 1984), Introduction, Conclusions.
2 Acheson, *Present at the Creation*, 214.
3 *FRUS*, 1947, vol. 3, 240.
4 Gaddis, *The U.S. and the Origins of the Cold War*, 344.
5 For text of Truman's February 21 speech, see *FRUS*, 1947, vol. 1, 1034–5; Jones, *The Fifteen Weeks* (New York: Harcourt, Brace, World, 1964), 198–9; Acheson, *Present at the Creation*, 221.
6 Jones, *The Fifteen Weeks*, 198–9.
7 Acheson, *Present at the Creation*, 219.
8 For Acheson letter, see *FRUS*, 1947, vol. 3, 197–8. For Clayton memo, see Dobney, *Selected Papers of Will Clayton*, 198–200.
9 For Clayton's appearance before the House Foreign Relations Committee, see Dobney, *The Selected Papers of Will Clayton*, 190–5. Clayton did not mention communism or the USSR, stressing rather that military security against the insurgents was "an essential prerequisite to economic stability."
10 See William Reitzel, *The Mediterranean, Its Role in American Foreign Policy* (New York: Harcourt, Brace, World, 1948), Chapter 10.
11 See the Tarchiani letter to Clayton, March 3, 1947, RG 59, 865.61311/3–347, CS/V, NA. See also *FRUS*, vol. 3, 874, 876–7.
12 See Foa, *Monetary Reconstruction*, 103; Gambino, *Storia del dopoguerra dalla liberazione al potere DC* (Bari: Laterza, 1975) 319; Daneo, *La politica economica della ricostruzione*, 200, 210.
13 Baffi, "Memoria sull'azione di Einaudi," cited by Daneo, *La politica economica della ricostruzione*, 219.
14 See Banca d'Italia, *Relazione Generale*, Anno 1946, Considerazioni finali, 222–57. *Notiziario*, April 5, 1947, and April 20, 1947.
15 For Morandi program, see Daneo, *La politica economica della ricostruzione*, 216, 217. Campilli informed the embassy of the bankers' threats. See Dunn to Secretary, March 4, 1947, RG 84, 851–Italy, CF, NA. For Costa program, see Angelo Costa, *Scritti e discorsi* (Turin: UTET, 1980), 385–90.

Cigliana handled foreign exchange operations on the New York market and was Einaudi's "eyes and ears" on Wall Street. Some of his correspondence with Einaudi including the letter of April 16, 1947, is found in the Paolo Baffi Archive, Bank of Italy, "Crediti all'Italia" file.

16 *FRUS,* 1947, vol. 3, 880. Dunn to Secretary, April 14, 1947, RG 84, 851–Italy/US, CF, NA.

17 On this point, I am indebted to Paolo Baffi, letter to the author, June 28, 1983.

18 When Dunn received word that Tasca had been offered the job of alternate director of the IMF in May, 1948, the ambassador cabled the department, "I feel very strongly Tasca should not leave Italy at this time, and it would be a serious loss to the U.S. with respect to the implementation of its foreign policy in Italy. As you know, Tasca is familiar in a unique way with the Italian picture and Italian personalities in the financial and economic field to the extent that it is impossible to substitute him at this time. . . . I wish to emphasize that I attach the greatest importance to his remaining at this time." Dunn to Secretary, May 10, 1948, RG 84, 851–Italy, CF, NA. Tasca's departure was delayed for some months, but he was eventually replaced as treasury representative by Andrew Kamarck, former AC finance officer.

19 Dunn to Secretary, April 22, 1947, RG 84, 851–Italy, CF, NA. On position of Gronchi et al. during April–May 1947, see Andreotti, *Intervista,* 80.

20 Daneo, *La politica economica della ricostruzione,* 221; Andreotti, *Intervista,* 81.

21 For text of Marshall's April 28 speech, see Department of State *Bulletin,* May 11, 1947, 919–24. On PPS action, see *FRUS,* 1947, vol. 3, 20 (footnote 2). For April 25 cable to Rome, see *FRUS,* 1947, vol. 3, 886–7.

22 See, for example, Gambino, *Storia del dopoguerra,* 330–60; Collotti, "La collocazione internazionale," 106–10; Faenza and Fini, *Gli americani in italia,* 180–6; Scoppola, *La proposta politica di De Gasperi,* 297–9; Moscati, "Nota sulla 'svolta' dea giuguo 1947", pp. 584–8; Giovagnoli, *Le premesse della ricostruzione,* Chapter 8; Simon Serfaty, "The United States and the Communist Parties in France and Italy, 1945–47," *Studies in Comparative Communism,* 18 (Spring–Summer 1975): 140–5. Each account uses *FRUS* documentation.

23 *FRUS,* 1947, vol. 3, 889–92.

24 Ibid., 893–4.

25 Ibid., 895–7.

26 Ibid., 708–09.

27 For text, see Department of State *Bulletin,* May 26, 1947, pp. 991–4.

28 Matthews to Dunn, May 26, 1947, RG 59, Matthews–Hickerson Records, "Ambassador, Italy," Box 16, NA.

29 Quoted in Acheson, *Present at the Creation,* 220.

30 Tasca's report is divided into two sections, "Current Economic and Financial Policies of the Italian Government," and "Recommendations." The first section is printed in *FRUS,* 1947, vol. 3, 898–901. For the remainder of the document, see Dunn to Secretary, May 7, 1947, RG 59, 865.51/5–747, A/FLH, CF, NA.

31 The document was sent to all major State Department offices as well as to the Departments of War and Commerce. Presumably, Tasca discussed the report with his own department, the treasury.

32 For notations, see p. 3 of Dunn to Secretary, May 7, 1947, RG 59, 865.51/5–747, A/FLH, CF, NA.

33 *FRUS*, vol. 3, 1947, 224–5.
34 The conference convened on April 11. See *FRUS*, 1947, vol. 1, 909–1025. For Clayton's memo, see *FRUS*, 1947, vol. 3, 230–2.
35 *FRUS*, 1947, vol. 3, 221.
36 Giovagnoli, *Le premese della ricostruzione*, 388–9.
37 *FRUS*, 1947, vol. 3, 904–8.
38 *FRUS*, 1947, vol. 3, 908–9.
39 *FRUS*, 1947, vol. 3, 908–9.
40 "1) A general pledge of US support for Italy, to be made on formation of new government. 2) Consultations to be undertaken UK and French Governments to urge them to lend support to Italian Government . . . including any possible treaty revision in Italy's favor . . . 3) Contemplated Italo-US agreements, including commercial treaty, bi-lateral air agreement and trade agreement, to be negotiated soon as possible to derive full psychological value. US to urge Italian government to take immediate effective steps to improve economic conditions. 4) Every available source of economic assistance to Italy to be utilized, including post-UNRRA relief. Congress to be urged to pass promptly enabling legislation for return of Italian assets in US, including seized ships; Eximbank to be urged to expedite availability $100 million earmarked loan; War Department to be asked to expedite final settlement of suspense accounts. 5) Surplus military equipment, recommended by SACMED for transfer to Italian armed forces, to be made available at lowest possible cost. 6) Every opportunity to be taken to advertise to Italian people US support for Italy and US appreciation of Italian progress." *FRUS*, 1947, vol. 3, 909.
41 See Gambino, *Storia del dopoguerra,* 352; In addition to Italian assets in the United States, Lombardo's agenda included the settlement of prewar Italian commercial debts, occupation costs, IBRD and ITO membership, and a new treaty of commerce and navigation. See Embassy to Secretary, April 23, 1947, RG 84, 851–Italy/US, CF, NA. Shortly after the formation of the new government, the Italian Foreign Ministry told the U.S. embassy that Lombardo's latest reports were "couched in optimistic terms as contrasted with some of his earlier reports; 'The Americans,' he is said to have reported, 'are showing a very sympathetic understanding of Italian problems.'" See Dunn to Secretary, June 5, 1947, RG 84, 851–Italy–US, CF, NA.
42 *FRUS,* 1947, vol. 3, 911.
43 Dunn to Secretary, May 28, 1947, RG 84, 851–Italy, CF, NA.
44 *FRUS*, 1947, vol. 3, 912–14.
45 Dunn to Secretary, May 28, 1947, RG 84, 851–Italy, CF, NA.
46 Sforza and Scelba remained at foreign affairs and interior, respectively. Amintore Fanfani made his first appearance in the cabinet as minister of labor, and Giulio Andreotti emerged as under secretary to De Gasperi.
47 *FRUS*, 1947, vol. 3, 232.
48 *FRUS*, 1947, vol. 3, 235; Acheson, *Present at the Creation,* 232.
49 *FRUS*, 1947, vol. 3, 238–9.
50 *FRUS*, 1947, vol. 3, 920.
51 *FRUS*, 1947, vol. 3, 232–3; Acheson, *Present at the Creation,* 232–5.

9. THE DILEMMAS OF DEFLATION

1 De Cecco, "Economic Policy," 180.
2 De Cecco observes, "The propulsion generated by the Korean War should

have made clear to the Italian leaders the same Keynesian truth which the Second World War had opened before the eyes of Anglo-Saxon neo-classical die-hards. It certainly proved by sending production figures so high in so short a time, how much spare capacity there had been in the three years of squeeze and the spiteful comments the Italian authorities had reserved for foreign critics of their conduct appeared in all their vanity." "Economic Policy," 179.

3 George Hildebrand observes, "The theory of demand deficiency was designed for the depression phase of the standard Anglo-American business cycle, where it fits very well. . . . The Italian case of 1948–1949 does not fit this model, and that was what the stabilization of the currency was all about. The first discrepancy is that Italy is a nation extremely dependent on foreign trade – as much so as the United Kingdom. Two-thirds of its imports consist of food, fuel and raw materials, paid for traditionally by exports, emigrants' remittances, and tourist expenditures, aided at the time by U.S. grants in aid. If in 1948–49 output were to be increased at an even faster rate, money demand for output would have had to be expanded still more rapidly. Imports would have then promptly gone up to provide the needed complementary raw materials and fuels and to supply the increase in consumer demand. The shortage of internally available complementary goods was the heart of the production problem, as proponents of stabilization well knew. In other words, the working reserves of foreign exchange – then largely inconvertible sterling – were still too small to cover the risk to the balance of payments implicit in a policy of the Keynesian type." Hildebrand, *Growth and Structure in the Economy of Modern Italy* (Cambridge: Harvard University Press, 1965), 41–2.

4 Foa, *Monetary Reconstruction in Italy,* 104.

5 Ugo Ruffolo, "La linea Einaudi," *Storia Contemporanea,* 2 (December 1974): 651–6.

6 Gambino, *Storia del dopoguerra,* 365–6.

7 Foa, *Monetary Reconstruction in Italy,* 118.

8 Pietro Griffone, *Il capitale finanziario in italia* (Turin: Einaudi, 1971), 56–7.

9 Pietro Armani, "La scelta occidentale dell'italia," in Aga Rossi-Sitzia et al., *Italia e stati uniti,* 104–5.

10 Gambino, *Storia del dopoguerra,* 362–74. For a similar view, see Vittorio Foa, "Movimento operaio e ricostruzione," in *Italia 1945–1975.*

11 The shred of evidence used by Gambino is Marshall's May 20 message to the Rome embassy. Marshall, it will be recalled, cabled a list of six steps the department was prepared to take in order to support a new government. Point 5 ended with the passage, "US to urge Italian Government to take immediate effective steps to improve economic conditions." Gambino (he translates "US to urge . . ." as "pressioni degli stati uniti," or "US pressures") reaches the odd conclusion that, since the phrase appears as part of a program of support, such pressures must have been requested by the Italians themselves. Gambino, *Storia del dopoguerra,* 374. For text of Marshall message, see *FRUS,* 1947, vol. 3, 909.

12 On June 12, Einaudi told the embassy ". . . the present ministry is a political experiment in governing without the Marxists, and in view of the precarious voting strength which will support it, it needs the backing of the United States. . . . To get present government well-started and to demonstrate its ability to inspire confidence internally and abroad, he [Einaudi] made a strong appeal for quick extra aid from the United States, for instance, in form of an additional Exim Bank line of credit, sufficient to carry Italy into next year without completely exhausting its dollar resources," Dunn to Secretary, June 12, 1947, RG 59 865.50/6–1247, CF, NA.

13 Kolko, *Limits of Power*, 428.

14 For Clayton remark, see *FRUS*, 1947, vol. 3, 287.

15 Dunn to Secretary, June 17, 1947, *FRUS*, 1947, vol. 3, 922–3.

16 Truman's February 21, 1947, aid request was passed on May 31. On AUSA and proposed surplus property deal, see *FRUS*, 1947, vol. 3, 930–1, 934–41. For the text of the financial agreement, see Department of State *Bulletin*, August 24, 1947, 371–6. See also, Kamarck, 217–28. The United States did not waive its claim for the massive amounts of supplies and services requisitioned directly from firms and individuals at Italian government expense. The settlement also provided for the restoration of the position of U.S. property holders as of June 1940, and their compensation for war damage (in lire) at a rate of two-thirds of the original value, and the rescheduling of Italy's prewar dollar debts (largely the Morgan loans of 1926) amounting to about $136 million in unpaid principle and interest.

17 On Clayton visit, see *FRUS* 1947, vol. 3, 945–9. For Einaudi memo (mentioned but not printed in the *FRUS*), see Dunn to Secretary, July 25, 1947, RG 59, 865.50/7–2547, NA, "Enclosure 1."

18 For documentation, see *FRUS*, 1947, vol. 3, 43–93.

19 See Secretary to Embassy, August 27, 1947, *FRUS*, 1947, vol. 3, 957; memo of conversation between Tarchiani and Lovett, August 28, 1947, see *FRUS*, 1947, vol. 3, 957–62.

20 Embassy to Secretary, October 8, 1947, RG 84, 851–Italy, CF, NA. *FRUS*, 1947, vol. 3, 982.

21 *FRUS*, 1947, vol. 3, 919.

22 La Malfa quoted in Faenza and Fini, *Gli americani in italia*, 201; Gambino, *Storia del dopoguerra*, pp. 358–9, 423.

23 For September 4 message, see *FRUS*, 1947, vol. 3, "Editorial Note," 965.

24 For discussion of Tasca's plan, see Chapter 8.

25 For summary of De Gasperi's June 9 speech, see Dunn to Secretary, June 10, 1947, RG 59, 865.50/6–1047, NA. For Tasca's comments, see Dunn to Secretary, June 12, 1947, RG 84, no. 1520, 850–Italy, CF, NA; Dunn to Secretary, June 12, 1947, RG 84, no. 1513, 850–Italy, CF, NA.

26 Dunn to Secretary, June 12, 1947, RG 84, no. 1520, 850–Italy, CF, NA. For Del Vecchio's view of IRI and Italian industry, see Dunn to Secretary, June 17, 1947, RG 84, 850–Italy, CF, NA.

27 On price increases, see Daneo, *La politica economica della ricostruzione*, 233. For data on foreign exchange and stock market developments, see Foa, *Monetary Reconstruction in Italy*, 109–10.

28 For Tasca conversation with Del Vecchio, see Dunn to Secretary, June 20, 1947, RG 84, 851.2–Italy, CF, NA.

29 Dunn to Secretary, July 9, 1947, RG 84, 850–Italy–Marshall Plan, CF, NA.

30 Wool exporters were granted 75 percent outright. Cotton exporters were henceforth granted $1 for each kilo sold to free-exchange countries. This provision served, in effect, to place 70 percent to 75 percent of earned hard currency in their hands. For Del Vecchio and Einaudi views – as expressed to Tasca – of Merzagora policies, see Dunn to Secretary, September 5, 1947, RG 84, 851.51 Italy–Export–Import Foreign Exchange Regulations (EXFER), CF, NA; see also Dunn to Secretary, September 24, 1947, RG 84, 851–51 Italy/EXFER, CF, NA. For Tasca's own views, see Dunn to Secretary, August 15, 1947, RG 84, 851.51 Italy/EXFER, CF, NA. For State and Treasury Department orders to approach

the Italian government on the matter, see their joint cables to Tasca, numbers 1559 and 1560, both dated August 29, 1947, RG 84, 851.51 Italy/EXFER, CF, NA. Merzagora defended the preferential measures in a conversation with Tasca on September 4. Tasca was not convinced but persuaded the State and Treasury Departments to permit the Italian government to study the matter further. See Embassy to Secretary, September 4, 1947, RG 84, 851.51 Italy/EXFER, CF, NA.

31 Foa, *Monetary Reconstruction in Italy*, 107.

32 Embassy to Secretary, "Effects of Italian Government Credit Controls on Industry, Labor Unions, Etc.," October 2, 1947, RG 1947, 865.51/10–247, NA.

33 On creation of FIM, see Mariuccia Salvati, *Stato e industria nella ricostruzione*. (Milan: Feltrinelli, 1982), 354–72.

34 *Corriere della Sera*. December 9, 1947.

35 See *FRUS*, 1948, vol. 3, 825–7.

36 *FRUS*, vol. 3, pp. 973–5.

37 *FRUS*, 1947, vol. 3, 976–81, 983–5, 986–7, 989–91. For Truman statement of December 11, 1947, see 746.

38 For Kennan view, see *FRUS*, 1947, vol. 1, 771. On Togliatti speech, see *New York Times*, September 7, 1947; James Edward Miller, "Taking the Gloves Off: The United States and the Italian Elections of 1948," *Diplomatic History*, 6 (Winter 1983): 41.

39 *FRUS*, 1947, vol. 3, 976. See also Secretary to Rome Embassy, October 1, 1947, RG 84, 851 Italy/Gold., CF, NA.

40 *FRUS*, 1947, vol. 3, 988–9.

41 See Dunn to Secretary, November 1, 1947, RG 59, 865.51/10–3147, NA; Dunn to Secretary, November 7, 1947, RG 84, 851–Italy, NA; Dunn to Secre-Secretary, December 1, 1947, RG 84, 851.51–Italy, CF, NA.

42 *FRUS*, 1947, vol. 3, 994–7. Dunn to Secretary, November 1, 1947, RG 59, NA.

43 See Dunn to Secretary, October 15, 1947, RG 59, 865.5043/10–1547, NA. Baget-Bozzo, *Il partitio cristiano al potere*, Vol. I, 176–7. For unemployment figures and additional information on the "sblocco dei licenziamenti," see Rome Embassy Economic News Airgram, November 28, 1947, RG 59, 865.50/11–2847, NA.

44 The ASC met for the first time on September 9, 1947, and included representatives of State, Army, Navy, Commerce, Interior, Treasury, Agriculture, Federal Reserve, Budget Bureau, and the White House. For September 29 memo, see, *FRUS*, 1947, vol. 3, 470–7.

45 "Local Currency Proceeds of US Foreign Aid," by Tasca and Walmsley, transmitted to State Department, October 2, 1947, RG 59, 865.5151/8–3047, CF, NA.

46 Secretary to Rome Embassy, December 20, 1947, RG 59, 800.48 Foreign Assistance Act (FAA)/12–2047, CF, NA.

47 Embassy to Secretary, October 18, 1947, RG 59. 865.515/10–1847, CF, NA.

48 Embassy to Secretary, December 31, 1947, RG 59, 800.48, FAA/12–3147, CF, NA. This cable is very briefly – and somewhat inaccurately – summarized in *FRUS*, 1948, vol. 3, 825, footnote 2.

49 The U.S. campaign is documented in *FRUS*, 1948, vol. 3, 724–882. The most recent and thorough treatment of the subject is James Miller, "Taking the Gloves Off."

50 Embassy to Secretary, January 16, 1948, RG 84–Italy, CF, NA. Embassy

to Secretary, April 2, 1948, RG 84, 851–Italy, CF, NA. Embassy to Secretary, January 13, 1948, RG 84, 851–Italy, CF, NA.

51 Dunn to Secretary, January 28, 1948, RG 59, 865.6362/1–2848, CF, NA.

52 Embassy to Secretary, February 3, 1948, RG 59, 865.5151/2–348, CF, NA.

53 On January 29, Dunn advised the department that the embassy was taking steps to ensure the security of U.S. personnel in the case of a Communist uprising. On February 7, he warned, "There will be an aggressive, violent, well-organized campaign by the Communists and their fellow travellers, the PSI. Should prospects of their electoral success diminish further, there may well be a resort to force. In any event, throughout Italy, a vast emotional upheaval will take place in the next few months." *FRUS*, 1948, vol. 3, 824.

54 Dunn to Secretary, February 4, 1948, RG 59, 800.48, FAA/2–448, CF, NA.

55 *FRUS*, 1948, vol. 3, 825–7.

56 Secretary to Embassy, February 6, 1948, RG 59, 865.6362/1–2848, CF, NA.

57 See *FRUS*, 1948, vol. 3, 775–9.

58 For Marshall speech, see Department of State *Bulletin*, March 28, 1948, 422–5. The speech was delivered on March 19. On the immigration ban, see Department to Secretary, March 24, 1948, RG 84, tel. no. 812, CF, NA.

59 Dunn to Secretary, February 21, 1948, RG 59, 800.48, FAA/2–2148, CF, NA.

60 The article by Luigi Federici appeared on the January 1948 issue of the Banca Nazionale del Lavoro *Quarterly Review*. See Embassy to Secretary, March 15, 1948, RG 84, 851–Italy, CF, NA. Henry Tasca to Representative Herter via Frank Lindsay, Herter's Italian specialist, March 17, 1948, RG 59, Records of the Office of Western European Affairs, Italy File, 1948, NA.

61 Embassy to Secretary, March 27, 1948, RG 59, 800.48, FAA/3–2748, CF, NA.

62 Secretary to Embassy, April 3, 1948, RG 59, 800.48, FAA/3–2748, CF, NA.

63 On the radio broadcasts from Hollywood, see *FRUS*, 1948, vol. 3, 875. For a summary of the pre-electoral measures – military, economic, and propaganda – taken by the United States, see embassy cable of June 16, 1948, *FRUS*, 1948, vol. 3, 879–82.

64 *FRUS*, 1948, vol. 3, 793–4.

65 Tasca letter, March 17, 1948, RG 59, NA.

66 The eminent Catholic economist Pasquale Sarceno is properly skeptical of the liberals' basic design to recast the Italian economy and deeply critical of their refusal to use available controls during the 1945–47 period. He acknowledges, however, that given the situation prevailing in mid-1947, Einaudi and his colleagues had no choice but to proceed as they did, despite resistance of both local Italian forces and American officials. See *Intervista*, 115–18. It also seems safe to presume that had he been alive at the time, Pietro Grifone would have had no difficulty in grasping the logic of Einaudi's effort to balance the budget and foreign accounts.

10. CONCLUSION: THE MARSHALL PLAN AND AFTER

1 See Kennan, *Memoirs, 1925–50,* Chapter 17, "The North Atlantic Alliance."

2 ACS, Segreteria Particolare Presidenza del Consiglio, De Gasperi, fasc. 21, busta 62.

3 The fifth De Gasperi government was formed May 23, 1948. In addition to De Gasperi, the key ministers included Saragat, vice-premier; Sforza, foreign minister; Scelba, interior; Pacciardi, defense; Vanoni, finance; Pella, budget; Lombardo, industry and commerce; and Fanfani, labor and social services.

4 See Pier Paolo D'Attore, "The ERP in Italy. Problems of Research," draft copy courtesy of the author. See also Salvati, *Stato e industria nella ricostruzione*, Part III.

5 D'Attore, "The ERP in Italy."

6 Embassy to Secretary, May 12, 1948, RG 84, 851–Italy, CF, NA.

7 NAC Staff Document, no. 232, May 28, 1948, RG 286, Records of the Agency for International Development, Box 166, S–2, Local Currency, NA.

8 Foa, *Monetary Reconstruction in Italy, 126.*

9 Saraceno, *Intervista,* Chapter 6. On the limited influence of Keynes in Italy, see Piero Bolchini, "La Fortuna di Keynes in italia (1930–50)," *Miscellanea storica ligure* 1 (1982): 37–72. Also, Paolo Baffi, "Via nazionale e gli economisti stranieri, 1944–53," 1–50, draft article, 1983, copy courtesy of the author.

10 Byington, charge, to Secretary, August 11, 1948, RG 59, 865.516/8–1148, CF, NA.

11 According to the embassy, Pella had assured the United States "he would fight the battle and irrespective of any personal sacrifice involved would not yield." Embassy to Secretary July 9, 1948, RG 84, 851–51–Italy, CF, NA. On Italian policy, see Daneo, *La politica economica della ricostruzione*, 256–8; Milward, *The Reconstruction of Western Europe,* 197–8.

12 ECA, *Italy Country Study* (Washington, D.C.: Government Printing Office, 1949), 21, 46.

13 Charles Maier, "The Politics of Productivity: Foundations of American International Economic Policy after World War II," 31 *International Organization,* (1977): 607–34.

14 Quoted in Ruffolo, "La Linea Einaudi," 666.

15 CIA report cited in James Edward Miller, "Chaos or Christian Democracy: The ERP as a Factor in Italy's 1948 Elections," (paper delivered to conference, The Marshall Plan and Europe, Rome, May 28, 1980), 13. See memo Conversation between Acheson and Tarchiani, December 5, 1949, RG 59, 865.52/12–549, NA.

16 On CIA operation, 1953–58, see William Colby, *Honorable Men: My Life in the CIA* (New York: Simon & Schuster, 1978), Chapter 5. Colby was station chief in Rome and directly responsible for the program.

17 See Guido Carli, *Intervista sul capitalismo italiano* (Bari: Laterza, 1977), Chapters 3, 4.

18 See Alan Platt and Robert Leonardi, "American Foreign Policy and the Postwar Italian Left," *Political Science Quarterly,* 93 (Summer 1978): 211–12.

19 Luigi Barzini, "Italy's *Own* Elections," *New York Times,* May 22, 1979. See also Rome embassy mimeograph, "The Strategy of Cooperation, A Progress Report," January 1980.

20 For Stone's June 1945 proposals, see *FRUS, Conference of Berlin,* vol. 1, 688–94.

Bibliography

ARCHIVES

Archivio Centrale dello Stato, Rome
   Carte della Delegazione Tecnica Italiana (Italian Purchasing Mission) in
      Washington, D.C.
   Carte Ugo La Malfa
   Segreteria Particolare Presidenza del Consiglio, De Gasperi, 1945–49.
   Presidenza del Consiglio Gabinetto, 1945–49
Banca d'Italia, Rome
   Archivio Paolo Baffi
Franklin D. Roosevelt Library, Hyde Park, N.Y.
   The Henry Morgenthau, Jr., Diary
Harry S. Truman Library, Independence, Mo.
   The John Snyder Papers
National Archives, Washington, D.C.
   Record Group 59, Records of the Department of State
   Record Group 84, Rome Post Files
   Record Group 169, Records of the Foreign Economic Administration
   Record Group 286, Records of the Agency for International Development
   Record Group 331, Records of the Allied Control Commission, Italy, Allied
      Operational and Occupation Headquarters, World War II
   Record Group 407, Records of the Adjutant General, Foreign Occupied
      Area Reports
United Nations Archives, New York, N.Y.
   Record Group 17, Records of the United Nations Relief and Rehabilitation
      Administration, Italy Mission, 1944–1947.

PUBLISHED DOCUMENTS AND REPORTS

Banca d'Italia. *Adunanza Generale Ordinaria dei Partecipanti.* Rome: Tipografia
   della Banca d'Italia, 1944, 1945, 1946, 1947, 1948.
Coles, H., and Weinberg, A., eds. *Civil Affairs: Soldiers Become Governors.* In
   Special Studies of the US Army in World War II. Washington, D.C.: Government Printing Office, 1964.

Bibliography

Commissione Economica dell'Assemblea Costituente. *Rapporto Economico, Industria*, Part II. Rome, 1946.
Rapporto Economico, Problemi monetari e commercio estero, Part III. Rome, 1946.
Dobney, Frank J., ed. *The Selected Papers of Will Clayton*. Baltimore: The Johns Hopkins University Press, 1971.
Economic Cooperation Administration. *Italy Country Study*. Washington, D.C.: Government Printing Office, 1949.
Export–Import Bank. *Semi–Annual Report*. 1945, 1946, 1947, 1948.
United States Department of State. *Bulletin*. 1944, 1945, 1946, 1947, 1948.
Foreign Relations of the United States. 1943, 1944, 1945, 1946, 1947, 1948, 1949.
United States Department of the Treasury, *Census of US Assets Abroad*. Washington, D.C.: Government Printing Office, 1947.
United States House of Representatives, *Foreign Assistance Program, Historical Series*, Part I. Washington, D.C.: Government Printing Office, 1976.
United States Tariff Commission, *Italian Commercial Policy and Foreign Trade*. Washington, D.C.: Government Printing Office, 1941.
UNRRA. *Survey of Italy's Economy*. Rome, 1947.

FREQUENTLY USED PERIODICALS

Business Week. 1945, 1946, 1947, 1948.
Corriere della Sera. 1945, 1946, 1947, 1948.
Cotton Trade Journal, International Edition. 1945, 1946, 1947.
Fortune. 1945, 1946, 1947, 1948.
Notiziario della Confindustria. 1945, 1946, 1947, 1948.
Rinascita. 1945, 1946, 1947, 1948.
New York Times. 1945, 1946, 1947, 1948.
L'Unità. 1945, 1946, 1947, 1948.
UNRRA. *Economic Notes*. 1946–1947.

ARTICLES AND PAPERS

Aga Rossi-Sitzia, Elena. "La situazione economica e politica dell'italia nel periodo 1944–1945: i governi Bonomi." *Quaderni del istituto romano per la storia d'italia dal fascismo alla resistenza* 2 (1971): 5–60.
Amendola, Giorgio. "Riflessioni su un esperienza di governo del PCI (1944–1947)." *Storia Contemporanea* 5 (December, 1974): 701–736.
Baffi, Paolo. "Monetary Developments in Italy from the War Economy to Limited Convertibility (1935–1958)," *Banca Nazionale del Lavoro Quarterly Review*, 12 (December 1958): 401–35.
"Via Nazionale e gli economisti stranieri, 1944–53." (Draft article, courtesy of the author, 1983): 1–50.
Bolchini, Piero. "La fortuna di Keynes in italia (1930–50)." *Miscellanea storica ligure* 1 (1982): 37–72.
Cafagna, L., Caffè, F., Quazza, G., Salvati, M. "Interventi su 'Stato e industria nella ricostruzione.'" *Italia Contemporanea* 150 (March 1983): 73–88.

Articles and papers

Cattani, Leone. "Dalla caduta del fascismo al primo governo De Gasperi." *Storia Contemporanea* 5 (December 1974): 737–85.

Damascelli, Ester Fano. "La 'restaurazione anti-fascista liberista,' ristagno e sviluppo durante il fascismo." *Il movimento di liberazione in italia* 103 (July–September, 1971): 47–99.

Di Nolfo, Ennio. "Il Piano Marshall e la guerra fredda." Paper delivered to the conference, "The Marshall Plan and Europe," Rome, May 28, 1980.

"Problemi della politica estera italiana, 1943–50." *Storia e Politica* 1, 2 (January–June 1975): 296–317.

"The US and Italian Communism, 1942–1946, World War II to the Cold War." *Journal of Italian History* 1 (Spring 1978): 79–94.

Ellwood, David. "Ricostruzione, classe operaie e occupazione alleate in Piemonte 1943–1946" *Rivista di Storia Contemporanea* 3 (July 1974): 289–325.

"The Marshall Plan and the Process of Modernization in Italy." Paper delivered to the conference, "The Marshall Plan and Europe," Rome, May 28, 1980.

Foa, Vittorio. "La restaurazione capitalistica nel secondo dopo-guerra." *Rivista di Storia Contemporanea* 4 (October 1973): 433–55.

Gallerano, Nicola. "L'influenza dell'amministrazione militare alleata sulla ricostruzione dello stato italiano (1943–1945)." *Italia Contemporanea* 115 (April–June, 1974): 4–21.

Hirschman, Albert. "Inflation and Deflation in Italy." *American Economic Review,* 38 (April 1948): 598–606.

Legnani, Massimo. "Restaurazione padronale e lotta politica in italia, 1945–1948." *Rivista di Storia Contemporanea* 1 (January 1974): 1–27.

Maier, Charles. "Italy and the Marshall Plan." Paper delivered to the conference, "The Marshall Plan and Europe," Rome, May 28, 1980.

"The Politics of Productivity: Foundations of American International Economic Policy after World War II." *International Organization* 31 (Fall 1977): 607–34.

Miller, James Edward. "Carlo Sforza e l'evoluzione della politica americana verso l'italia, 1940–1943." *Storia Contemporanea* 7 (December 1976): 825–53.

"Chaos or Christian Democracy: The ERP as a Factor in Italy's 1948 Election." Paper delivered to the conference, "The Marshall Plan and Europe," Rome, May 28, 1980.

"The Politics of Relief: Italian Americans, the Roosevelt Administration, and the Reconstruction of Italy, 1943–44" *Prologue* 1 (Spring 1981): 54–75.

"Taking the Gloves Off: The United States and the Italian Elections of 1948." *Diplomatic History* 6 (Winter 1983): 35–55.

Moscati, Ruggero. "Nota sulla 'svolta' del giugno, 1947." *Storia Contemporanea* 5 (December 1974): 569–90.

Parri, Ferruccio. "La caduta del governo Parri." *Astrolabio* (January 1972): 57–61.

"La politica economica del CLNAI." *Il movimento di liberazione in italia* 48 (July–September 1957): 42–51.

Pelaja, Margherita. "L'industria di stato nel dibattito del secondo dopoguerra: il caso del'IRI." *Italia Contemporanea* 124 (July–September 1976): 49–76.

Piscitelli, Enzo. "Del cambio o meglio del mancato cambio della moneta nel secondo dopoguerra." *Quaderni del istituto romano per la storia d'italia dal fascismo alla resistenza* 1 (1969): 3–89.

Bibliography

Platt, Alan, and Leonardi, Robert. "American Foreign Policy and the Postwar Italian Left." *Political Science Quarterly* 93 (Summer 1978): 197–216.

Profumieri, Paolo. "Capital and Labor in Italy, 1929–1940, An Economic Interpretation." *Journal of European Economic History* 1 (Winter 1972): 680–702.

Ruffolo, Ugo. "La linea Einaudi," *Storia Contemporanea* 5 (December 1974): 637–70.

Sarti, Roland. "Mussolini and the Italian Industrial Leadership in the Battle for the Lira." *Past and Present* 34 (May 1970): 75–106.

Serfaty, Simon. "An International Anomaly: The United States and the Communist Parties in France and Italy." *Studies in Comparative Communism* 8 (Spring/Summer 1975): 123–46.

Spini, Valdo. "Il discorso sull'economia e le scelte politiche (1945–1947)." *Il Ponte* 11, 12 (November–December 1975): 1279–1327.

Sullo, Franco. "Il dibattito politico sulla programmazione economica in italia dal 1945 al 1960." *Economia e Storia* 3 (1960): 382–413.

BOOKS AND DISSERTATIONS

Acheson, Dean. *Present at the Creation.* New York: Norton, 1969.

Acquarone, A., and Vernassa, M. *Il Regime fascista.* Bologna: Il Mulino, 1974.

Aga Rossi-Sitzia, Elena, ed. *Italia e stati uniti durante l'amministrazione Truman.* Padua: Franco Angeli, 1972.

Andreotti, Giulio. *Intervista su De Gasperi.* Bari: Laterza, 1977.

Are, Giuseppe. *Industria e politica in italia.* Bari: Laterza, 1975.

Baffi, Paolo. *Studi sulla moneta.* Milan: Giuffre, 1965.

Baget-Bozzo, Gianni, Il partito cristiano al potere. Vol. I, *La DC di De Gasperi e di Dossetti, 1945–1954.* Florence: Vallechi, 1974.

Bairati, Piero. *Valletta.* Turin: UTET, 1983.

Balloni, Valeriano, ed. *Lezioni sulla politica economica in italia.* Milan: Edizioni di Communità, 1972.

Barca, Luciano, ed. *I comunisti e l'economia italiana, 1944–1974.* Bari: De Donato, 1975.

Blackmer, Donald L. M., and Tarrow, Sidney, eds., *Communism in Italy and France.* Princeton: Princeton University Press, 1975.

Bocca, Giorgio. *Palmiro Togliatti.* Bari: Laterza, 1973.

Bohlen, Charles. *Witness to History.* New York: Norton, 1973.

Borgatta, Gino, ed. *Ricostruzione dell'economia nel dopoguerra.* Pisa: CEDAM, 1942.

Byrnes, James. *Speaking Frankly.* London: William Heineman, Ltd., 1948.

Calleo, David, and Rowland, Benjamin. *America and the World Political Economy.* Bloomington: Indiana University Press, 1971.

Carli, Guido. *Intervista sul capitalismo italiano.* Bari: Laterza, 1977.

Castronovo, Valerio. *Giovanni Agnelli.* Turin: UTET, 1972.

Catalano, Franco, *L'italia dalla dittatura alla democrazia, 1919–48.* Milan: Feltrinelli, 1970.

Storia del CLNAI. Milan: Bompiani, 1975.

Clough, Shepard. *An Economic History of Modern Italy.* New York: Columbia University Press, 1964.

Books and dissertations

Colby, William. *Honorable Men, My Life in the CIA.* New York: Simon & Schuster, 1978.

Coles, Flourney. "The Postwar Italian Economy and Foreign Trade." Ph.D. diss., University of Pennsylvania, 1949.

Corbino, Epicarmo. *Discorsi elettorali e interventi parlamentari dal 1944 al 1958.* Naples: Istituto Editoriale del Mezzogiorno, 1965.

Costa, Angelo. *Scritti e discorsi.* Turin, UTET, 1980.

Dana, Julian. *AP Giannini: Giant of the West.* New York: Prentice-Hall, 1947.

Daneo, Camillo. *La politica economica della ricostruzione, 1945–1949.* Turin: Einaudi, 1975.

De Cecco, Marcello. *Saggi di politica monetaria.* Milan: Giuffre, 1968.

De Gasperi, Maria Romana, ed. *De Gasperi scrive.* Brescia: Morcelliana, 1974.

De Luna, Giovanni. *Il partito d'azione.* Milan: Feltrinelli, 1982.

Demaria, Giovanni. *Problemi economici e sociali del dopoguerra, 1945–1950.* Milan: Malfasi, 1951.

De Santis, Hugh. *The Diplomacy of Silence.* Chicago: University of Chicago Press, 1979.

Diggins, John. *Mussolini and Fascism, the View from America.* Princeton: Princeton University Press, 1972.

Di Nolfo, Ennio. *Stati Uniti e Vaticano, 1939–1952.* Milan: Angelli, 1978.

Edelman, Eric. "Incremental Involvement: Italy and US Foreign Policy, 1943–48." Ph.D. diss., Yale University, 1981.

Einaudi, Luigi. *Lezioni di politica sociale.* Turin: Einaudi, 1967.

Ellwood, David. *L'alleato nemico, la politica dell'occupazione anglo-americana in italia, 1943–1946.* Milan: Feltrinelli, 1977.

Faenza, Roberto, and Fini, Marco. *Gli americani in italia.* Milan: Feltrinelli, 1976.

Felice, Renzo de. *Le interpretazioni del fascismo.* Bari: Laterza, 1969.

Felice, Renzo de., ed. *L'italia fra tedeschi e alleati, la politica estera fascista e la seconda guerra mondiale.* Bologna: Il Mulino, 1973.

Fini, Marco, ed. *Italia, 1945–1975: fascismo, anti-fascismo, resistenza, rinnovamento.* Milan: Feltrinelli, 1975.

Foa, Bruno. *Monetary Reconstruction in Italy.* New York: King's Crown Press, 1948.

Gaddis, John Lewis. *The United States and the Origins of the Cold War, 1941–1947.* New York: Columbia University Press, 1971.

Gambino, Antonio. *Storia del dopoguerra dalla liberazione al potere DC.* Bari: Laterza, 1975.

Gardner, Lloyd. *The Architects of Illusion.* Chicago: Quadrangle Books, 1970.

Gimbel, John. *The Origins of the Marshall Plan.* Stanford, Calif.: Stanford University Press, 1976.

Giovagnoli, Agostino. *Le premesse della ricostruzione, tradizione e modernità nella classe dirigente cattolica del dopoguerra.* Milano: Nuovo Istituto Editoriale Italiano, 1982.

Grassi, Gaetano, ed. *"Verso il governo del popolo," atti e documenti del CLNAI, 1943–1946.* Milan: Feltrinelli, 1977.

Graziani, Antonio, ed. *L'economia italiana, 1945–1970.* Bologna: Il Mulino, 1972.

Grifone, Pietro. *Il capitale finanziario in italia.* Turin: Einaudi, 1971.

Gualerni, Gualberto. *Ricostruzione e industria (1943–51).* Milan: Vita e Pensiero, 1980.

Bibliography

Harper, John L. "The United States and the Italian Economy, 1945–48." Ph.D. diss., Johns Hopkins University, 1981.

Harriman, Averell. *European Recovery and American Aid*. Washington, D.C.: Government Printing Office, 1947.

Harris, C. R. S. *Allied Military Administration of Italy, 1943–45*. London: HMSO, 1957.

Hildebrand, George. *Growth and Structure in the Economy of Modern Italy*. Cambridge: Harvard University Press, 1965.

Holbik, Karel. *Italy in International Cooperation*. Padua: CEDAM, 1959.

James, Marquis. *Biography of a Bank: The Story of The Bank of America*. New York: Harper Bros., 1954.

Jones, Joseph. *The Fifteen Weeks*. New York: Harcourt, Brace, World, 1964.

Kamarck, Andrew. "Allied Financial Policy in Italy." Ph.D. diss., Harvard University, 1951.

Kennan, George. *Memoirs: 1925–1950*. Boston: Little, Brown & Co., 1957.

Kogan, Norman. *Italy and the Allies*. Cambridge: Harvard University Press, 1956.

Kolko, Gabriel. *The Politics of War*. London: Widenfield & Nicholson, 1969. *The Limits of Power*. New York: Harper & Row, 1972.

Krock, Arthur. *Memoirs, Sixty Years on the Firing Line*. New York: Funk and Wagnalls, 1968.

La Malfa, Ugo. *La politica economica italiana, 1946–1962*. Milan: Edizioni di Communità, 1962.

Luperini, Romano. *Gli intellettuali di sinistra e l'ideologia della ricostruzione nel dopoguerra*. Rome: Edizioni di Ideologia, 1971.

Lutz, Friedrich A., and Lutz, Vera C. *Monetary and Foreign Exchange Policy in Italy*. Princeton: Princeton University Press, 1950.

Mack-Smith, Denis. *Mussolini's Roman Empire*. New York: Viking, 1976.

Mammarella, Giuseppe. *L'italia dopo il fascismo*. Bologna: Il Mulino, 1970.

Manzocchi, Bruzio. *Lineamenti di politica economica in italia, 1945–1959*. Rome: Editori Riuniti, 1960.

Markowitz, Norman. *The Rise and Fall of the People's Century*. New York: Free Press, 1973.

Mason, Edward. *Controlling World Trade, Cartels and Commodity Agreements*. New York: Arno Press, 1946.

May, Ernest. *"Lessons" of the Past. The Use and Abuse of History in American Foreign Policy*. New York: Oxford University Press, 1975.

Migone, Gian Giacomo, ed. *Problemi di storia nei rapporti tra italia e stati uniti*. Turin: Rosenberg e Sellier, 1971. *Gli stati uniti e il fascismo*. Milan: Feltrinelli, 1980.

Milward, Alan. *The Reconstruction of Western Europe, 1945–51*. Berkeley: University of California, 1984.

Morandi, Rodolfo. *Storia della grande industria in italia*. Turin: Einaudi, 1966.

Ortona, Egidio. *Anni d'america, La ricostruzione, 1945–51*. Bologna: Il Mulino, 1984.

Pallotta, Gino. *La costituente repubblicana, l'età verde della democrazia*. Turin: Societa Editrice Internazionale, 1976.

Pesenti, Antonio. *Ricostruire dalle rovine*. Milan: Picardi, 1946. *La cattedra e il bugliolo*. Milan: La Pietra, 1972.

Petrov, Vladimir. *Money and Conquest: Allied Occupation Currencies in World War II*. Baltimore: The Johns Hopkins University Press, 1972.

Books and dissertations

Quazza, Guido, ed. *Italia, 1945–1948, le origine della repubblica*. Turin: Giappichelli, 1974.

L'italia dalla liberazione alla repubblica. Milan: Feltrinelli, 1976.

Reitzel, William. *The Mediterranean, Its Role in American Foreign Policy*. New York: Harcourt, Brace, World, 1948.

Romeo, Rosario. *Risorgimento e capitalismo*. Bari: Laterza, 1959.

Breve storia della grande industria in italia. Bologna: Cappelli, 1972.

Rossi, Ernesto. *Lo stato industriale*. Bari: Laterza, 1953.

Rostow, Walt W. *The United States in the World Arena*. New York: Harper Brothers, 1960.

Salvati, Mariuccia. *Stato e industria nella ricostruzione, alle origini del potere democristiano (1944–49)*. Milan: Feltrinelli, 1982.

Salvemini, Gaetano, and La Piana, Giorgio. *What To Do with Italy*. New York: Duell, Sloan, and Pearce, 1943.

Sampson, Anthony. *The Sovereign State: The Secret History of IT&T*. London: Hodder and Stoughton, 1973.

Saraceno, Pasquale. *Ricostruzione e pianificazione, 1943–1948*, edited by Piero Barucci. Bari: Laterza, 1969.

Intervista sulla ricostruzione. Bari: Laterza, 1977.

Sarti, Roland. *Fascism and the Industrial Leadership in Italy*. Berkeley: University of California Press, 1971.

Schlesinger, Arthur M., Jr. *The Age of Roosevelt*, Vol. II. Boston: Houghton Mifflin, 1957.

Schurmann, Franz. *The Logic of World Power*. New York: Pantheon, 1974.

Scoccimarro, Mauro. *Il secondo dopoguerra*. Rome: Editori Riuniti, 1956.

Scoppola, Pietro. *La proposta politica di De Gasperi*. Bologna: Il Mulino, 1977.

Solari, Paolo, ed. *Liberismo e liberalismo*. Milan: R. Ricciardi, 1957.

Southard, Frank. *The Finances of European Liberation*. New York: King's Crown Press, 1946.

Spini, Giorgio, ed. *Italia e america dalla grande guerra a oggi*. Venice: Marsilio, 1976.

Spriano, Paolo. *Storia del Partito Comunista Italiano*. Turin: Einaudi, 1967–1975.

Stuart, Graham. *The Department of State*. New York: Macmillan, 1949.

Tarchiani, Alberto. *America-Italia: le dieci giornate di De Gasperi negli stati uniti*. Milan: Rizzoli, 1947.

Dieci anni tra Roma e Washington. Rome: Mondadori, 1955.

Toscano, Mario. *Dal 25 luglio all 8 settembre*. Florence: Le Monnier, 1966.

Valiani, Leo. *L'avvento di De Gasperi*. Turin: F. di Silva, 1949.

Varsori, Antonio. *Gli Alleati e l'emigrazione democratica antifascista 1940–1943*. Florence: Sansoni Editori, 1982.

Villari, Lucio. *Il capitalismo italiano del novecento*. Bari: Laterza, 1972.

Webster, Richard A. *Industrial Imperialism in Italy, 1908–1915*. Berkeley: University of California Press, 1975.

Weil, Martin. *A Pretty Good Club: The Founding Fathers of the US Foreign Service*. New York: Norton, 1978.

Welles, Sumner. *The Time for Decision*. Cleveland: World Publishing Co., 1945.

Westerfield, H. Bradford. *Foreign Policy and Party Politics, Pearl Harbor to Korea*. New Haven: Yale University Press, 1955.

Wheeler-Bennet, J., and Nicholl, A. *The Semblance of Peace, The Political Settlement after the Second World War*. London: St. Martin's Press, 1972.

Bibliography

Woodbridge, George. *UNRRA, the History of the United Nations Relief and Rehabilitation Administration.* New York: Columbia University Press, 1950.

Woodward, Sir Everett Llewellyn. *British Foreign Policy in the Second World War.* Vols. II, III. London: HMSO, 1970.

Woolf, S. J., ed. *The Rebirth of Italy.* New York: Humanities Press, 1972.

Yergin, Daniel. *The Shattered Peace, the Origins of the Cold War and the National Security State.* Boston: Houghton Mifflin, 1977.

Index

Acheson, Dean, 15, 17, 33, 77, 119, 120–1, 127, 130, 135, 171 n33; on Italian situation, 29, 42, 110, 123, 131, 164
Action Party (Pd'A), 9, 23, 29, 30, 37, 38, 50, 56, 59, 116, 131, 144
Aggradi, Mario Ferrari, 164
Agnelli, Giovanni, 9, 43, 69
agriculture, Italian, 1, 25–6, 39, 67, 74, 137, 156, 163; land reform, 9–10, 29, 164
aid, American, 25, 27, 28–30, 32, 34, 35, 38, 62–3, 66, 69, 92; credits, 27–31, 33, 44, 47, 50, 61; interim aid, 150–7; lend lease, 31–2, 41, 47; see also European Recovery Program
Alexander, General Sir Harold, 23, 38
Allied Control Commission/Allied Commission (ACC/AC), 11, 15, 38, 44, 45–6, 48–56, 60, 68, 71, 74, 79, 109; economic section of, 11, 26, 33, 39, 42–3, 50, 142–3; 1944 reorganization of, 23–7
Allied Financial Agency (AFA), 25, 32
Allied Force Headquarters (AFHQ), 23, 25, 28, 50–1, 53, 61–2
Allied policy, 2, 22–3, 26, 28, 30, 32, 37, 39, 41–3, 53, 56, 60–1, 68, 102, 148; invasion, 5, 22, 25–6; occupation, 2, 4–5, 15–16, 22–3, 25–6, 28, 35, 38, 42, 44, 50, 77, 81, 83, 88, 127, 159; see also Allied Control Commission (ACC)
Anderson, Clayton, and Company, 7, 46, 47, 48
Andreotti, Giulio, 55, 161
Ansaldo Company, 66
Antonini, Luigi, 63
Argentina, 122, 150
Armistice of 1943, 22–5, 28, 30, 35–6, 52, 69
autarchy, 3, 5, 8, 40, 65, 67
Automated Electric Company of Chicago, 70–1, 86–7

Badoglio, Marshall Pietro, 23, 38
Baffi, Paolo, 49, 88, 122, 165
Banca Commerciale Italiana, 29
Bank of Italy, 2, 29, 30, 32, 101, 103, 108, 114, 122–3, 134, 161, 164; and 1947 stabilization, 145, 147, 154; view of currency conversion, 49, 53, 55, 60, 89
banking, Italian, 3, 8, 11, 25, 29, 31, 34, 44, 64, 69, 73, 88–9, 95–6, 122, 129, 138, 144
Barucci, Piero, 4
Barzini, Luigi, 166
Bertone, Giovanni Battista, 103
Bevin, Ernest, 143
Blum, Leon, 81
Bohlen, Charles, 13, 14
Bonomi, Ivanoe, 27–8, 30, 35, 55
Braden, Spruille, 41
Bresciani Turroni, Costantino, 6, 50, 162
Bretton Woods Agreements, 31, 62
British Overseas Airways Corporation (BOAC), 84–5
Brosio, Manlio, 49, 57
Bureau of Economic Warfare (BEW), 11
Byrnes, James, 17, 38, 41–2, 76–7, 99, 119; and Italian policy, 57, 79, 80, 102, 112–15

Campilli, Pietro, 92, 98, 103, 114, 117, 124, 131, 133
Carli, Guido, 95, 114, 143, 165
Cattani, Leone, 56
Central Intelligence Agency (CIA), 164
Cevelotto, Mario, 71–2, 83–4
Christian Democratic Party (DC), 4–5, 12, 23, 30, 50, 59, 73, 100, 102, 103, 107, 116–18, 143, 166; economic policy of, 10, 20, 38, 90, 92, 131–4, 139, 141, 144–5, 150, 152–3, 156–8, U.S. policy toward, 21, 34, 105, 160–5
Churchill, Winston, 12, 23–4, 76–7
Cigliana, Giuseppe, 123

Index

Clayton, William, 7, 11, 16–17, 42, 75, 119–21, 134–5, 141, 178 n17, 190 n14; and Italian textile industry, 44–7; and U.S. aid to Italy, 29, 31–2, 36, 40–1, 47, 50, 52, 55–7, 62, 64–5, 67–8, 74, 78–80, 82, 85, 87, 90–1, 107, 110–15, 129–30, 142–3, 155

Cleveland, Harlan, 11, 39, 43, 74, 78–9, 90–4, 96, 111, 115

coal, postwar problem of, 1, 26, 42, 45, 94, 114, 126

Collado, Emilio, 85

Colombo, Emilio, 161

Colt de Wolf, Francis, 70

Combined Chiefs of Staff (CCS), 23, 33, 50–5, 62, 72, 83–4

Combined Civil Affairs Committee (CCAC), 23, 33, 72

Combined Liberated Areas Committee (CLAC), 27

Commerce Department, U.S., 16, 40

Committee of National Liberation (CLN), 9–10, 22, 30, 36–7, 57; see also resistance, North Italian Committee of National Liberation

Communist Party, Italian (PCI), 10, 12, 18, 21, 37, 39, 45, 50, 55–6, 59, 73, 91, 95, 102, 119, 144–5, 148–50; economic policy of, 9, 19, 43, 49, 65, 88–90, 99–101, 103, 117; U.S. policy toward, 61, 63, 73, 109–12, 116, 119, 124–32, 153, 155, 157, 159, 163, 166

Confindustria (General Confederation of Italian Industry), 12, 29, 59, 65, 100, 112, 122, 124, 129, 138, 149, 150, 164

Congress, U.S., 14, 17, 33; House Appropriations Committee, 35, 41, 81, 101; Joint Budget Committee, 120; view of Italy, 31–2, 42, 57, 74, 78, 80–3, 92, 104, 109, 110–12, 116, 120, 130, 135–6, 141–2, 151–3, 157, 159

Constituent Assembly, 5, 23, 56–7, 73, 75, 100, 116, 122, 127, 139, 148

controls: exchange, 2, 8, 18, 31, 40, 47, 50, 62, 74, 77, 89, 95, 96, 165; financial, 11, 18, 20, 34, 35; price, 2, 24, 95, 129

Corbino, Epicarmo: policies of, 6, 9, 20, 49, 59, 60–2, 64, 68, 72–3, 75, 87–91, 95–7, 99, 100–2, 107; relations with the U.S., 60–2, 64, 68, 72–3, 75, 87–91, 95–7, 99–103, 107; resignation of, 90–1, 100–1

Costa, Angelo, 65, 128, 138

Council of Foreign Ministers (CFM), 17, 79, 80, 100, 112, 118, 121

Cox, Oscar, 31, 32, 78

Crosby, Bing, 156

Crowley, Leo, 31, 41

Cuccia, Enrico, 29

currency, Italian, 24–5, 28, 29, 30, 32, 33, 35, 48–9, 52, 60, 101; Italian agreement with AC; 51–5, 60, 61; Allied Military (AMlire), 25–30, 35, 48,

51–3, 55, 60, 61; conversion of (cambio della moneta), 19, 48–9, 51–6, 60–1, 88–90, 95, 100; stability of, 139, 141–3, 146, 150–1, 154, 156, 158

Davies, Joseph, 14, 15

De Cecco, Marcello, 96, 137

De Gasperi, Alcide, 10, 20–1, 30–1, 37–8, 52, 55–7, 59–60, 68–9, 71, 73, 90, 96, 99–103, 123, 138–9, 145, 149, 150, 153, 154, 156, 161–3, 165, 182 n39, 188 n35, 191 n28; January 1947 visit to the U.S., 105–117; and May 1947 crisis, 118–134, 144

Deltec (Italian technical delegation), 31, 83

Del Vecchio, Gustavo, 6, 134, 145–6, 149, 153

Demaria, Giovanni, 5, 6, 8, 9, 12, 50, 64

Democracy of Labor Party (DL), 71, 116, 131

De Nicola, Enrico, 131

Dowling, Walter (Red), 109–10, 112

Dulles, Allen, 37

Dunn, James Clement, 13, 17, 114, 117, 124–28, 133, 135, 149–50, 152, 153–5, 164, 193 n18

Durbrow, Elbridge, 13, 17, 85

Eccles, Marriner, 80, 81

Economic Cooperation Administration (ECA), 140, 159, 162–4

economy, Italian: 1947 stabilization of, 126, 129, 130, 137–8, 141–8; postwar reconstruction problem, 1–4, 25–7, 42–8, 88–90, 121–5, 128–30; state control of, 3, 9, 11, 18–20, 34, 41, 43; see also currency, exchange rates, foreign exchange, industry, inflation, Instituto per la Ricostruzione Industriale (IRI), trade

Edison Electric, 163

Einaudi, Luigi, 6, 40, 49, 50, 51, 62, 64, 70, 83, 96, 103, 122, 123, 134, 136, 137, 138, 140, 144, 145, 147, 148, 153, 155, 161, 162, 163, 165, 170 n13, 195 n12, 198 n66; and currency conversion, 49, 51, 54, 88–90; and 1947 stabilization, 139, 141–3, 146, 154, 156, 158

Einaudi, Mario, 83, 170 n15

emigration, Italian, 6, 9, 129

Europe: economic recovery of, 16, 21, 32, 36, 125, 129–30, 135, 157, 159; U.S. policy toward, 11, 40, 91, 111, 118, 119–21, 125, 134, 151

European Recovery Program (ERP), 99, 118–19, 141; ERP in Italy, 138, 142, 148, 152, 153, 154–7, 159, 160–4

exchange rates, Italian, 25, 62, 95–101, 141, 145–6, 150

Fanfani, Amintore, 10, 130, 161

Fascist regime, 1, 4, 5, 6, 8, 10–11, 18–

Index

19, 21, 23, 31, 34, 37, 43, 49–50, 56, 58, 73, 88, 107, 110, 114, 139, 154, 165
Federal Reserve, U.S., 16, 80, 144
FIAT, 12, 43, 67, 69, 131, 163
Finsider Steel Co., 3, 65, 163, 165
Foa, Bruno, 31, 108, 137–9, 146, 162
Foreign Economic Administration (FEA), 15, 24, 26–7, 31–3, 36, 39–41, 74, 140, 142
foreign exchange, problem of, 9, 27, 45, 60, 61, 74, 78, 89, 90, 94, 95, 96, 101, 115, 129, 137, 142, 145, 146, 163, 165
Foreign Ministry, Italian, 79, 92, 123
Foreign Office, U.K., 34, 84, 120
Foreign Service, U.S., 13-14, 17–18, 41–2
Forrestal, James 76, 121
Fortune magazine, 15, 17, 41
France, 16, 47, 81, 118, 127, 131; Communist Party of, 81, 127

Gaddis, John Lewis, 76
Gambino, Antonio, 138, 140, 144
Gasparotto, Luigi, 117
Germany, 1, 37, 44, 62, 72, 77, 87, 118, 125, 131; occupation of Italy, 2, 12, 43; recovery of 77–8, 125
Giannini, A. P., 47, 48
Gimbel, John, 119
Great Britain: Anglo-American relations, 16, 34, 50, 84, 87, 118, 120, 136; Italian policy, 12, 15, 23–5, 27, 30, 33–5, 39–40, 42–3, 50, 69, 72, 74, 143; U.S. loan to, 41, 77–8, 116, 120
Greece, 36, 80, 100, 120, 123
Grew, Joseph, 13, 17, 36, 38–9, 41
Grifone, Pietro, 139
Gronchi, Giovanni, 10, 59, 78, 97, 124, 139, 153, 156

Halifax, Lord, 84
Harriman, Averell, 15
Henderson, Loy, 13
Herter, Christian, 156–7
Hickerson, John, 110, 112, 157
Hopkins Harry, 14–15
Hull, Cordell, 4, 7, 11, 14–17, 19, 20 26, 29, 40, 82–3, 87; economic doctrine of, 7–8, 18–20, 24, 40–1, 44, 77–8, 81–2, 87, 91, 105, 113, 136, 158, 165
Hyde Park Declaration, 27–8, 31

industry, Italian: confederation of, *see* Confindustria; prewar growth of, 5, 8, 9; Northern, 37, 44, 59; postwar recovery of, 20, 25–7, 37, 40, 42–3, 48, 55–6, 66, 74, 80, 106, 156, 163; state, *see* IRI; steel, *see* Finsider
inflation, Italian, 2, 11, 20, 24–6, 31, 37, 42, 48–50, 53, 75, 77, 88–90, 94, 96, 99, 107–8, 117, 122, 129, 137–8, 140, 144–5, 147, 149, 152, 163, 165; policies toward, 93, 96, 119, 136–8, 140–

2, 144, 147, 149–50, 152, 154, 162; *see also* currency
International Bank for Reconstruction and Development (IBRD), 16, 77, 82, 108, 123
International Monetary Fund (IMF), 7, 40, 77, 80, 106, 107, 108, 143
International Telephone and Telegraph Company (IT&T), 16, 69–71, 83, 85–7
International Trade Organization (ITO), 7, 80, 82, 107, 111, 114, 136
isolationism, U.S., 16, 77, 91
Istituto Mobiliare Italiano (IMI), 3, 115
Istituto per la Ricostruzione Industriale (IRI), 3, 103; U.S. policy towards, 64–8, 74, 145, 165
Italian Embassy in Washington, 16, 31, 63, 79, 107
Italian General Confederation of Labor (CGIL), 19, 43, 65, 138, 150, 161
Italian government, 37, 51, 52, 53, 54, 56, 58, 61, 74–5, 87, 91, 92, 94, 96, 130, 146; economic policies of, 25–8, 34–6, 40–2, 44–5, 62, 66, 68, 87, 91–2, 94, 96, 98–9, 122–7, 139, 141–3, 146, 154, 156, 158, 161
Italian Social Republic, 2, 43, 44

Jenkins, Thomas, 113
Jones, Joseph, 120, 128, 159
Jung, Guido, 95

Keeny, Spurgeon, Sr., 90–4, 98–9, 103
Kennan, George, 13–14, 76–7, 81, 119–20, 125, 126, 127, 129–30, 149
Key, David, 73
Keynesianism, 6, 90, 137, 140, 157–8, 162–5
Kirk, Alexander, 13, 17, 27, 33–4, 44, 46, 50, 53, 56–7, 61, 73
Kolko, Gabriel, 140

La Malfa, Ugo, 9, 54, 79, 93, 95, 131, 144
Leahy, Admiral William, 15, 17, 76
Lehman, Herbert, 91
Levi, Carlo, 37
Liberal Party (PLI), 18, 35, 45–6, 56, 59, 68, 100, 113, 131, 134, 156, 161, 163, 164, 165
liberalism, Italian classical school, 4, 6, 8–10, 12, 18–20, 49–50, 65, 70, 73, 87, 89, 100, 134, 137, 148, 161–2, 170 n13
Linee Aeree Italiane (LAI), 72, 83, 85
Lippmann, Walter, 121
lira, *see currency*
Lombardi, Riccardo, 9, 11
Lombardo, Ivan Matteo, 63–4, 93, 127, 132–3, 142
Long, Breckinridge, 12, 13
Lovett, Robert, 135, 143, 151
Luce, Henry, 7, 10
Luzzato, Bruno, 31

Index

MacMillan, Harold, 24
Marshall, General George, 15, 80, 113, 118–21, 125, 132, 133, 134–5, 141, 143, 151, 155; see also European Recovery Program
Martin, William McChesney, 80, 108, 114, 115
Mattei, Enrico, 165
Matthews, H. Freeman (Doc), 109–10, 128, 131–2
Mattioli, Raffaele, 29–32, 34, 38, 48, 51, 55
Mechanical Industry Fund (FIM), 147
Menichella, Donato, 103, 114, 135, 143, 145, 147, 153–4, 156, 161–3, 165
Merzagora, Cesare, 134, 139, 145–6, 150, 153, 156, 163
Molotov, V. M., 80
Monarchy (Institutional Question), 10, 12, 13, 19, 23, 50, 59, 73, 100; King Victor Emmanuel III, 12, 13, 23
Montecatini Company, 68, 69
Montini, Giovanni, 107
Morandi, Rodolfo, 9, 97–8, 122, 150
Morgenthau, Henry, 7, 11, 14–15, 23, 30, 34, 73, 77, 124
Moro, Aldo, 161
Mussolini, Benito, 5, 12, 13, 22, 139

National Advisory Council (NAC), 47, 77, 78–9, 80, 82, 108, 111–15; and Italian loan, 16, 81
Nenni, Pietro, 9, 37, 39, 56, 58, 59, 73, 110, 116, 117, 148
New York Times, 106, 197, 113, 115, 148
Nitti, Francesco, 59, 126, 131, 132
North Italian Committee of National Liberation (CLNAI), 10, 36, 37, 43, 44; see also resistance, Committee of National Liberation
Norton, Gerald, 84, 85

O'Dwyer, William, 27
Orlando, V. E., 59
Ortona, Egidio, 29

Pacciardi, Randolfo, 144
Paratore, Giuseppe, 68
Parri, Ferruccio, 9, 37, 49, 51, 53, 54, 56, 58, 60, 62, 66, 67; fall of government, 46–7, 50, 55–7
Peccei, Aurelio, 69
Pella, Giuseppe, 134, 139, 163
Pesenti, Antonio, 49
Phillips, William, 13, 15, 39, 45
Piaggio, Rocco, 65, 67
Piccardi, Leopoldo, 65, 68
Piccioni, Attilio, 124, 161
Pirelli, Leopoldo, 9
Piscitelli, Enzo, 50, 54, 55
Potsdam, Conference of, 36

Quaroni, Pietro, 160
Quintieri, Baron Quinto, 29
Quintieri–Mattioli Mission, 29–32, 38, 48

Rayburn, Sam, 82
Reale, Eugenio, 45
reparations, Italian, 77, 80, 100
resistance, Italian, 1, 10, 18, 22–3, 37, 59, 106, 124; see also Committee of National Liberation
Reston, James, 107
Ricci, Federico, 49, 53–4, 60–1
Romita, Giuseppe, 59
Roosevelt, F. D., 7, 11, 14–15, 17, 72, 78; and Italian policy, 12–13, 16, 24, 27–8, 30
Rostow, Eugene, 32
Ruini, Meuccio, 66

Sacerdoti, Cesare, 79
Salvemini, Gaetano, 38
Saraceno, Pasquale, 10, 25, 198 n66
Saragat, Giuseppe, 63, 116, 117, 124, 131, 144
Scelba, Mario, 59, 71, 117, 122, 149, 164
Scoccimarro, Mauro, 49–55, 59, 61, 95
Secchia, Pietro, 149
Sforza, Carlo, 30, 38, 117, 123, 143, 160
Shafer, Paul, 113
Sinigaglia, Oscar, 67, 69, 165
Snyder, John, 15, 143
Socialist Party (PSIUP, PSI after January 1947), 9, 12, 21, 23, 30, 37, 39, 50, 59, 63, 67, 73, 90, 92, 117, 141, 145, 166; economic policy of, 30, 65, 89; U.S. policy toward, 102, 119
Socialist Party of Italian Workers (PSLI), 116, 130, 143, 144, 149, 153, 156, 161
Soleri, Riccardo, 35, 49, 51
Soviet Union, 7, 13, 14, 17, 19, 21, 38, 40, 41, 42, 76–7, 99–100, 102, 107, 120–1, 123, 149, 156; and Italian situation, 36, 39, 72, 74, 80, 82, 87, 102–3, 119
Stalin, Joseph, 76, 77
State Department, U.S., 7, 13, 14, 15, 16, 17, 21, 38; Economic Development Division (ED), 64, 66; International Resources Division (IR), 64, 66; Office of Foreign Development Policy, 40; Office of International Trade Policy, 40; Office of Transportation and Communications, 40, 69; Policy Planning Staff, 119, 129; Western European Division (EUR), 13, 14, 17; EUR policy toward Italy, 21, 36, 40, 45, 56–7, 73, 81, 85, 103–5, 109–10, 112, 114, 119, 124, 128, 143
Stevenson, Adlai, 25, 26
Stimson, H. L., 26
Stone, Admiral Ellery, 23, 33–4, 38–9, 43, 46, 51, 60–2, 94, 166; and IT&T contract, 71

212

Index

Storoni, Enzo, 45–7, 93
Sturzo, Don Luigi, 124
Switzerland, 122, 154

Taft, Robert, 106, 113, 121
Tarchiani, Alberto, 32, 38–9, 56, 78–9, 81, 83, 110, 114, 116, 143, 149–50, 157; May 1947 crisis, 121–3, 127, 131–2
Tasca, Henry J., 11, 34, 35, 50, 53, 55, 60–1, 63, 66–8, 72–3, 79, 91, 101–3, 105, 111, 116, 126, 128–30, 145, 149, 157, 163–4, 175 n36, 193 n18; and 1947 stabilization, 146, 150, 154, 156, 158; role in spring of 1947 crisis, 123–7, 133–4, 144
Taylor, Myron, 12, 15
Terracini, Umberto, 149
Tesoro, George, 31
textile industry, 9, 12, 44–7, 64, 67, 75, 96, 97–8, 101, 115, 150; cotton, 1, 44–6, 63–4, 67, 95–6, 103
Thorp, Willard, 41, 114
Togliatti, Palmiro, 23, 37, 59, 73, 99, 109, 117, 133, 148, 149, 161; and PCI economic policy, 19–20, 55–6, 60–1
Togni, Giuseppe, 139, 161
trade, Italian, 6, 25, 31, 40, 47, 50, 55, 95; exports, 44–8, 63–4, 67, 74, 89–90, 95–8, 145, 165; protectionism, 6, 8, 9, 40, 77, 100, 106–7, 113, 118
Transcontinental and Western Airways (TWA), 16, 69, 71–2, 83–4, 85–7
treasury, Italian, 20, 91, 93, 96, 98, 101, 102, 108, 117, 122, 134, 147, 151, 164
treasury, U.S., 7, 15, 16, 27, 30, 34–5, 49, 53, 56, 62, 77, 80–1, 96–7, 101, 108, 127, 147, 154
Treves, Peter, 31, 96
Truman, Harry, 14, 15, 17, 38, 40, 41, 42, 77–9, 82, 91, 99, 103, 106, 112–13, 118, 120, 121, 122, 130, 136, 148, 151, 159

Ufficio Italiano dei Cambi (UIC), 45, 62, 95, 114, 150
unemployment, 1, 26, 44, 129, 137, 153, 162
l'Unità, 100, 132
United Nations, 7, 14, 15, 36, 91, 106, 107, 111, 121, 132; see also United Nations Relief and Rehabilitation Administration
United Nations Relief and Rehabilitation Administration (UNRRA), 11, 15; Lira Fund Control Committee, 94, 97, 98; relations with Italian government, 20, 26, 33, 40, 57–8, 60–2, 74–5, 78, 82, 87, 90–9, 103, 105, 107, 109, 120, 132, 133, 134–5, 142, 151, 162, 163; Tessile (textile) program, 97–8
United States Export–Import Bank, 16, 40, 47, 62, 64, 70–1, 78–83, 86, 105–6, 108–10, 112, 114–15, 123, 132, 133, 148
Uomo Qualunque Party, 100, 103, 107, 110, 112, 134

Valletta, Vittorio, 43, 69, 131
Vandenberg, Arthur, 15, 76, 106, 113, 120, 121, 155
Vatican, 4, 10, 12, 103, 107, 116, 130, 157, 161–2, 166; Lateran Pacts, 116–17, 123; Pope Pius XII, 12, 107, 108
Venezia-Giulia province, 51, 54, 60
Vinson, Fred, 15, 41, 79, 81

Wallace, Henry, 4, 10, 11, 14–15, 40, 81, 99, 121
Ward, Barbara, 103
Welles, Sumner, 15, 133
White, Harry, 15, 29–30, 80
Wilcox, Clair, 70
Wilson, Tom, 71–2, 84

Yalta Conference, 14
Yugoslavia, 54, 80, 100, 102

213